P9-CLO-091

# MONEY AND THE PEOPLE YOU LOVE

# Money and the People You Love

A NEW APPROACH TO FINANCIAL PLANNING
BASED ON WHAT MATTERS TO YOU MOST

## Bruce Helmer

SYREN BOOK COMPANY
MINNEAPOLIS

Most Syren Books are available at special quantity discounts for bulk purchases for sales promotions, premiums, fund-raising, and educational needs. For details, write

Syren Book Company
Special Sales Department
5120 Cedar Lake Road
Minneapolis, MN 55416

Copyright © 2006 by ELEW, LLC

All rights reserved. No part of this publication may be reproduced in any manner whatsoever without the prior written permission of the publisher.

*Published by*
Syren Book Company
5120 Cedar Lake Road
Minneapolis, MN 55416

Printed in the United States of America on acid-free paper

ISBN-13: 978-0-929636-52-8
ISBN-10: 0-929636-52-X

LCCN 2005934772

Cover design by Kyle G. Hunter
Book design by Wendy Holdman

To order additional copies of this book see the form at the back of this book or go to www.itascabooks.com

# CONTENTS

■ ■ ■

# HATS

■ ■ ■

We all wear many different hats in our lives. For example, I wear the hats of financial adviser, radio talk show host, founder and president of a financial advisory company, mentor to younger advisers, baseball coach, soccer coach, basketball coach, husband, and father. Wow, when you list them on paper that is a lot of hats! The most important hats I wear are the last two. Nothing in my life is as important to me as my family. They are always my top priority. I think I am a good financial adviser, but I am an even better husband and father (at least I hope I am—maybe you should ask my wife and kids). I believe the single most important responsibility I will ever have in my lifetime is to help my wife raise honest, ethical, responsible, productive children who become adults that contribute to society. The only thing I like about getting older is watching my kids blossom and flourish. By most measuring sticks I have been blessed to achieve a certain level of financial success. However, if I were not happily married, with the greatest spouse and kids in the world, I would still probably be playing softball every night and earning just enough money to live on beer and pizza. Getting married and being blessed with happy, healthy children (and I do count my blessings every day—it is easy to take good health for granted) changes one's perspective and priorities and what they want out of life. At least it did for me. That in a nutshell, is why it was important to me to write this book.

# THANK YOU

■ ■ ■

There are so many people I should be thanking that I can't list them all here, but you all know who you are. The one person I must single out to acknowledge is my wife, Laura. Without her I would be nothing (some would argue that even *with* her I am nothing).

Let me tell you a little bit about Laura. Laura is probably the smartest person I have ever known. She is a career A student with undergraduate degrees in economics and Spanish. She earned a master's degree in strategic management and once took the MENSA entrance exam just to see if she could qualify. The required score for eligibility was 140; Laura scored 157. Laura worked outside the home when we were first married in 1987. In 1993, we were blessed with our first child. In 1995, when our second child was born, Laura was on the fast track to partnership for an international human resources consulting firm specializing in employee compensation, She resigned to be a stay-at-home mom. She determined that it was more important to her to be the primary caregiver to our children than to be a partner in an international human resources consulting firm. We both believe it is better for children to have a parent at home. As much as I try to be an involved, engaged, and hands-on dad, I could never be as good a primary caregiver as Laura. Whatever success I have had in my career would not have been possible without Laura. This book would not have been possible without her, either.

Thank you, Laura. I love you.

# Introduction

■ ■ ■

## What's Really Important

We are social beings. Our lives revolve around others. For most of us our identity is inextricably linked with others: I am Joe's son, I am Sally's mother, he is a friend of mine. Having grown up in a small town in central Minnesota, perhaps I feel those personal connections more acutely than those who are from larger worlds that contained more anonymous faces. Growing up in Olivia, Minnesota, population about 2,500, I knew everyone and, like it or not (and sometimes I did not), everyone knew me. People knew my lineage and family history, and I knew theirs.

I have learned since living outside that protective cocoon that almost everyone from any environment or culture, privately if not publicly, describes themselves by their relationships to other people—those with whom they laugh and cry, work and study, play and worship. We dream with others. We hope with others. We mourn with others. We are nurtured, protected, and defended by grandparents, parents, siblings, spouses, children, and friends, and in turn we nurture, protect, and defend them. Our eyes mist up, our throats tighten, sometimes tears flow just on seeing an image of others—even unknown others—in pain or sorrow.

When we are confronted with a tragedy such as the events of September 11, 2001, or Hurricane Katrina in 2005, and the faceless threat they implied, our instinct is to gather around us those we love. The travel and tourism industry was deeply affected by 9/11 as air travel dropped off the table. But many resort owners on Minnesota's thousands of lakes reported an *increase* in their autumn business. Those who in calmer times would have vacationed in distant lands—or been too busy to take a vacation—packed their families into their cars and drove to a quiet place to spend time together. Why? The response to the tragedy became a refrain, echoing through our televisions, radios, and newspapers. "It makes you realize what's really important in your life," said one person after another, whether speaking from Nantucket, Dubuque, or Carmel. Invariably, what was really important was the people they loved.

That response has likely not varied since a prehistoric family huddled around a fire for warmth and protection. It reflects who we are at our core. Events that shake our world remind us of our true selves. Then, we profess publicly what we know in our hearts that we are. Some would say it's regrettable that it takes a cataclysmic event to evoke that outpouring of recognition and the emotions it summons.

You may be surprised to learn that in my profession, I see this response all the time. I am not a doctor, pastor, or counselor to whom people reveal their bodies, their souls, or their secrets. Instead, as a financial adviser, I hear people's hopes and dreams. And with very few exceptions, when people talk about their hopes and dreams, they talk about the people they love. Their future, the life they wish to live, is always full of the people most important to them. They don't talk first about dollars and cents, Dow Jones averages, or bond yields. They talk about a spouse, a parent, a child. Even those without family often focus on others when imagining their financial futures. Employees, friends, faith communities, and charities all have been the focus of planning efforts with my clients.

One of the simple truths my work has taught me is that relationships are the single greatest influence on how we use our money or plan to use it. Few people I advise are thinking only of themselves when they consider the possible uses of money. How they spend their *time* reflects many other priorities—and it was those scheduling priorities that were affected most by the tragedy of 9/11. But I don't think their realization of "what's really important" changed many people's *financial* priorities.

Perhaps my view of people's priorities is influenced by the very nature of financial planning. Those most inclined to seek professional assistance may be those who are most concerned about providing for or helping others. Put differently, those with the greatest sense of responsibility for others may be those who are most willing to take what I consider the most responsible course of action, namely, seeking professional expertise in how to fulfill those responsibilities.

Maybe. But I don't think the sampling of people I see is that much different from the population as a whole. I believe the inclusion in our financial planning of the people, institutions, and causes we love is widespread and consistent. Those who do not seek professional advice regarding their financial futures are no less concerned about their loved ones than those who do. The people that I and my colleagues do *not* see have a variety of reasons for not getting professional assistance. I have no qualms, however, in speculating that those people plan in their own way, some way, and that one of the keys to their planning is providing for the people they love. We do not live our financial lives in a vacuum. We live and plan with and for others.

Based on more than 20 years' experience as a financial adviser, I don't believe we can think about money without also thinking about the people we love. The two are inseparable—which is one reason I decided to write this book.

## ANOTHER BOOK ABOUT MANAGING MONEY?

You probably found this book nestled on a library or bookstore shelf among many others with financial planning or personal money management themes—or listed on a Web site with numerous related titles. (I *hope* it was listed with other books on financial affairs instead of books of advice to the lovelorn.) Why have I added to the jumble of titles on the subject?

Those who are not willing to work with a financial adviser have the same needs and concerns as those who are. They face the same financial dilemmas and uncertainties; they struggle with the same financial issues; they must choose from among the same dizzying array of options for what they do with their money. If you are willing to spend the money for this book, but not the fee for a planner's services, you will at least have some solid information on which to base some of your financial decisions.

I want people to succeed financially. Maybe it's due to the pride I take in my work and my profession, but I get a bit defensive when I hear people without credentials giving advice that I believe is misguided. And I get downright angry when I see some of the self-appointed gurus of personal finance dispensing repackaged conventional wisdom that, if followed, could be detrimental to your financial future. Invariably they say, "You don't need professional assistance with your personal finances—*if* you buy my book or tapes for three easy payments of . . ."

I have learned a few things in my 20-plus years as a financial adviser and I have strong beliefs about the most efficient use of money. I want to pass on some of what I've learned in the hope that you will benefit from it—just as I have benefited from so many others sharing their knowledge with me. If that sounds kind of sappy, blame it on my small-town upbringing and the values I learned in that environment. Not a bad place to be from. And not bad values to hold.

My views on personal finance are time-tested with real people who have real dreams, real futures, and real families. Thousands of people hold me accountable for my opinions—and that provides a powerful incentive to weigh options carefully and choose positions wisely.

I have written this book, first of all, because the principles of sound financial planning and personal finance management are constant. However, they have taken a lot of wrongheaded hits from people who should know better, but apparently do not. I believe my analysis returns personal financial planning to solid fundamental footing. Because that is my objective, I have not devoted space to telling you how to cut expenses by using coupons or how to save a few extra dollars a week by putting your spare change in a cookie jar. Those kinds of "how-to" tips I will leave to others.

I do not get into the stock-picking game—not even which categories or industry sectors may be hot in the near future. I am neither futurist nor prognosticator. My work is devoted to creating personal financial plans that take into account the specific dreams, goals, objectives, and finances of individuals. Without knowing the details of your finances, dreams, and therefore strategy, I cannot recommend specific investment vehicles. But I can provide a solid framework for you to make those decisions based on your circumstances. I can provide context for many of your financial decisions. You might still call on your uncle Wilbur for tips on the hottest stocks, but after reading this book I hope you'll understand why you shouldn't—unless, of course, he knows precisely your plans and investment strategy and how that hot stock would fit perfectly into your portfolio, which is not true of most uncles I have known.

The second reason I have written this book is that the psychology of money has changed in the past couple of years. Money's place in our lives has shifted. Trust in financial institutions and confidence in business have eroded. The boundless optimism for our financial prospects that ruled the end of the 1990s lies in tatters. (Or was it shredded or deleted in some accountant's office?)

In the late '90s almost anyone could be a financial genius. Any investment you made was almost certain to rise in value. Almost any job you considered came with a significant increase in pay. Who needed well-reasoned financial advice in that climate? Buy, buy, buy. Spend, spend, spend. The spectacular returns on investment in that era were unsustainable by any economic measure, yet they conditioned many people to harbor unrealistic expectations and spawned dreams of riches that were illusions. A few years later, investment portfolios were halved in value or much worse. Jobs were slashed in industry after industry. Having a job or finding a job, any job, became the goal, not doubling your pay. I hope that in this book I provide a realistic foundation for expectations about your financial future in an unsettled and sometimes scary economic and employment climate.

The economic events both before and after millennium celebrations have frightened almost everyone. Those who survived the recession and bear market unscathed financially have to determine whether their survival was due to their strategy or dumb luck—and how to continue to dodge the pitfalls that claimed so many others. Those who took a beating need to reexamine their financial futures more realistically. Almost everyone should take a serious look at their finances in light of the much-altered economic prospects for coming years.

So I have written this book because the time is right for everyone to take a serious look at their plans, their progress, and their prospects. The "irrational exuberance" noted by Federal Reserve board chairman Alan Greenspan shortly before the stock market topped out is gone and not likely to return soon. (Fortunately, the irrational gloom that pervaded the stock market recently has not lasted either.) New circumstances and new rules require new plans and new strategies.

The third and most important reason for this book is precisely the close relationship between our money and the people we love. I have tried to examine personal finance from the perspective of our relationships. You may not be interested in reading every chapter of this book, because not everyone will have the same concerns or demands. Perhaps you do not have children but rather are facing financial issues with a spouse. Perhaps your primary financial concern is helping to care for your parents as they become less able to care for themselves. Or maybe you are in the position to begin planning for gifts to a charity, faith community, or school.

This book is organized to help you learn about some of the critical financial issues you may need to address at different stages in your life with those you love in mind. In that regard, I believe this book is unique in meeting an important need. Our lives are entwined with the lives of others, the people we love. This book is about how money intersects with those lives.

In a nutshell:

- The fundamentals of personal finance are consistent, but they have been badly or erroneously presented by many in recent years.
- Everyone should take a new look at their personal finances as we emerge from a time of extraordinary economic upheaval.
- We organize and plan our finances largely around our love for others, so it makes sense to examine our options in that light.

Thus, *Money and the People You Love: A New Approach to Financial Planning Based on What Matters to You Most.*


## MONEY CAN'T BUY ME LOVE

Because I make certain assumptions about financial planning as it affects both you and your loved ones, it is only fair that I clarify those assumptions and my use of certain words early on.

As a child I listened to the Beatles sing "money can't buy me love." It certainly can't, and nothing in this book should be taken to imply otherwise. What money might help you do is provide a better life for those *you* love. The efficient use of money to provide for, protect, and care for loved ones is one expression of our love for them. Do you have to have money and give it away or spend it lavishly on those you love to prove your love? That's absurd. Spending time together, giving of ourselves, and being present are often more valuable to our loved ones than anything money can buy. You can probably lead a rewarding life if all you have is love, but your life would be quite hollow if all you had were money.

I make no value judgments concerning the role of money in your life. I do, however, place great importance on using whatever money you have most *efficiently*. Using money efficiently has no relationship at all to how much you have (that is, your net worth). The judicious use of money means getting the most from whatever dollars you have to help you achieve your personal goals. You can use $1,000 as wisely or foolishly as you can use $1 million or $100 million. Some people do not value material possessions highly. They choose to live without a lot of possessions and see no need to amass monetary wealth. Those people have their own priorities, and they love no less and no more than others. But even those people and their loved ones have basic needs that must be met, both now and down the road.

The point of this book is to help you establish priorities for the money you have and to make suggestions for using that money efficiently to achieve your goals. Money is only a tool. It can be used to do whatever you want. And money is one tool among many. Wisdom, intelligence, discipline, persistence, compassion, empathy, talent: These are other tools that each of us uses to achieve our goals. The difference with money is that there are exterior constraints and limits imposed. Many of those tools can help you acquire money, but money cannot acquire any of those other things.

Finally, when I write about "wealth," I am not referring to money per se. In my view, wealth refers to the richness of life. My philosophy is that wealth can mean many things: a wealth of wisdom, happiness, love, experience. We all know that money is not a measure of any of these qualities of life. But money can be used in the pursuit or expression of these things. No two people have the same view of money and wealth. Each person establishes individual goals and works toward them in his or her own way. It's a bit like biology. Some biologists specialize in the minute functions of small parts of human cells. Others choose to study global ecology. But both disciplines begin with biology. Personal interests take biologists in different directions. Likewise, each person will use money differently as a tool. The goal is not money but living a better life—however *you* define it.

Let me tell you a story about the role of money in my life. I am not driven by money, although I have done well financially. For me and for those I work with, money is secondary to doing a good job for our clients. We have a lot of fun, we really enjoy what we do, and, oh, by the way, we even get paid for it. Isn't this a great world?

It's a lesson that I learned from one of my early mentors. When I first got into the financial services industry I was not a "superstar," but I was doing well for a neophyte by most measures. After I had been in the business a couple of years, the real superstar of my company pulled me aside one day and said, "Helmer, I've been watching you. I think you've got what it takes to be successful in this business. I think you're going to last. I'm going to tell you the secret to success in this business."

As I anxiously awaited his words I thought, I've got the superstar, my mentor, giving me the secret to the business.

"You have to put your client's needs before your own," he said.

I gave him a perplexed look, I am sure, and he could see I was puzzled. "I mean that you can't worry about yourself," he explained. "You have to worry about your client. That has to be your top priority."

"Are you saying that I'm doing something wrong for my clients?" I asked.

"No, you're an honest guy, you're a nice guy," he said. "I'm sure you're trying hard to do what's right for your clients. But that's not where your focus is."

I still didn't understand what he meant.

"I'm not sure how to explain it," he said. "But let me ask this. How long is it after you consummate a deal and your client leaves your office before you reach for the calculator to figure out what your compensation will be or how much money you made?"

"Well, as soon as they're gone I do that. Doesn't everybody?"

"I never even think about what I make on a deal," he replied. "It's not part of my thought process. I just know that if I do the best job I can for each and every client, my income takes care of itself. When I figured that out, I tripled my income."

I wish I could tell you I was smart enough to have taken his words and applied them from that moment on. I wasn't. But gradually, I can't say exactly when, I realized that I wasn't paying any attention to what I made. Often I didn't even know what the compensation rate was on the strategies and products I was using. Fortunately, I have a team that does pay attention to those things, so we get paid what we're supposed to get paid. But they would tell you that I have no idea how much I make from the various things we do and I don't want to know.

Am I unusually unmotivated by money? I don't think so. I would be willing to bet that of my twenty most successful clients financially, without exception their financial success was never their primary motivation. Financial success was the consequence of doing what they did better than other people in their chosen field. They had a commitment to excellence. They had some intrinsic motivation. They wanted to do what they did better, smarter, work harder, do it more efficiently, be the best at what they did. And when they became the best, financial rewards followed. In the world of sports, Michael Jordan is a very, very wealthy man, but his goal, I'm sure, was to be the best basketball player in the world—not to be the wealthiest man in the world. When he became the best basketball player in the world, wealth came along with it. When Tiger Woods is walking down the 18th fairway at Augusta on Sunday with a one-shot lead, I bet he's not thinking about the size of the purse. He's thinking about the green jacket. Hitting the perfect shot and winning the tournament are what drive him. The financial rewards follow.

I tell this story not to convince you that I'm a great guy. Instead, I tell it to underscore my belief that money should not be the force behind your financial planning and strategy. If you begin with a number, a net worth figure that you desire, you are less likely to achieve your goal than if you start with a goal for your life, how you want to live, what you want to do. Then you can calculate what role money can play to help you reach your goals. You will also keep money in its place. Some of the saddest people I know are those who gave up their passion to take a job with better pay.

Do what you love, plan to do more of it, and determine how a more efficient use of money can help you achieve your dreams.

## SLAYING DRAGONS

My positions on many financial issues are controversial. My advice may be especially unpopular with the powers that be in the financial world. Most financial institutions place a greater priority on their success than yours and may give advice that is contrary to your interests. Recent history bulges with examples of people who have acted in their narrowest self-interest and flagrantly disregarded the interests of those they were supposed to be serving, from savings-and-loan directors and accountants, to corporate boards and CEOs. Those people were in many cases criminals. Optimists could rightly claim that those people have been and will always be the exception rather than the rule. My experience in the financial and business world is that the vast majority of people do behave ethically.

Ethical behavior does not necessarily mean, however, that others will always be right or have your best interests in mind. Honest people still make mistakes. And honest people still sell products, financial and otherwise, that it may not behoove you to buy or use. For instance, do passbook savings accounts serve a useful purpose? Yes, they do, and banks will compete for your deposits by telling you how smart it is to save. But is that where you should put your life savings? For most people that would be a bad decision. Even though the product is good in the right situation and the bank is ethical and the bankers would like you to deposit all of your money in their institution, it may not be in your interest to do that.

Another example would be term life insurance. Many insurance companies make a greater effort to sell term insurance policies than permanent policies. Why? Because it's a better product for you? Not necessarily. The companies promote those policies because they know you will likely never make a claim on a term policy. In fact, you probably won't continue paying premiums for the life of your policy—in which case it lapses and whatever money you've paid in is the insurance company's to keep without further obligation to you. Is that unethical? Not in the least. Term life insurance is a valuable product for some people, and while you pay your premiums you receive a valuable benefit. Just because it's a good product for some people, however, does not make it a good product for you. Is the insurance company likely to tell you that it's not a good product for you? Perhaps they will if they can get you to buy a different insurance product instead. But if the choice for them is selling a term policy or nothing, they'll sell you the term policy whether it makes any sense for you or not.

Many of you have experienced yet another practice that may not be in your best interest. Those of you who use stockbrokers are periodically encouraged to sell one stock and buy another. Are those decisions in your best interest? Or do the stockbrokers who receive commissions on transactions benefit more than you do? Is it unethical to encourage you to sell one stock and buy another? Certainly not, at least not if the sole motive is to improve the performance of your portfolio. One must be cautious, however, to scrutinize, more carefully than most stockbrokers do, how one stock or another fits with your investment strategy and goals. The stockbroker could be recommending an investment because he thinks it is a tremendous opportunity for you. That still doesn't mean it is good advice for you because it may be in a class of investments that doesn't fit with the rest of your portfolio, overexposes you to one asset class, or otherwise doesn't maintain the allocation of assets you desire. Ethical and well-intended advice? Yes. Advice that's good for you? Maybe not.

Fortunately, you are not forced to buy or use any products that do not meet your objectives or further your interests as you see them, just as no one insists that you buy the Fanny Lifter of infomercial fame. Throughout this book I will encourage you to use your independent judgment in determining your financial future instead of relying on the marketing and promotion departments of financial institutions. Some of those institutions will tell you I'm full of beans. You decide. I will try to give you some solid information on which to base those decisions.

A final thought on who you should listen to when your money is involved: You would be well served to maintain a healthy suspicion of financial advice provided by anyone. I do not exempt myself or other authors. Think critically of any advice that has anything to do with money. Skepticism is a valuable item in your financial planning toolbox.

In almost every discussion of money, someone has something to gain. Obviously, if you bought this book, I made money. And if you take my advice and hire a professional to help you create a financial plan or manage your money, some of you might choose to hire my firm. I also make money in that case. But as I noted a few paragraphs back, the pursuit of my own financial goals is not the only reason I'm writing this book. When you hear advice from anyone, including me, think first whether he or she has anything to gain if you act on that advice.

Next, consider where they got their information or opinions. Have they ever been held accountable by people who took their advice? Or did they become "experts" because they saw an opportunity to sell a few books and conducted a few cursory interviews to obtain their "knowledge"?

Finally, consider whether their books, TV shows, or opinions are popular because they make getting ahead financially sound easy. It's not. Just like miracle diets that promise to take off pounds and inches without any effort—"burn calories while you watch Andy Griffith reruns"—some personal finance authors and lecturers are selling miracle cures that are untethered to the real world. Their books could be described in utopian terms: three pounds of paper surrounded by reality. The charlatans of personal finance imply that money is easy to get, while the diet quacks claim fat is easy to lose. The truth is the opposite in both cases. Whenever the term "easy" is mentioned or implied when the topic is money, grip your checkbook tightly and, like a child in stranger danger, scream, "You're not my father." Unless he is, of course. In either case, run immediately in the opposite direction.

Many of the opinions I express in the following pages are not conventional wisdom. In fact, my positions will often contradict those of popular personal finance authors. A few examples:

- Life insurance *is* a good investment for many people.
- Prepaying your mortgage is usually *not* an efficient use of money.
- Contributing money to a 401(k) plan may be *detrimental* to your financial future.

And, many more, all just the opposite of what many others will tell you.

Many opinions pertaining to personal finance are neither right nor wrong, black nor white, but rather gray. I welcome challenges to any of my opinions. I am confident that I can defend them both theoretically and in the real world of the people I advise.

Like all licensed securities representatives and financial planners, I have to do more than tell you that I am fallible. I also have to tell you these important things. (If you have no intention of suing me because you wrongly inferred that I am making specific suggestions regarding any particular financial product or my ability to earn certain returns on your behalf, you may skip the following italicized print.)

*In this book, I discuss and sometimes compare different investment products. Each of these products is designed to address certain investor needs, and each has distinct risk and reward characteristics. Some of those differences are so marked that the regulators who supervise the securities industry require that financial professionals spell them out whenever we discuss these products—even in a book such as this, which does not purport to give advice about which products and specific investment strategies might be suitable for any specific individual.*

*With that said, here are some key facts about some of the investments I discuss in this book and about investments in general:*

- *Equity investments involve market risk, including fluctuating returns and possible loss of principal.*
- *Unlike equities, bonds offer a fixed interest rate and return of principal if held to maturity.*
- *High-yield bonds typically involve more risk of issuer default than investment-grade bonds.*
- *Government securities are backed by the full faith and credit of the United States and are considered to be among the safest investments.*
- *International investments involve special risks, including economic and political uncertainty and currency fluctuation.*
- *Small-capitalization stocks tend to experience greater volatility than large-capitalization stocks.*

- *Mutual funds and variable-rate contract investment subaccounts involve fluctuating returns and values so that an investor's shares, when redeemed, may be worth more or less than their original cost. In addition, early withdrawals from and loans taken against variable-rate contracts may involve additional fees, tax penalties, and/ or negative effects on death benefits.*
- *Money market mutual funds are neither insured nor guaranteed by the U.S. government and there can be no assurance that they will be able to maintain a stable net asset value of $1.00.*
- *Real estate and other sectoral investments may be subject to sectoral or regional economic downturns.*
- *Direct participation programs are generally illiquid and involve special risks. They may not be suitable for all investors.*
- *Unlike securities, CDs and other bank deposits offer a fixed interest rate and are FDIC-insured to $100,000.*
- *The Dow Jones Industrial Average, the Standard & Poors (S&P) 500, the Russell 5000, and other indexes are unmanaged and are provided for benchmark reference purposes only. Investors cannot invest directly in indexes.*
- *Periodic investment plans do not assure a profit, nor do they protect against losses in a declining market. Dollar cost averaging involves continuous investment in securities regardless of the fluctuating price of such securities. Investors should carefully consider their financial ability to continue their investments during periods of low price levels.*
- *Past performance does not guarantee future results. The reason is simple: The markets will never be exactly the same again.*

*Throughout this book I use many examples to illustrate financial concepts. These examples often use hypothetical rates of return for different kinds of investments. In all cases, these rates of return are for illustration only and do not represent any specific investment.*

Did you get all of that? Curiously enough, authors who do not hold the licenses and have the training and background I have can write whatever they please. They can and often do make outrageous claims and dispense horrible advice without anyone challenging them. It's as if they ran red lights and caused accidents, but the police had to let them go because they didn't have driver's licenses.

## DON'T TRY THIS ALONE

I hope that you will not read this book alone. I would rather you marked it up, wrote in the margins, and then discussed it with your spouse, parents, children, and friends. Although I'm sure your favorite bookstore (and I) would be happy to see them buy their own copy of this book, if you must, lend them yours.

Just as we don't live solitary lives in financial terms, neither should we attempt to plot our financial futures alone. In our culture it is often difficult to discuss personal finances. I know in Olivia it was unseemly to talk about money even with your family. The result was a lot of people who had no idea of the financial needs of their family or friends. It was rumored that Mr. Green had some money stashed away, that Mrs. White's pension no longer covered her expenses, that Daryl's family wasn't making ends meet on the pay from his new job—but no one knew for sure. Financial matters were an island of privacy in a world where everything else was exposed.

As much as I value where I came from and what I learned there, this is one case where I disagree with the social taboos of my hometown. I believe that for you to plan well to use your money efficiently you have to talk about your financial plans with those you love and with trusted advisers. You don't have to make your financial statements public, but you do need to discuss your financial future, especially as others' needs may impact yours, or vice versa. Discretion is one of the pillars of interaction in civilized society, but secrecy that breeds ignorance impedes social progress as well as personal financial progress.

Unlike many personal finance authors who claim you don't need professional expertise (only theirs!) in planning your financial future, I will tell you unequivocally that even after you read this book, you should hire a good financial adviser. There are too many details or alternatives you probably are not aware of and that I cannot fit into this book. Likewise, there are many arcane tax issues that could affect your financial future that no one in their right mind would try to master just for fun in their spare time. You need the input of tax professionals to efficiently manage, now and in the future. So many issues in planning for those you love are fraught with emotion, compounded by the complex bonds that unite families, that you need unbiased opinions from someone you trust to make the best decisions.

So why do you need this book, if you're going to hire a professional planner anyway? First, some readers will not take the step of working with a planner, and they'll give the excuses they always have for not doing so. They may, however, look at some personal finance issues in a new light or follow some of my advice, even if they ignore the part about using professional resources. In that case, their efforts should still be rewarded. Second, even if you decide to seek professional help, you will be more comfortable hiring and working with someone if you have a solid foundation in the concepts and issues that you will address together.

In Chapter 22, I share my thoughts on how you should go about selecting and working with a financial adviser. No, I do not expect your adviser to become someone you love—although some of us are pretty lovable. But he or she will become someone who makes an important contribution in your efforts to focus your financial future on "what's really important."

Ultimately, I will consider this book a success if, after reading these pages, you take effective steps to align your finances with your heart. The answer to "what's really important to you?" is almost always a person, a *who*. That one person—or many—is the starting point for most financial planning. The what, why, where, when, and how are just details to be worked out. Complex details? You betcha, as a caricature of my people would say, but they're a whole lot more meaningful, and much easier to deal with, once you have your starting point. If that's what you're looking for, start here.

# PART I

# *Money and You:*
# *Financial Fundamentals*

The only logical place to begin a discussion of money and the people you love is with you. Without an understanding of the fundamentals of money and your money behavior, most steps to using money to protect and provide for others will be inefficient.

Your options for what to do with your money seem as boundless as the prairie sky I grew up under. But in truth your options are limited, because you can really do only five things with money:

1. Spend it
2. Save it
3. Invest it
4. Pay taxes with it
5. Give it away

Slice the pie however you'd like, but those are your options—five pieces. Only two slices are mandatory: spending and paying taxes—for most people. We all have basic needs that require spending. I don't know anybody, and have never heard of anybody, who is completely self-sufficient, who produces everything they need to live or makes enough of anything that they can barter for everything else they need. Everyone spends something.

Despite the talk of zillionaires who pay no taxes, it is almost impossible not to pay some income tax. Your income will almost certainly be taxed. But taxes are not as ironclad as many think either. The U.S. tax code provides many opportunities to reduce the taxes you have to pay.

It is neither illegal nor unethical to reduce your tax bill in ways provided for by the tax code.

The other three categories—saving, investing, and giving—are completely voluntary. Many people have chosen, to their detriment, not to cut their pie into that many pieces no matter how big or small the pie.

Few of us have the resources to do everything we would like with our money, so we need to establish priorities. We have to understand our options, and how they interact, clearly. A bigger slice for spending reduces the size of all the other slices, except paying taxes. On the other hand, *less* spending may increase the size of the investing or giving slices, which may also decrease the size of the tax slice. The objective of financial planning is to increase our control of the size of each slice.

# 1

## SPENDING: WHAT DO YOU WANT AND WHEN DO YOU WANT IT?

■ ■ ■

For most people, spending takes up the major part of their income. Almost no one has so much money that they don't have to be concerned about spending. What about the super rich? Curious, isn't it, that some of the greatest corporate scandals of recent times have been perpetrated by people who were already wealthy beyond the imaginations of most of us. Why? Only they and their shrinks could make a good guess. I suspect it's partly because they wanted to spend more. Strange as it seems, there is always more to buy. Another yacht. Another chateau in France. Another Monet or Van Gogh.

You have probably played the game that most of us play. You ponder how much money you'd have to have before you quit working (or wanting more). I would bet that most of us set that limit far lower than the annual compensation of well-paid executives, entertainers, and athletes. Why? It's simple really: The more you have, the more you want. One of the flaws of the human spirit, I think, is this inability to be satisfied with what we have, to give up the quest for more. Throughout human history some people have amassed astonishing fortunes only to want more. If you need an example, picture Saddam Hussein hiding in his spider hole with a briefcase that contained nearly $750,000. To him it may have been pocket change, but he seemed to be trying for more even as he was toppled.

### NECESSITIES OR LUXURIES

Most spending falls into two simple categories: necessities and luxuries. Almost every dollar you spend could be divided in that way. The challenge of dividing our spending in such a way, however, is made more difficult because of the simple fact that most of us are not now and never have been in dire need.

Still, a "necessities versus luxuries" spending breakdown is useful for anyone trying to organize their finances and use their money efficiently. Most people spend most of their money, as opposed to saving, investing, or giving it away. Therefore, whether you are buying necessities or luxuries, spending has to be the starting point for any financial planning. A dollar not spent is a dollar that can be used in another way; a dollar not spent has the same future value as an extra dollar earned. You can increase the size of your financial pie only three ways: spending less, earning more, or, in some cases, paying less tax.

There is no baseline for needs or wants. One person's needs are another's luxuries. You just have to look at analyses of the "basics" of living in the United States to see the evolution in what we consider necessities. Necessities gradually include the modern conveniences that technology has made available. When did a telephone become a necessity instead of a luxury? Are cell phones now reaching the status of necessity in our scrambled lives? I would bet that many people who have become accustomed to their phones at their sides, in their pockets, or in their purses would have a very difficult time living without them—at least for a while.

Is a car a necessity or a luxury? In most parts of the country, a car is a necessity. You couldn't live in Southern California very easily without a car. The same is true in my home area, the Twin Cities of St. Paul and Minneapolis, Minnesota, although some people here still rely primarily on buses, bicycles, and walking. Many residents of New York or Boston, on the other hand, live quite comfortably without a car. How nice a car do you need to get to work or to carry the kids to piano lessons? Many people could spend $10,000 or $20,000 less on their vehicles and still meet their basic transportation needs.

We can look at food and drink in much the same way. We have to eat and drink to live, but what exactly are we choosing to eat and drink? The phenomenon of Starbucks and other coffee shops has amazed me. A stop for a cup of coffee on the way to work has become an important part of many people's day. A necessity—especially at a few bucks a cup? Try to take that coffee away from caffeine addicts and see what the response is. Is habit synonymous with need?

Is wine a necessity? For some people, a glass of wine with dinner is not viewed as a luxury. It is part of their cultural tradition. In parts of Europe especially, a meal without a glass of wine is not a meal—even apart from the health benefits that we've learned are conferred by a sip of the grape.

What about the vast array of specialty home appliances? How necessary are they? Certainly we can prepare food for ourselves and our families without microwave ovens. But what if the time we save cooking is spent with our kids, enriching their lives, or enriching our lives in other ways?

I have already mentioned cell phones as perhaps a line in the sand between what is necessary and what is not. What about a home computer? Television? If you believe TV is a necessity, does that include cable TV service? Some people believe that ESPN or CNN is essential to their lives.

Devices that deliver entertainment and information—radios, TVs, computers—are almost all in that space between luxury and necessity in our lives. Many people would consider being well informed not just a luxury but a responsibility for citizens in a democratic society. Does that mean we need cable television and fast Internet connections? I know people who eschew those "luxuries" but still subscribe to numerous magazines and newspapers. Some people can't start their day without reading the local newspaper or the *Wall Street Journal*. Do they need that information or do they just enjoy it? Don't we all need entertainment, a respite from the demands on our lives? How do we get that entertainment—and how do we pay for it?

And what about pets? Now we have huge pet-product supermarkets to meet the demand for pet food, toys, and health products. Do you *need* a dog? Some people would claim that their pets are important members of their families, providing companionship for the elderly and lessons in responsibility for children. Is having a pet the only way for a child to learn to appreciate animals and the delicate balance among all living things in the world? Or do we acquire pets simply for amusement and keep them out of guilt? I have seen homeless people with a pet dog. A choice was made. Who is to argue?

What about medical care and medicines? Is any drug or treatment that may increase our chance of long-term survival or decreases the severity of our indigestion a necessity?

I don't raise any of these potential expenditures as a means of chiding people for how they spend money. Rather, I mention them because it is necessary for all of us to understand our own spending patterns and habits. We need to understand without reservation that we have many more choices than we think when it comes to using our money.

Everyone will arrive at different conclusions as to what is a necessity and what is a luxury. The psychology of "need" is a far more complex subject than I am qualified to tackle. Some people, indeed, may have unusual needs. Ted Kaczynski, the Unabomber, lived in a shack in Montana that measured 10 by 15 feet, smaller than most of our kitchens. But given his lifestyle and beliefs, he probably considered his typewriter a necessity. It was what he used to communicate with the world, however twisted his methods and his message. Joe DiMaggio reportedly had fresh roses placed daily at the grave of his ex-wife Marilyn Monroe. Were those roses a necessity in his life? Probably.

Some people blame advertising for manufacturing "needs" in our society. All you have to do is observe a child watching public television without advertising and then notice the difference when that same child is exposed to commercial programs. That child will suddenly realize upon seeing the ads that there are many things he or she really must have. And try telling a five-year-old the difference between wants and needs once her mind is set on having a lightbulb-powered toy oven that bakes real cookies.

Our susceptibility to advertising and the needs it creates doesn't make advertising itself the culprit. What if someone develops a lifesaving device, but nobody knows about it? Or even a better mousetrap? Wouldn't you want to know? Advertising tells you about products you may actually need as well as those for which a need is created. And despite the ubiquitous advertising to which we are exposed, we all have the ability to resist the needs that it supposedly creates. We always have choices. How we make them is solely our responsibility.

This scenario distinguishing needs from wants is irrelevant for most of us because our affluence and our lifestyles are so far removed from actual survival. The question becomes not what we need to live but what we need to be happy. I am also confident that regardless of your attitudes about spending on luxuries now, your "needs" will inevitably grow with time, affluence, and invention.

Some people have chosen to opt out of our material world and live simpler lives. More power to them if they are happier that way. But even those people become dependent to a degree on the needs and wants of others.

A friend who spent several years working in Africa framed the challenge as follows. In many African societies there is a vigorous debate about the extent to which they should adopt "Western" customs or maintain their traditional cultures. But my friend says that the critical question becomes, "Do you want your children to live?" Do you then need hospitals, roads, schools, buses, basic hygiene, clean water, sewage treatment? If the answer is yes, you want your children to live—and who would answer otherwise?—then you need much of what modern technology offers and you move beyond an agrarian, barter economy to one that requires capital formation, skilled labor, and in many cases a significant step away from traditional means of governance.

The questions of what we need and what we want are not easy to answer. Each of us must answer them in ways that make sense to us individually. But how we answer them will tell a great deal about our view of money and our use of it to get what we want both now and in the future.

## NOW OR LATER

The second spending issue is not what we need, but when? Do we spend to keep ourselves alive and healthy today and save any remaining resources for future needs? Or do we spend on luxuries any resources above those needed to survive today?

An ancient fable tells the story of an ant and a grasshopper. The industrious ant saved for the winter, storing mounds of grain. The grasshopper did not, playing his fiddle all day instead of working to put away the harvest. When winter snows came, the ant had food and the grasshopper did not. Finally, the ant took in the grasshopper and fed him. The story had a happy ending when the grasshopper's fiddling provided entertainment for all the ants. He ultimately had a skill that earned him his keep. The fable is intended to emphasize the necessity to plan ahead, but some could view the story as redemption for the grasshopper: He developed a skill that, as luck would have it, he could barter for food. No doubt struggling artists and musicians everywhere see the story in a different light than many others of us would.

Choosing how and when we spend our money is not much different from the ant and the grasshopper choosing how to spend their time. We can live for today, or live for the rest of our lives. I am not suggesting that you live like a pauper today so that you won't have to in retirement. Neither option is very attractive. But if you have an understanding of your spending, you can begin to strike a balance that's right for you. You can learn to use money more efficiently given your habits, your foibles, and your strengths.

For many people, financial success will require delaying some gratification. And I don't think that comes naturally to a lot of people. I am convinced there is an innate personality trait, some gene, that determines our propensity to spend today or save for tomorrow. The evidence is in small children. Some very small children readily put aside some candy for another day, whereas that notion would be preposterous to other kids. Did the kids who delay gratification learn it from their parents' exhortations? I'm not so certain. I wouldn't be surprised to read someday that a geneticist has discovered a pinchpenny gene that sits not many twisted pairs away from the one that determines whether we can curl our tongues.

## The Propensity to Consume

Most people and most societies consume what they can. Americans are notoriously shortsighted, as demonstrated by a low personal savings rate by international standards. There could be many explanations, from a standard of affluence that has distanced us from the struggle for mere survival, to our propensity to invent and create that places a premium on spending whatever money we have in order to create more. We are the consumer society. Just look at the ads in magazines or newspapers and calculate the percentage of them that sell what for most people are luxuries.

I can give you an example from the financial planning business. A couple came to me to help them with their financial plan. They had a combined income of $70,000 a year and they had managed to save 10 percent of it each year for retirement. Their challenge was that they had both just gotten raises that increased their income by $7,000. Should they add all of that increase to their savings, save 10 percent of the additional amount or spend it and continue saving $7,000 a year as they did before, effectively reducing their savings rate to 9 percent? They decided to spend all the additional income on purchases they had put off when they were making less. They continued to save, just at a lower level, even though they had more disposable income.

> ▪ **EXERCISE: TRACK YOUR SPENDING.** You may be surprised to find that you are guilty of a habit that dooms you to never having money. Some people who constantly feel money pressure buy themselves little treats or rewards, in part because they never have the money to buy themselves what they really want. But it's precisely that accumulation of "little" expenses that prevents them from getting ahead. Many don't even realize they do this. The only way to find out is to keep track of what you spend. Do it for a week or a month. Try to remember every expenditure, no matter how small. Record everything in a little notebook each day. Add them up in different categories at the end of your test period: food and drink, entertainment, utilities, gifts, and so forth. Pay particular attention to the small expenditures on unnecessary items. See how they accumulate over time.

## Spending Money You Don't Have: Debt

Spending too much is one thing if you have the money to spend. Spending it when you do not have it—going into debt—is quite another. Debt can be the thief of dreams. Used wisely, debt can make your life richer. Used poorly, it may doom you to a life of money worries.

Consumer debt is like driving on a highway through Death Valley where you see signs that the next gas or services are 50-some miles away. Once you're on that highway, you don't have many chances to get off or get help.

I repeat this admonition, as do all other financial advisers, only because it is so critical to your financial success. If you can't pay off your credit card bills when they arrive each month, you shouldn't use credit cards. They are wonderful as a convenience, but that convenience has led many people down a road they cannot exit.

Don't even go into a store unless you have the cash in hand to buy what you are going to look at. And in these uncertain economic times, don't even assume that you will have enough to pay for an item as soon as you get your next paycheck. Your next paycheck might be your last if you are laid off. Cash in hand means dollars, hard currency, in your pocket, not the likelihood or expectation that you will have it.

Imagine the opportunity cost of consumer debt. You're not only paying interest but also forfeiting the ability to earn a return on those dollars if you could have invested them. The cost of consumer debt becomes staggering—and the only purpose it serves for most people is to enable them to buy things a few months earlier than if they had saved the money to pay in cash.

If you have consumer debt, with interest rates these days in the 10 percent to 20 percent range, you are essentially paying 10 percent to 20 percent more for every purchase you make until you pay off that debt. Any dollar you spend instead of applying it toward your balance is a borrowed dollar. If you're buying a loaf of bread priced at $1.50, it's actually costing you $1.80 if you have a credit balance at 20 percent interest on a credit card somewhere.

The craziest thing of all is that some people charge things to credit cards just because those things happen to be on sale at the moment. To save 15 percent on the purchase price of an item, they're willing to pay 20 percent in interest. Not even items on sale are worth buying if you have to borrow to do it. The interest you will pay on those purchases will, in the long run, make them no bargain at all.

Debt is the first matter any financial plan has to address. Millions of Americans have inefficient debt. Consumer debt and personal bankruptcies are at all-time highs. Millions of Americans carry balances on high-interest credit cards and never seem to gain ground. They cannot eliminate that debt—and they have a devil of a time even reducing it.

I have seen firsthand how deep a hole some people can dig for themselves with consumer debt. One of the more extreme examples was a couple I'll call Phil and Lil. They came to me because they wanted to purchase their dream home. The home cost $350,000, which wasn't out of their reach because they had a combined annual income of $150,000. But when they went to get financing for the house they were turned down by more than one lender. The reason? More than $100,000 of credit card debt—money for which they were paying 16 percent on average. Every month the interest cost alone on that debt, without paying a penny toward the principal, was more than $1,300.

Most Americans do not have that much of a problem with plastic money, but it's not unusual to see people with credit card debt at levels that will keep them from *ever* investing a penny unless they radically change their spending habits.

The first step in controlling debt is to control spending. Stop debt from growing. Cut off its fuel. You do not need to buy a new jungle gym for your kids just because your neighbor bought one for his children. Keeping up with the Joneses is dangerous and can cause irreparable financial harm. Remember that credit cards are not a replacement for cash. Waiting a few months for that new bedroom furniture or going without a vacation this year will not be easy, but postponing those purchases will better serve you in the long run.

The second step in controlling debt is to pay it off. I see some people who know they should be saving and investing for retirement or to buy a home, so they save a small sum from their paychecks for those reasons. But those same people have credit card balances on which they are paying relatively high interest. Every dollar those people save instead of using to pay off their credit cards loses money for them! Why? Because very few investments will consistently pay a return higher than many credit card rates. If you earn, as an example, 12 percent on your investments, a good return compared to the historical average for the stock market, but are paying 18 percent interest on a credit card, you are actually losing 6 percent a year on your investment—before taxes! Why would you invest in anything where you are so likely to see your money dwindle? That is inefficient, to say the least.

Pay off your consumer debt even if doing so means that you save nothing! It is the most efficient use of your money. You will be amazed at how fast you can save money—and see it begin to accumulate—once those monthly credit card payments are gone.

Of course, you will likely need to own a car and many people cannot afford to pay cash for a car these days. Buying a car is the one case when most people will take on some debt to purchase something that will not appreciate in value. But to my knowledge it is the only consumer purchase that justifies taking on debt.

## Good Debt: Mortgages

Is debt always bad? No. There is such as a thing as "good" debt, and it has four characteristics:

1.  Good debt has a lower interest rate than you may earn on other investments.
2.  Good debt is used to buy assets that will likely increase in value and you enjoy the full appreciation of that asset.
3.  Good debt interest payments may be tax deductible.
4.  Good debt is amortized over a long period of time.

The only type of debt I know that meets all these criteria is a home mortgage. The only other type of debt that comes close to meeting these criteria is student loans; you pay a low interest rate and they help you buy an asset that should increase your earning power for the rest of your life. Another possible exception is an investment in your business or profession, but that really fits into the category of business finance, not personal finance.

A home mortgage is one of the most efficient obligations you can make. The government makes it so. The mortgage-interest deduction is the biggest tax deduction most people can—and by far the biggest of all government subsidies. The tax deduction that you get from your home mortgage interest makes it an extremely efficient way to borrow and *invest* money.

Buying a home is not only a good debt for many people, it is also probably the best investment many people will ever make. A home enhances the quality of life for many individuals and families, and it is one of the surest investments in our world. Despite the recent run-up in housing prices, housing almost always continues to appreciate. Maybe not as fast as it has in the past few years, but steadily over time. Given the increases in house prices in the recent years, you may not enjoy the same appreciation as current homeowners have; prices may flatten out for some time, but in most areas homes are not likely to lose significant value either. Except in true "bubble" situations, usually restricted to areas that are experiencing an economic boom, housing prices usually do not drop significantly; instead, the rate of increase slows.

## Making "Good" into "Better"

Even if the house you buy does not appreciate in value, you are still able to enjoy the single greatest tax break available to you by deducting mortgage interest from your taxes while you live in your house.

Of course, even if you want to take advantage of the economic and "quality of life" advantages of home ownership, you still have many important decisions to make in the type of financing you buy.

What type of mortgage is best? *The longest term at the lowest rate with the lowest down payment without paying points.* A mortgage is the cheapest money you can borrow. Long term, investments in equities historically have earned higher rates of return than current mortgage interest rates. If you have the discipline to invest the difference between a longer-term monthly payment and the payment on a shorter-term mortgage, the longer mortgage should leave you in a better position for long-term investing.

Buying the use of money today through a mortgage is so efficient that I recommend making the smallest possible down payment when you buy a house and carrying the largest mortgage that you can. Consider this: In recent years you could get a 30-year fixed mortgage for about 6 percent to 7 percent interest. Depending on your tax bracket, after taking your interest deduction, your net "cost" of that money would have been 4 percent to 5 percent. Could you have invested the extra money not used for a down payment and averaged better than 5 percent net after taxes? You probably could have. Many people have.

A simpler way to think about this is to disregard taxes. In other words, you finance at 7 percent and don't consider the deduction. The historical average annual return of the S&P 500 from 1984 to 2003 is nearly 13 percent. Economically it makes sense to try to invest as soon as possible and apply less money to your mortgage debt. Using these hypothetical figures, you would have a net pretax gain on these dollars of almost 6 percent.

The price of borrowing money fluctuates, of course, as does the price of anything else. If mortgage interest rates were to rise above 10 percent again, as they did in the 1980s, you would have to compare carefully the potential net gain or loss of any down payment or prepayment plan. But if you are among those who financed or refinanced in recent years at under 7 percent interest, you may do better investing that money instead of paying down your mortgage.

But, you say, what if you figure in the appreciation of the real estate? That has to be worth something, too. It is—but your home will appreciate at the same rate regardless of how much equity you have in it. It does not appreciate faster if you have more equity. In fact, if your home does appreciate, you earn a far higher return on your investment if your down payment is *lower*.

Suppose you are going to purchase a home for $200,000. You can actually get financing with 5 percent down, or $10,000, but you're considering putting down $40,000 or 20 percent. What will happen if your home appreciates by 5 percent the first year? With $10,000 down, you would have a return on paper of 100 percent. With a down payment of $40,000, however, your return would be only 25 percent.

One catch in making lower down payments is that many lenders require mortgage insurance until the borrower has 20 percent equity in the property. Look carefully at the cost of that mortgage insurance to compare it with the cost of a lower down payment. Or better yet, find a mortgage lender that does not require mortgage insurance. Some home buyers have even found that it's cheaper to take out a second mortgage immediately to cover the difference between the down payment and the 20 percent equity requirement, just to eliminate the high premiums of mortgage insurance.

If you are paying mortgage insurance because you have less than 20 percent equity in your home, take a good look at how much your home may have appreciated in value since you financed it. If your home has appreciated in value enough that you would have 20 percent equity at your home's current market price, call your mortgage holder to find out what must be done to get rid of the mortgage insurance. They will likely only require a new appraisal of your home to establish its current value. In most parts of the country a full appraisal costs around $300. If you are paying $50 a month in mortgage insurance, you will pay for the cost of that appraisal in six months if you can eliminate your mortgage insurance. After that, you have an extra $50 a month to spend, save, or invest.

### A 15-Year versus a 30-Year Mortgage

The logic we applied to making the smallest down payment you can without incurring additional costs also applies to the term of your mortgage. Should you take a 15-year or a 30-year mortgage? With the low interest rates of recent years, many people have been able to afford the larger monthly payments of a shorter-duration mortgage. Therefore, they have opted for a 15-year mortgage to eliminate the debt twice as fast and save thousands in interest costs. That's a bad choice—at least if you have the discipline to take the difference in the monthly payments and invest it.

Even though a loan may be amortized over a 30-year period, nothing prevents us from paying it off early. If we take a 30-year mortgage and invest the difference between the smaller payment and what our payment would have been on a 15-year mortgage schedule, we actually need only a very modest rate of return in order to make a balloon payment on our 30-year mortgage after 15 years. (See Table 1.1.)

### Prepaying Your Mortgage

After going through this complicated explanation of how you could perhaps pay off your mortgage early and come out ahead by investing money

TABLE 1.1. THE ADVANTAGES OF A LONGER MORTGAGE

You might end up money ahead if you take out a 30-year mortgage instead of a 15-year mortgage—if you invest the difference in payments. This example is for a $200,000 mortgage at 6.125 percent for the 30-year obligation and 5.5 percent for the 15-year mortgage.

|  | 30-Year Mortgage | 15-Year Mortgage |
| --- | --- | --- |
| Loan balance | $200,000 | $200,000 |
| Interest rate | 6.125% | 5.5% |
| Annual payment | $14,500 | $19,608 |
| Principal owed after 15 years | $142,862 | $0 |

If you invested the difference between the annual payments, you would need to earn only 5.5 percent net (after tax) return to accumulate $142,862 after 15 years. That's the equivalent of roughly an 8.5 percent return before taxes if you were in a combined federal and state tax bracket of 35 percent. And keep in mind that the average annual return on the S&P 500 over the past 50 years is more than 10 percent. If you earned that return over the 15 years, you would be able to pay off your 30-year mortgage after 15 years *and* still have several thousand dollars left in your investment account. Moreover, you would have enjoyed the flexibility of smaller payments over that time in the event of an emergency such as disability or loss of employment.

for 15 years instead of increasing your monthly payments, I want you to disregard it. Why? Because I don't think prepaying a mortgage makes good financial sense anyway. For those with the discipline to invest the money they could use to prepay their mortgage, I recommend *against* prepaying the mortgage. We have already seen that you may come out ahead investing instead of taking a shorter-duration mortgage. We have seen that after 15 years of investment returns below historical averages for the S&P 500 you would be ahead by investing. Now double the period to 30 years. The argument for not prepaying your mortgage becomes even stronger.

Of course, all of these benefits disappear if you don't have the discipline to invest the difference in payments. In addition, you need to consider the risk involved in investing; the returns will fluctuate and there is the possibility of loss of principal. If you need the threat of foreclosure to force you to set aside the money each month, you're better off to take the shorter mortgage. And set this book down now, because without the discipline to invest you may never get far enough ahead to think about saving and investing anyway!

I mentioned in the introduction that you should beware of anyone who suggests that getting ahead financially, enhancing your wealth, is easy. That is why I become furious when popular financial advisers on TV tell you to take the shorter-term mortgage. Why? They look at the audience and ask for a show of hands of people who would probably spend instead of save the money that would accrue from having lower mortgage payments. Most in the audience raise their hands. And the adviser smiles and says, figuratively, "See, you're fools anyway, so take the shorter mortgage."

I believe that it is my *job* to help my clients become more efficient managers of their money, not to acquiesce to inefficient behavior. I am not here to tell you to do whatever seems easiest. Yes, the human inclination is to spend. We are consumers. But that does not mean consuming is good for you. I'm trying to describe smart money management, not easy money management. If I have to encourage you to change your money habits, I will. I can't smugly tell you to do what is not in your interest just because I have doubts about whether you can follow the harder road. I do not have such a low opinion of your ability to see what is in your longer-term interest and change your behavior as necessary to achieve your goals.

Financial advisers who tell you to take shorter mortgages because they don't believe you are smart or disciplined are supported by mortgage companies that know what's best for them, if not for you. A scam run by some mortgage companies is to have the borrower make biweekly payments rather than monthly, or 13 payments per year instead of 12. They then demonstrate how you will pay off your mortgage in 23 years instead of 30 and save thousands of dollars in interest. We have already seen the holes in that argument. But the kicker is that they often charge a fee to provide this service. What a joke!

This approach makes no sense, for at least two reasons. First, some companies are charging as much as $400 to set up this change in payments. Even if it made sense to accelerate your mortgage, you can pay extra on your principal anytime you like; you shouldn't have to pay a fee to increase your mortgage payment. Second, as we have already demonstrated, those same dollars invested have the potential to earn a higher return than the interest rate at which you are borrowing for your mortgage.

Debt is often the destroyer of dreams. But mortgage debt can help you realize your dreams, not only because of the house you can call home, but also because of how you can save and invest. Mortgage loans are different from all other types of loans, because the interest is typically lower than for other forms of debt and the interest payment may be tax-deductible. That combination makes mortgage debt very attractive. Rather than pay off your mortgage as soon as you can, invest the difference and you should come out ahead. The amount you earn on your investment may well exceed the amount you pay in additional interest.

## THE PSYCHOLOGY OF DEBT: HOW MUCH IS IT WORTH TO BE DEBT FREE?

An additional consideration for those considering prepaying a mortgage is the psychology of debt. Many people, particularly in the frugal Midwest, have an emotional aversion to debt that supersedes logic. I have seen it countless times in my career as a financial adviser.

An old friend of mine grew up in a town just four miles down the road from my hometown of Olivia. We were high school sports adversaries, but later became friends and I became his financial adviser. One day he called me and said, "Bruce, I'm going to sell my lake home. I'll walk away with about $200,000 in cash and that's precisely what I owe on my mortgage. I can pay it off and be debt free at age 32. What do you think?"

"I wouldn't do that," I told him. I knew his annual income was roughly $300,000, which put him in a combined state and federal tax bracket of about 50 percent. After his mortgage-interest deduction on his taxes, the net cost of his mortgage was just a fraction over 4 percent (this was in the higher mortgage-interest days of the early '90s). "Don't you think we could invest this $200,000 and do better than 4 percent after taxes?" I asked him. There was long pause, and when he finally spoke he said, "Man, that's a great idea! It's so simple! I don't know why I didn't think of it. That's why you're my financial adviser. It's so easy and so obviously makes sense." He gushed on and on for a couple of minutes and finally there was another pause, a lengthy one. When he spoke again he said, "You know, everything you said makes sense, but I think I'm going to pay off the mortgage anyway."

He understood the financial logic of my argument that he could invest that money and earn more than 4 percent after taxes, but the emotional side of his brain, the one that said, "I'm 32 years old and I'm debt free," won out. The postscript to the story is that numerous times through the years he has said, "Man, I wish I'd listened to you. If I had invested that entire $200,000 back in the early '90s, just look what it'd be worth today based on the stock market we had then."

Fortunately, when my friend paid off his mortgage, he began investing each month what he had previously paid on his mortgage, roughly $1,750. So he's still in very, very good shape, but if he had invested the entire $200,000 instead of $1,750 a month, he would have a lot more money today than he does. For him, as well as for many others, the emotion—and the ability to say, "I'm debt free"—was more powerful than the economic logic.

I can't prevent emotion from entering into financial decision making; it almost always does—for me and my clients. Our personalities and experiences condition many of our responses to money, often causing us to take actions we know intellectually are not the most efficient. But we choose them anyway because they make us more comfortable emotionally or psychologically.

Ultimately it is not my job, with clients or with readers of this book, to chastise or berate you for your financial behavior. Instead, I think it is my obligation to educate you so that you will understand why certain choices may or may not be in your best financial interest. Your range of choices for how you will spend, save, invest, pay taxes, and give away money is huge—and not one of those choices is always right for every individual. On paper there may be a right answer. In the real world of emotions, personalities, and circumstances, there are many appropriate answers depending on the individuals.

What I'm trying to do is provide you with some tools and insights so that you can better evaluate your options and make your choices. I hope that you will understand in many cases how you can use money more efficiently to accomplish your goals. Once you understand the fundamentals, you can choose to ignore them—for whatever reason. At least that choice is vastly preferable to listening to conventional wisdom and then realizing days, months, or years later that you had other, better options than you knew existed at the time.

Prepay your mortgage? Sure, if you don't have the discipline to invest the difference or if you have a psychological need to be rid of debt. But you will be using money more efficiently if you do *not* prepay that mortgage and invest it as part of your overall, diversified investment strategy.

The lower mortgage rates are, the more advantage you will get from taking out the longest-term mortgage possible. That seems counterintuitive and lenders are trying hard to get mortgage customers to buy 15-year instead of 30-year mortgages. They are tempting at less than 5 percent as I write. But locking in a rate of 6 percent or so for 30 years is too good to pass up. The historical average return on equity investments is nearly twice that. Depending on your tax bracket, the net after-tax cost of a 6 percent loan may be as low as 3 percent.

One reason mortgage rates are so low is that equity investments have not provided attractive returns in the past couple of years. More people put their investments into bonds, which forced interest rates down (along with a stimulative Federal Reserve Bank policy). Again, using history as a guide, returns on equity investments have never stayed as low as they have been in the past two years. History suggests that equity returns will return to historical averages over a term as long as 30 years. Yet, with a 30-year mortgage, even when equity returns pick up, you are locked into the lower mortgage interest rates of current times.

Now, don't go overboard and assume that borrowing money just to invest is a great idea. In fact, that is what you are doing by borrowing money for a mortgage, taking the longest term possible and investing the money that you would be paying each month on a shorter-term mortgage. For most people, borrowing to invest—such as commodity options or margin stock purchases—is usually not a good idea. It's a high-risk use of debt that does not have a place in the portfolios of most investors. Investors can make a fortune in a short time, but they can also be wiped out financially if one transaction goes bad.

## A Debt Like No Other

If you have incurred inefficient debt, one method of eliminating it is to transfer the debt to your home equity. Many people are reluctant to use their home equity to consolidate other debt. This reluctance really stems from a mind-set that is behind the times. Certainly, 30 years ago, if people refinanced their home or took out a second mortgage, you can be sure the neighbors were talking behind their backs about their financial woes. But using your home's equity is economically wise. It provides low interest rates, a tax deduction, and an extended amortization.

However, even this form of debt should not be used recklessly. Defaulting on a mortgage of any kind has greater consequences than defaulting on consumer loans. Mortgage loans are secured by your home, which means that if you can't make payments, you will lose your home. Consumer credit lenders cannot take such drastic remedies.

Avoid all other kinds of debt, including the high-risk debt of stock margin purchases and stock and commodity options. Leave those investments to the professional gamblers. Otherwise, buy only what you can pay for with cash.

Final words on debt. When to use it: rarely. How to use it: to increase your net worth or long-term quality of life, *not* to buy more things.

# 2

## SAVING: THE FIRST STEP

■ ■ ■

Basically, we save for three reasons:

- To meet emergencies. I recommend that people maintain liquid savings, which means money that is readily accessible in bank accounts or money market funds, to cover six months of basic living expenses;
- To spend; and
- To invest.

Saving is quite different from investing, although the two are often confused. We can save without investing, but we usually cannot invest without saving. Investing presumes that assets have a reasonable expectation of producing earnings or appreciating in value. I do not believe most passbook savings accounts or even many certificates of deposit that pay fixed interest meet this definition.

Your savings for emergencies and to invest should be, at a minimum, equal to 10 percent of your income—and it should be the first 10 percent of your income. Save first, spend later. Saving for other purposes, such as the new plasma TV or a vacation trip, should be *in addition to* the 10 percent for emergencies and investing. All money you take in should be subject to this 10 percent rule. If you get a gift or a windfall, such as an inheritance, at least 10 percent should go into long-term savings. If you get a raise, increase your savings to match.

Where emergencies are concerned you should also keep up with advances in your own lifestyle. Your $5,000 emergency savings account may have been sufficient when you were in your 20s. But as you age, acquire more obligations, such as children and mortgages, and your income goes up, it may no longer be sufficient. A close look at your potential emergency needs should be a part of at least an annual review of your finances. Be sure you have enough on hand to cover a medical emergency, a loss of income, or some other catastrophe. Your bills won't stop arriving just because your paychecks do.

When we save to meet emergency needs, the most important factor in deciding how to do that (i.e., which savings vehicles to use) is liquidity. Any funds set aside to meet emergencies should be available to you immediately or within a couple of days. I would recommend, however, that you do not keep your emergency money in your regular checking account. Keep it separate from your other money so that you can't accidentally, or in a moment of weakness, spend it.

The rate of return you earn on that money is not nearly as important as your ability to get it quickly. Some people worry that if their savings are not earning a good rate of return inflation will wipe out their purchasing power. They are worrying about the wrong thing with their savings. Inflation is a factor in the types of *investments* you choose, but not the type of savings you choose. If you think there is no difference, read on.

Yearly fluctuations in inflation rates are not a major concern for me as I work with clients. To begin with, you can do nothing about inflation. It is sufficient to know that nearly everything you buy will cost more tomorrow than it does today. Beyond that we can't predict very far into the future. All we know for sure is that the historical rate of inflation runs about 3–4 percent. But that's just a number.

Even government measures of inflation such as the Consumer Price Index (CPI) are not relevant to many people. The CPI measures the cost of a "basket" of consumer items, many of which you may never purchase, such as cigarettes. It is, therefore, simply a very broad indicator of whether prices are rising at a faster or slower rate, not whether *your* cost of living is increasing by a certain percentage each month or year. Just because the Federal Reserve Board and economists focus their attention on inflation, and every slight change in their opinions invites frenzied analysis, does not mean that it has great significance for you.

One negative result of tremendously expanded coverage of financial markets, such as CNBC on cable TV and MSN Money on the Internet, is that every bit of financial and economic information is treated as important news and analyzed to death. The fact that financial news outlets have to fill their time or pages does not make every piece of economic news they cover relevant to most of our lives. Very few of us need to know the most recent reading on consumer confidence or manufacturing activity, yet the release of one report or another—there's one just about every day—is treated as a momentous event by nearly breathless reporters. Most of them really are not relevant to the average investor. So it is with minor fluctuations in rates of inflation.

Accept the fact that any savings you have that earn short-term fixed-interest rates will barely keep ahead of inflation. But your savings accounts are not really investment vehicles anyway, so that is not your primary concern or reason for having those accounts.

Instead of worrying about the effect of inflation on your savings, I would suggest that you do two things that will be more productive:

1. Control your spending; and
2. Create an efficient investment strategy.

# 3

## Investing: Financial Progress

■ ■ ■

The goal of investing is quite different from saving. Saving makes money available to you in a secure place; investing makes that money grow for some future use.

Two rules of thumb: Invest 10 percent of your income, and pay yourself first. Your deposit into your investment account should be the first check you write each time you get paid, not the last. If you pay yourself first, you'll be able to manage on what remains. If you instead plan to invest what remains from your paycheck after you've met other needs (and wants), you'll find that you have little or nothing left for investing most months.

### The Grand Illusion

If you're thinking that we've finally gotten to the juicy part of this book, the part where I give you hot stock tips, you're going to be disappointed. Trying to pick hot stocks is the greatest mistake that most people make with their investments. It is a willy-nilly search for outrageous returns. Perhaps it comes from the lottery mentality that seems to have taken over the country.

Investing has nothing in common with winning a lottery. Successful investors are not speculators or gamblers. There is no sure way to get rich quick through investing. Those who try are deluding themselves and more often than not will end up poorer for the experience.

## STEP 1: DEVELOP A STRATEGY

Successful investing begins not with scouring the financial pages for the next big thing; it begins with creating a sound strategy for achieving your financial goals.

Successful planning strategies are not usually stumbled across. This is not Columbus setting sail for India and bumping into America. Investment strategies are constructed with goals and objectives in mind, proper planning, discipline, and the right investment products. You worked very hard for your money over your lifetime, and you deserve a plan of action that can help assure that you have a comfortable retirement.

The two great sins of investing are fear and greed. Either can be your downfall. Greed in the 1990s drove people to be in the market or in small-cap stocks who should not have been. Fear drives people today, after the market losses we saw from 2000 through 2002, to be afraid of the market and remain on the sidelines. There has always been turmoil in the world, and we can always point to events that created fear or panic and caused people to stay out of the market (such as those depicted in Table 3.3). But investors who remain focused, even during times of war and crisis, have been rewarded with growth to their principal. The greatest value of a good investment strategy is that it will help you overcome any tendencies you may have toward fear or greed. A sound strategy will help you remain patient and confident—and let time work for you.

Your investment strategy should *not* be built on hitting home runs. You don't have to be Barry Bonds to get into the Hall of Fame. Singles and doubles over a long period of time are just fine in the world of investing—as they are in baseball, which is why players with 3,000 hits over their careers, like Rod Carew and Paul Molitor, are in baseball's Hall of Fame. They didn't hit a lot of home runs, but year after year they hit a lot of singles and doubles.

It is possible for most investments to earn a combined return (appreciation plus dividends) of 8 percent to 12 percent a year. If you earn that consistently over a long period of time, your money will appreciate nicely. The world's most famous billionaire investor at the moment, Warren Buffet, is well known for his goal of earning annual returns of

8 percent a year. It may not seem much compared to the returns on stocks in the late 1990s, but it sure looks better than the losses many people suffered in the first years of this millennium. Just remember that most home run hitters in baseball also have a lot of strikeouts.

Let me give you another hypothetical example to illustrate the value of consistency and stability over volatility in your investment portfolio. Table 3.1 compares a steady, modest return to more volatile returns. Returns of 25 percent a year are very attractive, but they come at the risk of seeing significant losses in other years. History proves that 25 percent returns are unsustainable over a long period of time.

TABLE 3.1. STABILITY VERSUS VOLATILITY

| | Rate of Return Investment ABC (in %) | Balance | Rate of Return Investment XYZ (in %) | Balance |
|---|---|---|---|---|
| Initial Amount | | $100,000 | | $100,000 |
| Year 1 | 7.5 | $107,500 | 25 | $125,000 |
| Year 2 | 7.5 | $115,563 | 25 | $156,250 |
| Year 3 | 7.5 | $124,230 | 20 | $187,500 |
| Year 4 | 7.5 | $133,547 | 20 | $225,000 |
| Year 5 | 7.5 | $143,563 | -15 | $191,250 |
| Year 6 | 7.5 | $154,330 | -20 | $153,000 |

A good investment strategy begins by identifying your specific individual goals and the time you have to achieve them. Those highly personal decisions, very often driven by your love of others, will suggest your strategy. Your strategy may include shorter- and longer-term objectives. Are you investing to buy a house, pay for college, or to retire with sufficient income to support the lifestyle you desire? How much money will you want for each objective? When will you need it? How can you get there? Will you have to make trade-offs to achieve those goals? Which take the highest priority? When? The answers to all of those questions will help you determine your individual strategy. Without that strategy it is nearly impossible to know how to invest.

## STEP 2: ALLOCATE YOUR ASSETS

Your individual strategy will determine your asset allocation. Asset allocation determines how much of your money, as a percentage of your total investment, you want to invest in different asset classes. This is the "diversification" you hear so much about. It doesn't mean owning one high-tech stock, one biotech stock, and a handful of shares in General Electric. It means dividing your portfolio into different types of investments depending on your goals, how long you will hold your investments, and when you may need to withdraw your money.

Creating an investment strategy, building a portfolio, and selecting investments are a lot like building a house. You start by determining how much you can spend and choosing the location and size of house. Then you design just the right number and type of rooms to suit your lifestyle. Only when the house is built do you furnish it in a way that complements everything else you have done.

A portfolio is not just a collection of assets, any more than a house is merely a collection of rooms. If you own a bunch of assets without proper asset allocation, you may, so to speak, have a house with two dining rooms and four living rooms, but no bathrooms or kitchen. Allocating assets is like saying, "I need a house with four bedrooms, one big kitchen, three baths, a living room, and a family room, and here's how big I'd like them each to be." Now you've got a functional house—a dwelling that meets your specific needs.

What you have done is allocate space. A portfolio is your allocation of investment space. Instead of doing it by rooms or square footage, you do it by percentages of your resources in asset classes: 10 percent in this type of asset, 40 percent in that, 15 percent in another, and so on.

Modern Portfolio Theory demonstrates that a proper mixture of assets provides an optimal combination of risk and return. And when planning your life, your future, you have to think of risk and return in their broadest terms. Risk may not mean losing money; it may mean losing *opportunities*—in financial or personal terms. Reward may be more than making more money; it may mean increasing *financial security* or enhancing your *enjoyment of life*. The goal is to earn the highest return possible over a period of time in a variety of unpredictable market conditions, rather than chase the highest possible return at any one given point in time.

Investing should not be a guessing game—at least not for those who want to make money consistently. Modern Portfolio Theory is based on research that demonstrates that market timing and stock selection—combined!—account for less than 10 percent of a portfolio's success. The rest is due to asset allocation.

Only after you have determined a strategy and allocated space in your portfolio is it time to consider the merits of specific products. Buying those products is like putting the furniture in each room of your investment house.

Maybe you want a big old overstuffed easy chair in your living room, very comfortable—similar to an annuity or insurance that provides security. Maybe you want an entertainment wall in your family room, with all the latest electronic gadgets—like high-flying equities. Maybe you want to make room in your study for the big oak desk you inherited from your grandfather—like a trust for the education of your grandchildren.

The options are practically endless. The first requirement is that the furniture fit in the rooms of your house—the asset classes in your portfolio—that's located in the neighborhood, city, and state that offer everything you've ever wanted—your strategy.

To access the full return potential of the financial markets and reduce risk, portfolios must be diversified within each asset class as well. The stock and bond markets are composed of numerous styles and sectors (large value, small growth, international equities, government bonds, corporate bonds, etc.). An efficient management philosophy will have carefully designed strategies for the domestic equity market, international equity market, fixed income market, and so on.

To conclude the asset allocation–house analogy, I want you to remember one thing above all else. I call it the "investing corollary of the real estate rule." What are the three most important things to remember about investing? Allocation, allocation, allocation.

## Three Critical Factors in Asset Allocation

It is easy to allocate space in a house based on the size of your family, your needs, and your lifestyle. But how do you decide to allocate space in your investment house? Investment professionals look at three basic components of each asset class: expected rate of return, expected risk level, and expected correlation with other asset classes:

- *Expected rate of return* is simply a historical calculation: how the asset class has performed on average over an extended period of time.
- *Expected risk level* is a mathematical calculation of the average variance from the expected rate of return. The greater the average variance, the greater the likelihood that performance will be significantly different from the expected rate of return in any given year.
- *Expected correlation with other asset classes* is determined by comparing historical performance for various asset classes. Over time, we learn that some asset classes tend to perform similarly or quite the opposite of other asset classes.

## Rate of Return and Risk Level

I address rate of return and risk together because they are so closely linked. When you consider the issue logically, risk and return have to be correlated. You wouldn't take a greater risk unless the potential return or reward for taking that risk were also greater. If the potential return weren't greater, why would anyone take the risk?

Most people get into trouble with investments because they don't know how to balance risk and reward. Successful investing is actually reasonably predictable for those who do it right. I will outline for you how predictable investments in stocks have been historically. If you don't yet appreciate the difference between saving and investing, I hope you will read this discussion carefully. I have encountered many people who are afraid of investing, especially in stocks, because of the risk they perceive that they will lose some of their principal. I have tried to convince them, usually successfully, that *a greater risk may be outliving their invest-ments*. (I return to this topic later.)

If you have already embraced investing in stocks, I suggest you read on as well. Many investors are not getting the returns they could, and perhaps should, because they are willing to take too much risk—or they do not take a long enough view of the stock market. In any event, I think you will find the historical performance of the stock market as portrayed in the data I present very interesting. I hope it gives you food for thought about how to allocate your assets to achieve the goals you have for your-self and those you love.

## The Stock Market Benchmark: Remarkable Consistency Over Time

The benchmark for many discussions of investment returns is the Stan-dard & Poors (S&P) 500. The S&P 500 is an index that includes the 500 largest companies in the United States. Because it includes the 500 largest U.S. companies (companies are added and removed each year as they grow, shrink, or go out of business), the S&P 500 is widely considered to be a good yardstick for overall stock market performance. From 1962 through 2004, the average return of the 500 companies in the S&P index was about 12 percent.

*A word of caution is in order.* The S&P 500 is an unmanaged index, and you cannot invest directly in that index—although some mutual funds attempt to approximate the performance of the index. The average return does not reflect the impact of any management fees, transaction costs, or expenses. And, of course, past results do not indicate future performance. Also keep in mind that the S&P 500 returns cited are an *average* of 500 companies. An individual company may have fared better or worse in any year or over the course of several years, and therefore the return on investment in its stock may have been better or worse than the average.

Still, it is useful to have some idea of how the broader stock market has done over time. What I find most interesting is that although the average return on the S&P 500 since 1962 is about 12 percent, only four years had returns near the average (between 10 percent and 15 percent). The returns

TABLE 3.2.
S&P 500 ANNUAL INVESTMENT RETURNS, 1962–2004

| Below -20% | -20% to -10% | -10% to 0 | 0 to 10% | 10%-20% | Over 20% |
|---|---|---|---|---|---|
| 2002 | 2001 | 2000 | 1994 | 2004 | 2003 |
| 1974 | 1973 | 1990 | 1993 | 1988 | 1999 |
|  | 1966 | 1981 | 1992 | 1986 | 1998 |
|  |  | 1977 | 1987 | 1979 | 1997 |
|  |  | 1969 | 1984 | 1976 | 1996 |
|  |  | 1962 | 1978 | 1972 | 1995 |
|  |  |  | 1970 | 1971 | 1991 |
|  |  |  |  | 1968 | 1989 |
|  |  |  |  | 1965 | 1985 |
|  |  |  |  | 1964 | 1983 |
|  |  |  |  |  | 1982 |
|  |  |  |  |  | 1980 |
|  |  |  |  |  | 1975 |
|  |  |  |  |  | 1967 |
|  |  |  |  |  | 1963 |

Source: Wealth Enhancement Advisory Services, LLC.

varied greatly from year to year, ranging from a low of -26 percent to a high of 37 percent. (See Table 3.2.)

I want you to remember one thing from this information: Returns on stocks, the most widely used form of investing, do not go in a straight line up or down. The stock market, and therefore investors in stocks, will have some years that are better, or worse, than others. The key is that over longer periods of time, such as the 40+ years I have used here, stocks show a consistent appreciation as measured by a broad indicator.

Get used to reading this principle because I will repeat it often: Time is an investor's friend. Over time, the stock market has always gone up. I have no reason to believe that trend will change over the next 10 or 20 or 30 years. There has never been a 10-year period since 1926 in which the S&P 500 has shown a negative return.

Even in the wake of war, assassination, and other crises you could have done quite well in the stock market. If you had invested $10,000 in the S&P 500 Index (remember, though, that such an idea is technically impossible) on the very day of some of the most calamitous and ignominious events in U.S. history, you still would have enjoyed gains within 10 years—and could have a considerable nest egg by now. (See Table 3.3.) Stocks have appreciated, over time, even in the worst of times. Perhaps Dickens was right: The best of times and the worst of times may occur simultaneously.

TABLE 3.3. FROM TURMOIL COMES OPPORTUNITY*

| Event | Value End of 2002 | Value End of 2004 |
|---|---|---|
| The Great Depression (November 1932) | $16,263,296 | $22,402,098 |
| Pearl Harbor Bombing (December 1941) | $11,072,447 | $15,251,892 |
| Cuban Missile Crisis (November 1962) | $449,706 | $619,454 |
| JFK Assassination (November 1963) | $605,716 | $834,352 |
| Nixon's Resignation (August 1974) | $321,287 | $442,561 |
| Crash of 1987 (October 1987) | $50,248 | $69,215 |
| First Gulf War (January 1991) | $34,120 | $46,999 |

*These are hypothetical examples for illustrative purposes only.
Source: Wealth Enhancement Advisory Services, LLC.

I cite this historical data to underline what investing truly is: a reasonable expectation that your money may earn money, the balance of risk and reward. I hope you see that despite the disclaimers, investing in stocks provides that "reasonable" expectation over time. Of course, no well-planned portfolio will ever be made up *entirely* of investments in stocks. Proper asset allocation has the capability to enhance returns and reduce risk. Done properly, asset allocation levels out the highs and lows of equity investing, making investing more a train ride through gently rolling foothills instead of the steep climbs and hair-raising, zero-gravity drops of a roller coaster.

## Now Inflation Matters

Inflation is not a major concern with your savings, but with investing it takes on greater importance. The primary investment objective of most Americans is to provide for their retirement. With the life expectancy of American males reaching 74.7 years and American females, 80.4 (83.2 years for people who have reached age 65), many people will be living off their retirement investments nearly half as long as it took them to accumulate the money to invest for retirement. The big question is, will you outlive your investments? Inflation will likely play a big part in how you ultimately answer that question.

Once again, I would discourage you from worrying about monthly or yearly changes in the inflation rate. Even for investment purposes those fluctuations have little importance. What matters is that over many years the rate of inflation has remained consistently at 3 percent to 4 percent on average. You can use this number with some confidence in any financial plan.

The greatest impact of inflation on investing is that it can turn "low risk" investments into "high risk" investments. Many people like to invest in what they consider "low risk" investments, such as certificates of deposit (CDs), savings accounts, money markets, and other fixed-interest investments. These vehicles provide ways to protect your principal—but for many that's not enough. If your nest egg doesn't grow faster than your cost of living, your purchasing power actually steadily decreases and it will have a detrimental impact on your lifestyle, especially if you're retired and don't have a source of income outside of your investments.

Let's look at a hypothetical example of the high risk of a low-risk investment philosophy. When it comes time to retire, it's very important that you understand whether or not the amount you've saved will be sufficient to provide the retirement income you want for as long as you may live while also protecting your principal and allowing it to grow at a higher rate than inflation. We'll use the Andersons and the Bensons to demonstrate how inflation will affect their life savings based on the investment choices they make.

### Low Risk, High Risk: The Andersons and the Bensons

At the end of 1982, the Andersons and the Bensons retired. Each couple had saved $200,000 for their retirement years. The Andersons thought they would just play it safe and put their $200,000 in a 20-year Treasury Bond that paid 10.6 percent per year. Back in 1982, you could live pretty nicely on annual earnings of $21,200, which is what the annual interest would be on the Andersons' account. But the Andersons did not take into account that inflation over the years would increase their cost of living. It takes more than $39,000 today to purchase what $21,200 bought back in 1982 and 1983. The Andersons experienced another setback when their Treasury Bond matured at the end of 2002. Remember that they took out a 20-year bond, so they had that dividend rate for 20 years. They were shocked to find that the interest rate at the end of 2002 was only 5 percent—less than half of what they received for the first 20 years! So their "safe investment plan" was now forcing them to live on less than $10,000 per year. There was always the original $200,000 that they could use for expenses, but they were now in a very precarious situation because they didn't have any growth in their investment portfolio. The Andersons' "safe investment" paid the same amount year after year. So after earning that consistent amount for 20 years, let's look at a breakdown of what actually happened. Their original investment was $200,000. Over the 20-year period of time, they earned $424,000 in interest that they used for lifestyle.

I am assuming that if the Andersons continued to take out the same amount of money each and every year in this example—$21,200—they actually had a decrease in their standard of living because $21,200 does not go as far in 2005 as it did in 1982. But, in any event, in this example they continued to take $21,200 for 20 years, meaning that they spent roughly $424,000 over that 20-year period of time and at the end of 2002 they still had $200,000.

Now let's look at the Bensons' strategy. The Bensons invested their $200,000 in the stock market. For the purposes of this hypothetical example

I am again using the S&P 500 Index.[1] When they retired at the end of 1982, their plan was to withdraw 6 percent from their portfolio annually, deriving that 6 percent figure from the portfolio value at the end of the prior year. So in 1983 they spent $12,000 because that was 6 percent of the $200,000 they started with at the end of 1982. The amount varied in subsequent years because the stock market went up and the stock market went down, but their withdrawal was always 6 percent of the total value of the previous year. In the beginning of their retirement years, the Bensons lived on less than the Andersons did, but over time the Bensons' income grew substantially. By allowing their principal amount an opportunity to grow in the equities market, the Bensons benefited more than the Andersons, who sought the safer features of the bond market. The Bensons accepted greater volatility and were rewarded with principal growth.

At the end of the 20-year period the value of their investment had grown to $721,292. (Let me caution you again that these hypothetical examples are based on past performance and are not meant to indicate future performance of any equity investment.) The Bensons had tripled their investment in 20 years and reaped greater income rewards simultaneously. Let's summarize. The Bensons' original investment, like the Andersons', was $200,000, but over the 20-year period they actually took distributions of $743,777—in other words, over $300,000 more than the Andersons. The value of their account at the end of 2002 was $721,292, a whopping $521,292 more than the Andersons' account. Which investment strategy would you have chosen, the Andersons' or the Bensons'? Which was the more prudent strategy?

To keep inflation from reducing a nest egg to near nothing most people probably need to allocate at least some portion of their investment assets into something that has the opportunity to beat inflation. Low risk investment vehicles play a role in a well-diversified portfolio or asset allocation, but low risk investments alone may not provide the investment

---

[1] The S&P 500 Index is an unmanaged, broad based index and is not available for direct investment. The calculation includes the reinvestment of dividends. Past performance is no guarantee of future results, and investment results and principal values will fluctuate so the shares, when redeemed, may be worth more or less than their original cost. There is no assurance that the investment process consistently leads to successful investing. Each investment vehicle has unique risks and potential for rewards.

returns that one needs to keep up with inflation. The most likely way that most people are going to be able to keep up with inflation is by having some part of their investment allocation in equities or stocks. History proves that equities provide an effective means to outpace inflation.

## FIXED-INTEREST INVESTMENTS: SECURITY, PROTECTION OF PRINCIPAL

Fixed-interest investments are more appropriate for saving than investing, yet I'm sure you've heard that most brokerages advise their clients to maintain an asset allocation of, say, 50 percent stocks, 30 percent bonds, and 20 percent cash, to give but one example. Am I saying they are wrong? No. Fixed-interest investments, such as bonds, are an important asset class that should be part of most portfolios because they often provide "negative correlation" (we'll get to that concept in a moment) with equity or stock investments. For instance in 2002, the S&P 500 index declined 22 percent while bonds increased in value by 15 percent. In this instance there was negative correlation. As stock prices dropped, bond prices rose. That increase in the value of bonds in portfolios helped offset the decline in stock prices.

My opposition to fixed-interest investments is when they comprise all or too much of someone's portfolio. As an intricate part of a portfolio, they are essential. As a substitute for an investment strategy, they are sadly and perhaps dangerously inefficient.

### Final Words on Risk

How do you know if any of the fixed-interest investments I've described is appropriate for you? Your personal tolerance for risk should help you determine an asset allocation you can live with. If you lie awake worrying about your investments, you should probably invest your money in vehicles that are less risky. Don't forget, however, the risk the Andersons took of outliving their money because they did not earn competitive returns. I think that is a much scarier risk than making some investments that could, in the worst case, lose money, but on average should provide better returns.

I believe my primary duty as a financial adviser is to educate people about the true risks of investing—or not investing at all. To put it simply, even for the most risk-averse people, risk tolerance increases with greater knowledge of investment options and strategies.

One way to help you strike the balance between risk and reward is to look more closely at how various assets perform relative to others. It's time to examine the third important element of asset allocation: the correlation of each asset's historical performance.

## CORRELATION: A NEGATIVE IS POSITIVE

If we fill our portfolio with only asset classes that tend to perform alike, we maximize our risk. If market and economic conditions favor those asset classes, we could do very well. But if any of those asset classes performs badly, they probably will all go into the tank. Our other option, a much smarter option, is to balance asset classes: In other words, find the best combination of asset classes to get optimum performance while minimizing volatility.

Even if one asset class tends to be very risky, meaning that it can fluctuate wildly over time, we can balance that asset class with another that also appears risky but tends to move in the opposite direction. That balance reduces the risk in our portfolio and increases the returns over time. That's an example of negative correlation—which is positive in asset allocation. Ideally, the asset classes you choose will have this "negative" correlation built in.

### TABLE 3.4. SAMPLE ASSET CLASS PERFORMANCE, 1998–2004

| Index | 1998 | 1999 | 2000 | 2001 | 2002 | 2003 | 2004 |
|---|---|---|---|---|---|---|---|
| Standard & Poor's 500 | 28.58 | 21.04 | -9.10 | -11.88 | -22.10 | 28.68 | 10.87 |
| Lehman Bros. Aggregate Bond Index | 8.70 | -0.82 | 11.63 | 8.44 | 10.26 | 4.10 | 4.34 |
| MSCI Europe, Asia, & Far East | 20.00 | 26.96 | -14.17 | -21.44 | -15.94 | 38.59 | 20.24 |
| Russell 2000 | -2.55 | 21.26 | -3.02 | 2.49 | -20.48 | 47.25 | 18.32 |

Each of the four asset classes selected shows a loss in at least one year, but in no year did they all show losses. Moreover, you can see that stocks turned around sharply in 2003. If you had been sitting on the sidelines waiting for the market to recover before you put your money back into stocks, you would have missed a powerful market move.

### A LOVE STORY: THE SUNNY SHORES OF RAINY LAKE

To put negative correlation in simple terms, consider this love story. A young woman opened a resort on beautiful Rainy Lake in northern Minnesota. She was a smart businessperson and her guests adored her. Her problem was that her business depended on the weather. In a hot, sunny summer, she made a 50 percent return on her investment. But in cold, damp summers, she would typically lose 25 percent. The ups and downs were a little unsettling for her.

As luck would have it, however, a regular guest at her resort was a bachelor who owned an umbrella company. His business had the opposite problem: In clear, sunny weather, he lost 25 percent, but when the weather was blustery and wet, he enjoyed a hefty 50 percent return on his investment.

Perhaps it was inevitable that the resort owner and the umbrella maker would fall in love, get married, and pool their assets. Now neither of them worries about the weather because, rain or shine, they make a nice, steady 12.5 percent on their combined investments.

That is negative correlation—and it's the objective of asset allocation as well as diversification within a portfolio. This story is clearly an oversimplification to make a point, but my money management philosophy *is* very simple. With a well-diversified, actively managed portfolio, we reduce performance peaks and valleys and achieve competitive long-term performance with less risk.

Of course, if the resort owner and umbrella maker were extremely good at guessing which summers would be sunny and which would be rainy, they could take full advantage of both conditions, shifting their assets as appropriate, and really make a killing. But anyone who could predict whether a summer will be bright and warm or cold and damp would have a gift they could use to such financial advantage that they wouldn't need advice from me on how to create wealth.

Guessing the ups and downs of the stock market is a bit like predicting the weather. Not even the professionals are right all the time—in weather or stocks—and they're smart enough to know it. So they minimize their risk and maximize the potential for return by using percentages. The meteorologist says we have a 60 percent chance of rain. The money manager says we have 60 percent of our portfolio in stocks, 30 percent in bonds, and 10 percent in cash.

Your individual circumstances will determine how you should allocate your assets. People with a longer time horizon, such as someone who is only 30 years old, are probably best off significantly invested in equities. Over the length of time that they are likely to be invested, stocks will almost certainly outperform all other asset classes. As people get older, their asset allocation should weigh two factors: their dependence on income from their investments and the amount of debt they have. Those who have higher net worth and low or no debt will likely want to remain fully invested in stocks or maintain a high percentage of their portfolio in equities. Those who will need to depend on their investment returns for living expenses will likely want to choose a different mixture of assets, keeping in mind the Andersons, whose "safe" strategy wasn't really so safe.

## MOON SHOT MONEY: WHEN YOU CAN'T RESIST SPECULATING

For many people picking stocks is a game, a hobby, an avocation, something to get them up in the morning to check the newspaper or Internet to see how they've done. If you insist on scratching that itch, set aside a small percentage of your portfolio to invest in individual speculative stocks—not more than 10 percent of your portfolio. That's what I do. I call it my moon shot money. Or, to mix metaphors, I try to hit home runs with that money. It's fun to play around with and gives me a chance once in a while to pick a stock that can appreciate more dramatically than most assets I maintain in my investment portfolio. But trust me, I don't rely on my moon shot investments to provide for my retirement or my children's education. If one of my moon shot picks does well, I put the profits back into my general portfolio and maintain the asset allocation I have chosen.

I don't keep trying to hit home runs with all of my gains. Home runs are nice, but singles and doubles produce a lot of wins.

## STEP 3: SELECT YOUR INVESTMENTS

After you have established a strategy based on where you want to go and determined the ideal asset allocation to get you there, the next step is to select individual investments within your portfolio. As you build your portfolio you determine which investments in each asset class will give you the ideal mixture of assets to reduce risk and enhance return.

Finally, you are ready to select individual investments, such as buying shares in Microsoft or General Electric. While most investors jump straight to selecting investments, it really must come after a great deal of planning and careful consideration.

Within each asset class you want to pursue competitive returns for that asset class. In other words, once you have determined that you want to invest in a particular class of assets that gives you diversification and negative correlation, you want to find specific investments that provide returns equal to or better than the average within that class. But be sure you are comparing apples to apples. Don't compare returns in one asset class with those of another. If you do, you will be tempted to throw out your strategy and just chase the highest returns, which means you may in turn be chased by the highest risk. Stick to your plan and accept the best returns you can get in a balanced portfolio.

### Equity Investing: Appreciation, Growth of Principal

You should be well aware of the risks of investing in stocks, and I hope you are also now aware of the consistency of historical returns over several years. But before you begin selecting stocks to meet your asset allocation criteria, you need to consider more than market risk—the risk that your stocks will decline in value. Also keep in mind the following risks inherent in equity investing:

- **Currency risk.** Currency risk is the risk that the value of currencies will fluctuate widely. For example, if the euro declines against the U.S. dollar and you own a European stock fund, the euro, when translated back into dollars, could have a negative impact on fund performance.

■ **Economic risk.** This is risk associated with economic uncertainty. For example, the recent U.S. economic downturn had a dire effect on many cyclical business such as airlines and steel, where earnings fell below levels of prior years.

■ **Financial credit risk.** Inherent in all business is the uncertainty of the future of the corporation issuing a security. For example, if a company finds itself in financial straits, it may not be able to meet its payments to its bondholders.

■ **Inflation risk.** Inflation risk is the danger that rising prices will cut into a company's margins. Do they have pricing power—the ability to raise their prices as the cost of their materials increases? This is especially true of companies that rely heavily on a single commodity. Airlines, for instance, are impacted greatly by changes in oil prices, which hit all-time highs in 2004.

■ **Interest rate risk.** Changes in interest rates may hurt a company's performance. Do they need to go to credit markets often for working capital? Does the company need to borrow money regularly to build or update new facilities?

■ **Management risk.** This risk relates to the quality and stability of a corporation's management and its impact on business and security prices. For example, poor management choices can have an effect on the company's underlying security or share prices.

### The Most Common Method of Stock Ownership: Mutual Funds

Many people invest in equities primarily through mutual funds, which is a much easier way to acquire diversity in your portfolio than buying all the stocks yourself. Very few people actually have the assets to diversify strictly through ownership of individual stocks. Mutual funds, therefore, should be a significant part of almost every portfolio.

One of the basic decisions facing many fund investors is whether to buy a load fund or a no-load fund. A load fund has a sales charge that is paid either at investment or withdrawal; thus the terms "front load" and "back load." Many investment advisers glibly discourage people from buying load funds, but I'm not so quick to disqualify them.

I recommend mutual funds that I think will provide the greatest net return in their asset class. I do not disqualify a fund because it has a load, or sales commission, if it provides the likelihood of superior performance. That said, I recommend load funds only for longer-term investments. In the shorter term, the load may dilute the net return on your investment. Over time, however, some load funds may be worth it. I would recommend no-load funds, for example, if you have a teenager who is saving for college. Because you'll need the money in three or four years, a no-load fund makes more sense. Anytime you anticipate redeeming shares within a few years, look at no-load funds. If you plan to leave the money invested for a longer time, find the best fund regardless of "load."

I am often asked what I would recommend people do with underperforming mutual funds. It's hard to give one simple answer. There is so much I need to know to give good advice. For instance, is the fund performing poorly against the market as a whole? Or is it underperforming similar funds? Does the fund represent an asset class that you want in your portfolio? Does it provide the asset allocation your strategy dictates?

How long you hold funds that don't perform well depends on why you bought them and where they fit in your overall strategy. If you carefully selected funds to provide good asset allocation, I would recommend that you be patient—with one caveat. Compare the performance of your funds with others in the same asset class, such as large-cap growth, international, or small-cap value. If your funds consistently underperform similar funds that buy the same type of assets and have the same investment philosophy, then you might consider changing funds. If your funds are not performing well, but neither are others in that asset class—and it's an asset class you want in your portfolio—I would hang on to them.

## STEP 4: MANAGE YOUR INVESTMENTS

You are not done yet. You have a brilliant strategy in place, asset classes that suit your personal goals to a T, a portfolio you are quite sure will enhance your returns over many years, and carefully researched investments within your chosen asset classes. Now you sit back and watch your portfolio grow, right? I hate to break it to you, but investing doesn't work that way. Perhaps the hardest work is done, but successful investors never just walk away from their investments and let them manage themselves. If left untended, portfolios have a bad habit of going seriously off course. Any investment plan requires continuous management to achieve long-term success.

## Continuous Management and Rebalancing

Your asset allocation was just right when you started your investment plan, but what happens after six months or a year? Your goal was to balance asset classes that tend to perform differently as a group, so if one performs poorly, the others are likely to perform better. Over time that should increase average returns. But if one asset class performs better than others, it changes the percentage of your investment in each. The time has come to rebalance your portfolio.

Rebalancing means buying and selling assets to bring the percentages of assets in your portfolio back in line with your asset allocation strategy. However, rebalancing your portfolio to maintain your asset allocation can be complicated, especially in taxable accounts. Capital gains taxes, surrender charges, and back-end loads on mutual funds may make rebalancing too expensive to do quarterly. If this is the case, I would recommend rebalancing once a year. It's still in your interest to rebalance your account at least annually, even if you incur some costs. Of course, if your assets are in tax-deferred plans, you don't have to worry about capital gains. The ease of rebalancing is one advantage of variable annuities and variable universal life insurance, which I will discuss later. Those products usually make it easy to transfer money from one subaccount to another within the plan at no cost.

Because I consider asset allocation and, therefore, rebalancing the linchpins of successful investing, I want to present three strategies to illustrate the concepts hypothetically. For our purposes, we'll choose two imaginary mutual funds, one a "large cap" fund and another a "small cap" fund. We'll start with $10,000 in each, because that represents a rudimentary form of asset allocation, and see what happens.

Let's say that in the first year, the large cap fund doubles in value, and the small cap fund loses half its value. Clearly, those are extreme returns used to make a point. Few funds will double in value or lose half their value in a year—although both extremes have actually occurred in the last decade. Then, for the purposes of comparing strategies, we'll say that the funds reverse performance the second year: The small cap fund doubles in value, and the large cap fund loses half its value.

### Strategy #1: Buy and Hold

The first strategy, if we can call it that, is to "buy and hold." You'll hear many investment advisers and TV talking heads recommend that you buy a stock or mutual fund and put it away, ignore it. That may be a fine idea if you're looking at an isolated equity investment. But I hope I have convinced you that looking at any investment outside of your overall portfolio is not a good idea. Table 3.5 indicates what happens to our investments if we buy and hold—in other words, if we don't manage our investments at all.

### TABLE 3.5. YOUR INVESTMENT WHEN YOU BUY AND HOLD

|  | Large Cap Fund | Small Cap Fund | Total Value | Return (in %) |
|---|---|---|---|---|
| Investment | $10,000 | $10,000 | $20,000 | |
| 1st year | x    -0.5 | x     2 | | |
| Value | $5,000 | $20,000 | $25,000 | 25 |
| Hold | $5,000 | $20,000 | | |
| 2nd year | x     2 | x    -0.5 | | |
| Value | $10,000 | $10,000 | $20,000 | 0 |

The problem with buying and holding is that it does not maintain an optimal asset allocation. Investments that perform well become a larger percentage of your portfolio. In this example, after the first year, clearly your asset allocation is skewed. You now have only 20 percent of your assets in large cap and 80 percent in small cap investments. That is not the asset allocation you chose at the start, so why would you accept that asset allocation after one year? Your approach is out of whack if you follow a buy-and-hold strategy instead of rebalancing. The portfolios of people who follow this course can become overweighted in a few asset classes. If the market turns against those asset classes, those portfolios can go downhill fast. It is much better in my opinion to manage your portfolio continuously with regular rebalancing to maintain the asset allocation you want.

### Strategy # 2: Chase the Hot Fund

The second option—I hesitate to call it a strategy because emotions have taken control of investing—is to chase the hot fund. Unfortunately, this is typical investing behavior. You think that because the value fund is doing so well, you should put all of your money into that fund. Table 3.6 illustrates what happens if you do.

#### TABLE 3.6. YOUR INVESTMENT WHEN YOU CHASE THE HOT FUND

|  | Large Cap Fund | Small Cap Fund | Total Value | Return (in %) |
|---|---|---|---|---|
| Investment | $10,000 | $10,000 | $20,000 |  |
| 1st year | x   -0.5 | x     2 |  |  |
| Value | $5,000 | $20,000 | $25,000 | 25 |
| Chase | $-5,000 | $+5,000 |  |  |
| Value | $   0 | $25,000 |  |  |
| 2nd year | x     2 | x   -0.5 |  |  |
| Value | $   0 | $12,500 | $12,500 | -37.5 |

What this decision represents is complete abandonment of your asset allocation, and in this hypothetical example it would cost you. Too many people try too hard to figure out when to get into and out of markets. Morningstar, Inc., a company that tracks performance of mutual funds, monitored the performance of 219 growth funds for five years ending in 1994 and then researched how well the investors in those funds had done. Over those five years the average aggregate performance of the funds was 12.5 percent appreciation per year. That's a five-year performance most people would be happy with. Were the investors in the funds during that time happy with the performance? Not likely! Why? The actual return for investors in those funds for that period of time averaged minus 2.2 percent.[2]

The average investor in the funds lost money in the same time period that the funds were appreciating in value. How could that be? Because more investors jumped on board when the funds were doing well and then got off when they were doing badly. Hot funds had attracted investors, but when they cooled off, investors abandoned them for other hot funds. The investors in those funds, on average, were buying high and selling low—exactly the opposite of every investor's intention.

### Strategy #3: Rebalance

As Table 3.7 illustrates, the third and best option is to rebalance the portfolio after the first year, bringing your asset allocation back in line with what you wanted from the start, namely, 50 percent in each type of fund.

#### TABLE 3.7. THE BENEFITS OF REBALANCING

|  | Large Cap Fund | Small Cap Fund | Total Value | Return (in %) |
|---|---|---|---|---|
| Investment | $10,000 | $10,000 | $20,000 | |
| 1st year | x   -0.5 | x   2 | | |
| Value | $5,000 | $20,000 | $25,000 | 25 |
| Rebalance | $12,500 | $12,500 | | |
| 2nd year | x   2 | x   -0.5 | | |
| Value | $25,000 | $6,250 | $31,250 | 56.25 |

---

[2] Securities Data Publishing, June 1, 1998.

As I said, the hypothetical returns in this example have been exaggerated to make a point. In reality, there is no way to predict returns, and the differences in the strategies are likely to be less dramatic than shown here. But I hope you see the point: If you maintain the asset allocation you deem optimal, rebalancing your portfolio regularly, you are less likely to fall victim to the shifts in market sentiment and to wild swings in performance. Keep in mind what I said at the start of this discussion: Our objective is to achieve optimal long-term performance rather than pursue the highest possible returns at any one point in time. Rebalancing is an essential component of long-term success.

### Rebalancing Applies across the Board

Rebalancing applies to your entire portfolio of investments, whatever that may be, whether stocks, bonds, real estate, or other investments. I used mutual funds to demonstrate rebalancing in the preceding example largely because they are the most common form of equity investing. Investors achieve diversification much more easily through mutual funds than they can through owning individual stocks.

I would caution, however, that rebalancing mutual funds requires an additional step. You also have to monitor your funds to be sure that they are giving you the asset allocation you thought you were getting. In the competition for investors, fund managers are tempted to fudge their investment discipline a bit in pursuit of stocks that are hot, even if they are slightly outside the stated investment "style" of the fund. This "style drift" is very common. So you need to monitor the buy and sell decisions of your funds to ensure that they are not drifting into asset classes that don't meet your asset allocation target. If a fund begins to invest in assets outside its professed targets, your asset allocation may be skewed.

---

■ **EXAMPLE:** You choose to allocate some of your investments to a "value" mutual fund that invests in companies that are considered undervalued. But then you learn that the fund managers have begun to invest in some faster "growth" companies to improve their returns. That should not please you if you chose that fund precisely because it did *not* invest in faster-growth companies, which are often more volatile. You may already own shares in another fund that has growth as its stated objective. Now you have more of your assets than you might have wanted invested in "growth" companies. During your annual rebalancing you may want to shift your funds allocated to "value" investments to another value fund that has maintained its discipline.

---

The only way to check for this style drift is to read carefully the reports that your fund sends you. You need to examine closely the type of stocks the fund holds to be sure that they are staying true to their goals. Style drift became very common in the late 1990s as managers struggled to achieve higher returns as some funds—especially tech funds—soared. The greater danger in the early years of the millennium is that managers of more aggressive funds may pursue more of a value strategy than you would like in order to avoid losses in the same type of stocks that once were over-pursued.

## Timing Your Investments

In these days of detailed and ubiquitous reporting on stock markets one of the great dangers facing individual investors is the temptation to time the market. Never forget that *time, not timing,* is the investor's greatest ally.

If your biggest concern is *when* to invest your money, you're worrying about the wrong thing. Investing a set amount each month is fine as a *saving* strategy, but as an *investing* strategy, it's flawed. The best time to invest is as soon as you can. If you have created your asset allocation strategy, invest now!

But many people don't follow this advice, or they try to beat the market by picking the right time to invest. The two most popular methods of trying to beat the market that way are dollar cost averaging and market timing.

### Dollar Cost Averaging Is Overrated!

Many investment advisers suggest that one way to get the best of all worlds in investing is to "dollar cost average" your investment. Dollar cost averaging is an excellent way to invest regularly. It requires you to set aside money each month for investing. But I do not recommend dollar cost averaging if you have a lump sum of money to invest. In most cases, the sooner you invest, the better.

Dollar cost averaging is a nugget of misguided "wisdom" that seems to be promoted primarily by mutual fund companies—although it has its advocates among TV financial news readers whose qualification for giving investment advice seems to be good hair or a friendly smile.

Here's how dollar cost averaging works: Rather than investing money in stocks or mutual funds in one lump sum, you invest a set amount of money every month. The thinking is that since the dollar amount remains consistent, the investor acquires more shares when prices are low and fewer when share prices are high. The supposed advantage is that the average price the consumer pays is less than the average price at which the security is offered.[3]

In successive months we invest $100 into a mutual fund. The first month the share price is $10. Therefore, we buy 10 shares. The second month, the share price is only $5. Consequently, we buy 20 shares. To calculate the average share price of the fund at the time we made our purchases we add the prices the fund was offered at and divide by the number of purchases ($10 + $5 ÷ 2 = $7.5). The average share price is $7.50. However, we spent $200 to acquire 30 shares, meaning our average purchase price per share was only $6.67 (200 ÷ 30).

That seems like a pretty good deal—if that's as far as you care to go in analyzing your costs. But the fact remains that your 30 shares are not worth $6.67 a share; they are now worth only $5 each. If the share price

---

[3] "Periodic investment plans do not assure a profit or protect against loss in a declining market. Dollar cost averaging involves continuous investment in securities regardless of the fluctuating price of such securities. Investors should carefully consider their ability to continue their investments during periods of low price levels."

then bounces back up, your purchase at $5 a share will look good. But what if it goes down further? Then would you not have been better off to have just kept your money in the bank until you *knew* share prices would go up? But if you did know the price would go up from $5, why did you buy only 20 shares at that price?

Conversely, what if the original share price increased by 50 percent from one month to the next, instead of decreasing by that amount—and continued to go up every month after that? Then dollar cost averaging wouldn't look so good, either. If you had had the money to invest, you would have been far better off investing it all at the beginning.

The people who recommend dollar cost averaging say, "You don't know what the market will do, and you're crazy to guess, so hedge your bets by investing a little at a time. You won't miss out on long rallies or get hurt as badly by a big crash."

It is true that markets are as likely to go up as down on any given day, but we do know that over time markets have consistently gone up. Although, again, past performance does not guarantee future results, the average annual increase for the S&P 500 historically is over 12 percent. It seems that if you really want to play the law of averages, you would want your money in the market sooner rather than later.

Although the popular perception of markets is that they increase steadily and plummet suddenly, research provides an interesting counterpoint. The most precipitous collapses of markets have occurred on single infamous days such as Black Monday in 1929 and Black Tuesday in 1987. But research demonstrates that one-day rallies can have an enormous impact on overall performance as well.

If you take just the best 30 days away from the 2,500-plus trading days in the 10-year period from 1995 to 2004, the average annual return drops—from 10.19 percent to -2.04 percent per year. (See Table 3.8.) That's if you missed, on average, only three trading days a year for that 10-year period! Dollar cost averagers are going to miss some of these big days, too, just as they avoid some of the big down days. Dollar cost averaging is guessing with a hedge, but with no real rationale at all for the guessing. Perhaps a consistent investment plan such as dollar cost averaging gives some people the illusion of an investment strategy where none really exists.

---

### TABLE 3.8. DON'T MISS THE GOOD DAYS

| | S&P 500 Annualized Returns (in %) |
|---|---|
| 1/1/1995–12/31/2004 (2,519 trading days) | 10.19 |
| Minus the 10 best days | 5.11 |
| Minus the 20 best days | 1.26 |
| Minus the 30 best days | -2.04 |

Historically, if you miss out on the few days or months each year when stock prices rise sharply, you will experience much lower long-term returns.

---

*Source: Wealth Enhancement Advisory Services, LLC.*

*The S&P 500 is an unmanaged index; investors cannot invest directly in an index.*

*Remember: Past performance does not guarantee future results.*

---

So why do people recommend dollar cost averaging as an investment strategy? Mutual fund companies stand to gain the most if you follow the strategy. Of course, it would be in their interest, too, if you invested as much as you could with them as soon as you could. But a fund company also wants you to become a regular investor. They want you to get in the habit of adding to your account every month, and they don't want you to be scared off by a little downturn in the market.

Dollar cost averaging is a wonderful way to keep people invested even if markets are down for a time. It's a theory that encourages people to look at the bright side of bad markets: "Wow, look how cheaply I'm buying shares this month!" I can't prove it, but I would bet that people who dollar cost average are less likely to withdraw their money from funds when stocks plunge or those funds perform poorly.

Redemptions from mutual funds can get very expensive for those funds if enough shareholders redeem their shares at the same time. If mutual funds do not have enough cash reserves to pay off redemptions, they have to sell assets—and being forced to sell assets when prices are low is not very good for overall performance. Mutual funds are more profitable for their managers if people invest steadily and consistently over a long period of time, instead of jumping into and out of the funds, even with larger sums.

Dollar cost averaging is a defensive strategy—a saving strategy—not an efficiency strategy. It is for *accumulating* assets, not *allocating* assets already accumulated. It has the potential to work fine for saving $50, $100, $200 a month—and if you don't have any investments or savings, I would recommend that you start doing that. But if you already have $5,000, $10,000, or even $20,000 available, it is more efficient to invest that money in one lump sum as soon as possible—properly allocated, of course.

## Outthinking and Underperforming

The more aggressive method of trying to outguess the market doesn't even present the illusion of strategy—it's pure gambling. It's called market timing, which means putting money into or pulling it out of stocks based on whether one thinks the market is going up or down in the short term or even on a given day—or hour!

Those who reduce investing to guessing market moves are making investing far more complicated and potentially far less rewarding than it should be. You probably know people, as I do, who have picked the right time to make an investment. "I bought the sucker and it went up 30 percent the next week," they gloat. They probably mention it at all only because it was such a rarity in their investment experience. But, like me, I bet you know very few people, if any, who have consistently picked the right time to make an investment. It's tough to replicate good luck. It's tough to know when those three big days each year are going to fall.

If market timing were really so simple that your uncle Wilbur could master it, don't you think some Wall Street company with millions to spend on computers and software and mathematicians would eventually figure it out, too? Well, they haven't, and many high-flying companies and stock pickers have had their comeuppance in bankruptcy court when their theories crashed along with their portfolios.

## What Are You Waiting For?

I had a frustrating experience in the fall of 1998 with an investor trying to time the market. One component of the plan I prepared for her was an improved allocation of her assets. Before implementing the plan, however, and buying the assets I recommended, she wanted to discuss it with her brother. That was perfectly understandable, so I agreed to call her in a couple of days to answer any questions that might have come up in their discussion of the proposed plan.

I discovered that she was reticent to implement the plan at that time. You see, since mid-July of that year the market had been in a tailspin. The S&P 500 had depreciated about 20 percent. She was troubled by the markets at that time and wanted to wait until the markets "stabilized" before investing. By November, the market had regained virtually everything it had lost from July to October—and the potential investor was still standing on the sidelines, waiting for some magical point at which she would know that the markets had stabilized.

She had passed on the opportunity to buy stocks at about a 15 percent discount from where the price had been earlier in the year and to where they had returned while she was still waiting.

If you were considering buying something for $100 and you were confident it was a good purchase, and then you saw that it was on sale for $85, would you refuse to buy it just because the price had dropped? Of course not. You wouldn't be able to get out your checkbook fast enough. Conversely, if instead of going on sale, the item's price were raised to $115, would you think, "It's even more valuable now, so it's an even better buy"? Unfortunately, when it comes to investments, most people respond like that. They react emotionally, not logically.

One of the greatest benefits of a good financial plan is that it gives you something concrete to cling to when your emotions are about to carry you away. A timeless movie, *Casablanca*, gave us a timeless song that contains a line all investors should keep in mind. Play it, Sam. "You must remember this, a kiss is still a kiss, a sigh is just a sigh, the fundamental things apply as time goes by."

I do not see any changes in the fundamentals of investing and markets that came out of the supercharged markets of the 1990s, even though the decade did give us an unprecedented bull market. That was followed by three years of terrible equity performance, but pretty good returns on bonds. Anything is possible in financial markets. Some people think that the fundamentals have changed, first for the best, then for the worst. I doubt that opinions on either extreme will be correct. I think the fundamental things apply—and will continue to for years.

Although there is no guarantee, I would expect that the average annual returns on money invested in equities will remain not too far from the historical average of between 10 and 12 percent. That means at some point we will certainly have a couple of years of lower returns and slower growth, then some good years. The investors who will be hurt the worst will be those who have no strategy, but just chase hot stocks. Investors who have proper asset allocation in their portfolios will have the potential to see a return on their investments that could exceed what they would be getting if they were totally invested in fixed-rate investments. Your asset allocation may give a prominent place to equity investments, but it will also balance those investments with others that are expected to have a negative correlation.

In truth, dollar cost averaging is an attempt at market timing—a pursuit better left to gamblers than investors. Of course, many in the financial industry encourage it because it commits people to investing money regularly and trading more often, which can generate commissions. But what may be good for them is not necessarily good for you. Invest regularly, but if you have more to invest than usual don't hold some of it back to dollar cost average. Put your money to work for you as soon as you can, but be sure to follow your investment strategy. Don't succumb to the siren song of whatever is hot at the moment. A friend likes to say that there are three things he won't chase: buses, women, and stocks. He is happily married and a successful investor.

Here's a personal anecdote about time—not timing—in terms of stock market investments. My wife and I got married in June of 1987. Shortly after we got married, I received a bonus on my job at that time and we decided to put that money, roughly $10,000, into a mutual fund. Now keep in mind, we were a newly married couple, and my wife was fresh out of college. Times were tight. We were wondering from month to month if we were going to have enough money to pay the rent. For one of the few times in our nearly 20 years of marriage I actually won the debate, and we put the money in a mutual fund. My wife wanted to leave it in the bank to have it more accessible. But I pointed out that I felt it would perform better in the stock market and would still be accessible if we really needed it.

A few months after our marriage and shortly after we invested this money, the Dow took a big hit on October 19, 1987. Our mutual fund fell from $10,000 to just under $6,000, a whopping decrease of over 40 percent. The question was, "What should we do now?" Should we take our $6,000 and put it in a bank? That's what my wife wanted to do. If we had done that and if we had averaged a 6 percent annual return over 15 years it would have accrued to roughly $15,000. We did not do that. We could have waited until we had some recovery in the market and gained back what we lost and got back to $10,000 and then put that in a CD at 6 percent. Then today we would have a little over $20,000. We didn't do that, either. What we did was hold on. We assumed it would be a long-term investment and we would only tap it in the short term if we were desperate. We sat tight and the mutual fund is now worth more than $60,000. So the moral of the story is that the equity investment, the mutual fund, over time significantly outperformed the fixed-interest alternative investments, although one could argue that we incurred a higher degree of risk. But, as I have noted, there is more than one way to measure risk.

## Start Investing Early

The key to any investment plan is to start soon. No time is better than now. If time is your greatest ally, and it is, the longer you invest, the better off you will be.

Let's assume that Jill at age 21 starts to put $4,000 per year into a Roth IRA with no income tax consequences whatsoever. She does this for only 10 years and stops. Now why she stops doesn't really matter, but she does. And let's assume that she can earn 10 percent each and every year on her account. So she starts at 21, invests for 10 years until age 30, then stops. The account continues to accrue until she's 65. The total value of her account at age 65, earning 10 percent every year, would be $1,970,674. (See Table 3.9.)

Now, her identical twin, Jack, doesn't start to fund his Roth IRA until he's 31. Jack puts away the same $4,000 per year, and he puts it away in the same investment Jill does and earns the same 10 percent each and every year. Furthermore, Jack makes these contributions for 35 years—from 31 until 65. So Jack's total amount of contributions is $140,000 over a 35-year period of time. Jill's total contribution was $40,000 over a 10-year period of time. Jack invested $100,000 more than Jill, but he started 10 years later.

His account at age 65 accrues to $1,192,507, or $778,167 less than Jill's. The moral of the story: Start saving as soon as you can, as much as you can, as consistently as you can. Don't wait. Pay yourself first and you may be rewarded long-term. There is a huge cost in waiting.

TABLE 3.9. THE BENEFITS OF INVESTING EARLY

| Age | Jill's Contribution | Total Balance at End of Year | Jack's Contribution | Total Balance at End of Year |
|---|---|---|---|---|
| 21 | $4,000 | $4,400 | - | - |
| 22 | 4,000 | 9,240 | - | - |
| 23 | 4,000 | 14,564 | - | - |
| 24 | 4,000 | 20,420 | - | - |
| 25 | 4,000 | 26,862 | - | - |
| 26 | 4,000 | 33,949 | - | - |
| 27 | 4,000 | 41,744 | - | - |
| 28 | 4,000 | 50,318 | - | - |
| 29 | 4,000 | 59,750 | - | - |
| 30 | 4,000 | 70,125 | - | - |
| 31 | - | 77,137 | $4,000 | $4,400 |
| 32 | - | 84,851 | 4,000 | 9,240 |
| 33 | - | 93,336 | 4,000 | 14,564 |
| 34 | - | 102,670 | 4,000 | 20,420 |
| 35 | - | 112,936 | 4,000 | 26,862 |
| 36 | - | 124,230 | 4,000 | 33,949 |
| 37 | - | 136,653 | 4,000 | 41,744 |
| 38 | - | 150,318 | 4,000 | 50,318 |
| 39 | - | 165,350 | 4,000 | 59,750 |
| 40 | - | 181,885 | 4,000 | 70,125 |
| 41 | - | 200,074 | 4,000 | 81,537 |
| 42 | - | 220,081 | 4,000 | 94,091 |
| 43 | - | 242,089 | 4,000 | 107,900 |

TABLE 3.9. THE BENEFITS OF INVESTING EARLY (CONT.)

| Age | Jill's Contribution | Total Balance at End of Year | Jack's Contribution | Total Balance at End of Year |
|---|---|---|---|---|
| 44 | - | 266,298 | 4,000 | 123,090 |
| 45 | - | 292,928 | 4,000 | 139,799 |
| 46 | - | 322,221 | 4,000 | 158,179 |
| 47 | - | 354,443 | 4,000 | 178,397 |
| 48 | - | 389,887 | 4,000 | 200,636 |
| 49 | - | 428,876 | 4,000 | 225,100 |
| 50 | - | 471,764 | 4,000 | 252,010 |
| 51 | - | 518,940 | 4,000 | 281,611 |
| 52 | - | 570,834 | 4,000 | 314,172 |
| 53 | - | 627,917 | 4,000 | 349,989 |
| 54 | - | 690,709 | 4,000 | 389,388 |
| 55 | - | 759,780 | 4,000 | 432,727 |
| 56 | - | 835,758 | 4,000 | 480,400 |
| 57 | - | 919,334 | 4,000 | 532,840 |
| 58 | - | 1,011,267 | 4,000 | 590,524 |
| 59 | - | 1,112,394 | 4,000 | 653,976 |
| 60 | - | 1,223,634 | 4,000 | 723,774 |
| 61 | - | 1,345,997 | 4,000 | 800,551 |
| 62 | - | 1,480,597 | 4,000 | 885,006 |
| 63 | - | 1,628,656 | 4,000 | 977,907 |
| 64 | - | 1,791,522 | 4,000 | 1,080,097 |
| 65 | - | 1,970,674 | 4,000 | 1,192,507 |

Note: Assumes that contributions are made in January; also assumes 10 percent growth annually.

## Timing Your Withdrawals or Adjustments to Your Portfolio

One of the great mistakes of investing is that people plan only for the accumulation of investment assets, but not for the distribution of investment assets. I will address this issue in more detail in Chapter 10, "Planning for Retirement," but it also has a huge impact on your strategy and the timing of your investment.

As a general rule, I recommend that anytime you are within five years of needing to use the money in your investment accounts you shift your money into more conservative, lower-risk asset classes. Does this contradict my argument that exposure to stocks is necessary for most people? Not at all. You will recall that I stated that over longer periods of time, such as 10 years, stock markets have usually outperformed fixed-interest investments. Over time equities generally do better. But equities are subject to greater fluctuation in shorter periods of time. Inevitably stock markets do go through good and bad years. Some years equities most likely will lose money. If you don't have the time to wait out those dips in the market, they can pose more risk than I think is acceptable. That is why I advise anyone intending to spend money in an investment account within five years to shift at least some, if not all, of that money into assets that will not depreciate.

This applies to investing for almost any purpose. If you're investing to pay for college for your child, when your child reaches high school you should shift your investments into more conservative vehicles. If you intend to retire within five years and you will need income from your investments to pay living expenses, you should begin to shift some of your investments as well. The mistake many people make, however, is shifting into more conservative investments before they should.

---

▪ **EXAMPLE:** Let's say you are 55 and plan to retire in 10 years. You have 50 percent of your retirement investments in aggressive mutual funds. Is that too much? For many people in that situation, 50 percent of their equity investment in aggressive funds would not be too much—if they are allocated appropriately—because those funds have the greatest potential for appreciation and people of that age still have a long time horizon. Markets have ups and downs. A dip in the market is no reason to abandon a successful strategy, just as a spike in the market would not justify it. However, when people are within five years of needing that money for living expenses, I would recommend that they begin to reduce the percentage of their portfolio in aggressive funds, but not abandon them.

---

■ **EXAMPLE:** Let's say that you are 65 and you are already retired. You have 50 percent of your retirement investments in aggressive mutual funds, but you do not need income from those funds to pay your living expenses. You have other assets from which you pay your bills. Do you have too much risk in your retirement account? No. If you do not need to spend some of that money within five years, there would be no good reason not to continue pursuing greater returns with that money. If you will not likely need to use that money, those funds will probably be passed on to your heirs through your estate. The time horizon for those investments could be quite long, sufficient at least to weather the shorter-term ups and downs of equity markets and increase the size of your financial legacy.

---

I hope you see from these two examples that age itself has little to do with how you adjust your portfolio. The only factor that is important is your intended use for the money—your investment strategy.

## HOW DO YOU HOLD YOUR ASSETS?

I would like to address one final aspect of investing that is rife with false assumptions, myths, and misunderstandings. It is a subject that is very important to me, because my views are contrary to conventional wisdom. Many people are not using their money as efficiently as they could because they have accepted popular, but misguided, prejudices about three types of portfolio vehicles—the types of accounts in which they hold their assets. The first is tax-deferred retirement accounts, which may be inefficient if they are your only source of retirement investment. The second is variable universal life insurance, and the third is variable annuities—the scorned stepsisters of investing—which are too often overlooked as efficient investment vehicles.

## Myth #1: Tax-Deferred Accounts Are the Best Way to Invest for Retirement

This is one of the most pervasive myths in the world of personal finance, and for many people it is one of the more detrimental to their financial health. Tax-deferred accounts are for many people *not* the most efficient way to invest for retirement.

Tax-deferred accounts are all of those that permit a tax deferment on investments from the time the money is earned as income until it is withdrawn. These accounts include 401(k)s, IRAs, SEPs, and Keoughs.

Contributions to a tax-deferred account may be an excellent starting point if you are planning for retirement. But they do present some problems. For one, you are locking up your money for a long time. You cannot withdraw those funds without a 10 percent penalty until you are 59½. If you are saving to buy a home or if you have consumer debt that needs to be paid off, those may be wiser shorter-term uses of your money. The other potential drawback to tax-deferred funds lies in the assumption that you are deferring taxes until you are retired, have less income, and may be in a lower tax bracket. That may be a false assumption. Tax rates are at historically low levels, especially for those in higher income brackets. Are they likely to stay as low as they are now? Not with the deficits our federal and state governments are currently running. The quickest fix for deficits is to raise tax rates. You may be deferring taxes until they are higher than they are now.

Read more about the potential hazards of tax-deferred accounts in Chapter 10, "Planning for Retirement," where I lay out the pluses and the minuses of tax-deferred accounts in greater detail.

## Myth #2: Life Insurance Is Not an Efficient Investment

Life insurance can be much more than an important way to protect your family. It can also be an important part of an efficient *investment* strategy. The primary complaint about life insurance as an investment is that the cost is too high, that investing through life insurance is more expensive than buying mutual funds. While life insurance does have additional cost, I believe cost is not the primary issue when dealing with any investment. Our focus should be on value instead of cost. For many people the value of life insurance investments fully justifies the cost.

The prejudice against life insurance is based on the life insurance of your parents' time. Life insurance has changed dramatically in recent decades, and with those changes it has become an investment vehicle you should consider. Of course, I'm referring to variable universal life insurance (VUL), a type of permanent life insurance. A VUL is a quite different animal than term insurance, which is a policy you take out just to cover your life for a certain number of years, but has no investment value.

Permanent life insurance does have higher costs than mutual funds, but those costs may be justified by greater returns in some cases. Permanent life insurance also offers many tax advantages. Policy payouts to your beneficiaries are often not taxable, unlike IRA investments, which usually are taxable.

For a more detailed discussion of life insurance I suggest you read closely the pages I've devoted to the subject in Chapter 8, "Planning for Emergencies."

## Myth #3: Variable Annuities Are Too Expensive

Variable annuities, the second scorned stepsister of investing, have taken a bad rap. They are one of the most widely used investment vehicles by financial advisers, yet they are roundly criticized by many self-appointed media experts on personal finance. How can we explain this contradiction?

I am not alone in my belief that variable annuities can be part of a very efficient strategy for investors. My view of variable annuities has been influenced by the writings of Dr. Jonathan Huggard, a lawyer, certified financial planner, and faculty member of North Carolina State University. I have changed my thinking on variable annuities over the years in large measure due to his research and writing. If you want more information on variable annuities, I highly recommend Dr. Huggard's book *Investing in Variable Annuities*.

Just to be clear: I put my money where my mouth is. I personally own variable annuities. Why? Because they make good financial sense. They provide value in spite of their costs.

## Variable Annuities in Detail

Let's investigate the criticism of variable annuities—and why I believe those criticisms may have little merit for many investors.

The term "annuity" comes from the Latin word for "annual" and generally refers to any circumstance in which principal and interest are liquidated through a series of regular periodic payments over time. A tax-deferred annuity is an annuity in which taxation of interest or other growth in the account is deferred until distributions are actually made. A tax-deferred annuity is essentially a contract between an annuity company and a contract owner or an investor. In a typical situation the investor contributes funds to the annuity, the money is put into the contract and allowed to grow over a period of time. At a future date, distributions can be made from the contract either in the form of annuitization (an annual payout) or as general periodic distributions. Either way, distributions are taxed as ordinary income.

### Apples and Oranges

Variable annuities are frequently compared to mutual funds primarily because the mutual fund–like subaccounts in the variable annuity are often managed by the same people who manage mutual funds. Variable annuity contracts offer no guarantees and no specific investment return to the investor. The funds are contributed by the investor or contract owner and then placed in a potential variety of special annuity subaccount choices. Within these subaccounts, the owner can invest the funds in a wide variety of options. These equity- or stock-based subaccount options should perform comparably to their mutual fund cousins.

Variable annuities are criticized when compared to direct investment in mutual funds for two reasons. First, variable annuities are more costly. Second, they have a deferred sales charge, surrender penalty, or back-end load. Pick your term, but they all mean the same thing: If the annuity is withdrawn prior to a time specified in the contract, usually three to seven years, there is a penalty. In other words, if you don't leave your money in the variable annuity for a certain length of time you don't get full value. This feature obviously reduces the liquidity of a variable annuity when compared to mutual fund accounts that can be closed without penalty.

There is no arguing the first criticism: Variable annuities include fees that make them more expensive than mutual funds. I would submit, however, that comparing variable annuities to mutual funds is not accurate. Investors in mutual funds or families of funds usually have limited choices. Transferring money to other funds or families may involve transfer fees and more labor. Variable annuities and their mutual fund–like subaccounts provide access to a multitude of different money managers and a multitude of different asset classes among which you can shift money easily and without fees.

A more accurate comparison, in my opinion, for variable annuities would be brokerage wrap accounts or managed money services, in which an investor pays a professional money manager to select mutual funds and/or individual securities on his or her behalf and mix and match as the financial adviser deems appropriate to try to enhance returns and reduce risks using different investments in a variety of different asset classes. If we use that comparison the cost disadvantage actually disappears, since the managed money or brokerage wrap account fees would be comparable to the total cost to the investor in a variable annuity.

So, if we make the right comparison—not mutual funds, but a managed money or brokerage wrap account—the cost disadvantage disappears. Ironically, the same financial commentators who criticize variable annuities as too costly do not have the same criticism for managed money or brokerage wrap accounts, even though the cost is roughly the same.

The second disadvantage—reduced liquidity—certainly can be a disadvantage for many investors. With brokerage wrap accounts, which as I noted is a more apt comparison than mutual funds, you can withdraw your funds from the account on very short notice without penalty. It should be noted that some mutual funds also now have imposed surrender penalties, but they usually permit penalty-free withdrawal after a shorter period than most variable annuities.

In fact, however, surrender penalties are simply not an issue for many people. If you are 50 years old and plan to retire at age 60 and not spend any of your investment until you retire, then the surrender penalty is probably irrelevant to you because you don't intend to use the funds anyway. But, if you are 59 years old and ready to retire in a year and use those funds, then the deferred sales charge is a significant issue and may make the variable annuity inappropriate.

Many of the same people who are critical of the liquidity disadvantages of variable annuities are proponents of IRAs. That makes no sense. IRAs and variable annuities are alike in that any withdrawal before age 59½ incurs a 10 percent penalty. In other words, a 25-year-old putting money into an IRA cannot withdraw that money until age 59½ without a penalty. That young person, in essence, is facing a 34½-year surrender penalty. The restrictions imposed by federal tax law on IRAs are far more severe than the company-imposed surrender penalties on variable annuities. Yet critics of variable annuities do not attack IRAs for being illiquid.

For those who choose a variable annuity as part of their IRA (now I'm really ruffling feathers, but I'll return to this point in a moment), the surrender charge imposed by the variable annuity company is essentially meaningless. If you are 35 and cannot withdraw your money for nearly 25 years without a penalty imposed by the government, why would you care if the company that issues the annuity will penalize you if you withdraw it in less than seven years? It is highly unlikely that you will withdraw any of that money until you reach 59½ anyway.

The key is not whether a deferred sales charge is detrimental in general, but whether the financial adviser and the investor understand the reduction in liquidity and make the choice with open eyes.

### Cost versus Value

Let's take a closer look at the cost of variable annuities to see if critics exaggerate the cost disadvantage. I believe they do. There's no question that variable annuities cost more. On average, a variable annuity will cost about 0.6–0.75 percent more than a typical mutual fund. (Estimates vary depending on the source.) Obviously, the annual cost of mutual funds varies greatly from fund to fund, just as the cost of variable annuities also varies.

The question is, what does the investor get for the added cost? Is value provided for that cost? Do you get any bang for your buck? I think so—

and so do many of my clients, who, when they learn of the added value, very often opt for a variable annuity over other investment options. As I have said, I am so convinced of the added value of variable annuities that I personally own them. I and many others in this industry vote with our own dollars and futures.

For one, I would suggest that the sheer volume of choices in most variable annuities gives investors at least the opportunity if not the likelihood of enhancing their investment performance by more than the cost disadvantage. If, as an example, I could improve my gross performance by 1 percent, hypothetically that means my net improved performance would be 0.25 percent if my cost disadvantage were 75 basis points.

Some research has demonstrated that variable annuities do provide returns that often exceed those of other equity investment alternatives. Conning Research conducted a study of variable annuity returns in 1998 following passage of the 1997 Taxpayers' Relief Act. Their research was based on the speculation that because of the lower 20 percent capital gains rate under the Taxpayer's Relief Act of 1997 it would become much more advantageous for the majority of investors to invest in mutual funds rather than annuities. So, they asked, "Who would be better off with an annuity and who would be better off with a mutual fund?" They concluded that over a 20-year period, there is an 82 percent probability that a variable annuity will result in *more* assets for distribution after taxes than a mutual fund. Over a 20-year period, there is a 48 percent chance that the variable annuity will exceed the mutual fund after taxes by $50,000 or more and a 33 percent chance that a variable annuity will outperform the mutual fund after taxes by $100,000 or more. Further they determined that if the variable annuity does underperform the mutual fund over the same 20-year period, it does so by less than $5,000 and never more than $10,000 after taxes.[4]

---

[4] The Conning & Company variable annuity study, 1998, assumed variable annuity insurance charges of 1.87% and an annual maintenance charge of $30. The study also assumed a mutual fund load of 2% and a management fee of 1%. Keep in mind, there are significant differences between mutual funds and variable annuities, including fee, expenses, sales charges and liquidity. In addition, any withdrawals from a variable annuity prior to age 59½ may trigger a 10% IRS penalty.

Ric Edelman, whom I consider one of the best authors on matters of personal finance, examined the relative returns of variable annuities and mutual funds. He wrote: "Our research shows that annuities always win if you leave the money invested for at least 15 years. (Which makes sense since annuities are intended to be used for retirement savings.) They sometimes win even in shorter periods too, depending on the variables used in the analysis."[5]

Second, variable annuities typically offer features and benefits not available in mutual funds. One of the most important benefits is tax deferral. Earnings within a variable annuity are not taxed until they are distributed. All things being equal, it is better to defer or delay the payment of taxes than to pay them fully and immediately. So the annuity offers the investor tax deferral that the managed account or mutual funds do not.

## A Safety Net

Variable annuities also offer protection against market losses. These protections are usually in the form of a death benefit or a "die in a down market" clause. Although the contractual terms of annuities may vary, this type of clause typically guarantees that the survivor or beneficiary will never receive less than a specified return compounded annually. Usually that rate is about 4 percent.

For example, if you put $100,000 into a managed account or a mutual fund that invests in equities and the market drops 20 percent, as it did in 2001 and 2002, your account would be worth $80,000. If you died, your survivor would get that $80,000, the actual account value. However, a variable annuity with a die in a down market clause would pay your beneficiary $104,000 because of the minimum return guarantee—regardless of the underlying performance of the subaccount portfolio. This clause essentially establishes a floor for the value of your variable annuity portfolio. It does not, however, establish a ceiling. If your $100,000 initial investment increased to $120,000 before your death, your survivor would get that full amount.

---

[5] Ric Edelman, *Discover the Wealth Within You,* Harper Business Press (2002).

The 4 percent per year only comes into play if you did not do better than 4 percent annually in the marketplace. It's a safety net. Critics argue that it's a meaningless benefit because if people live to their statistical life expectancy their portfolios will earn better than 4 percent a year. They also claim that a person could get similar protection by simply purchasing term life insurance outside of the annuity for less money. I think those criticisms are misguided for two reasons, and I would like to stress that these criticisms come primarily from media commentators and regulatory agencies, not from financial professionals or their clients.

What these critics don't understand is that a benefit does not have to be used to have value. No one criticizes you for having homeowner's insurance, even if you never file a claim. Many of us would be nervous and unable to sleep at night if we did not have homeowner's insurance. So the peace of mind, or the "pillow power," of having the protection affects us emotionally and affects our quality of life and our lifestyle.

The same is true of the equity portfolio insurance on a variable annuity. I cannot tell you how many times in the down market between 2000 and 2003 I sat down with a client, looked at a depreciating portfolio value, but then reminded them, "By the way, if you passed away, your spouse or your beneficiary or the survivor of the contract, whoever it is, does not get this reduced account value. They actually get your original account value plus 4 percent compounded." It's amazing what a calming effect that has on my clients.

Psychologically, many investors are willing to take a more aggressive approach or agree to a higher percentage of assets in equities when they have the die in a down market clause in a variable annuity. I have had clients tell me, "I don't want any exposure to the stock market. I'm afraid of the stock market, and I don't want to invest in it." They come to us with, say, $100,000 and they want to spend $500 a month of their investment. That's $6,000 a year, which means they have to earn a 6 percent return on their principal if they don't want to eat into the principal. I have to look those people in the eye and say we can't earn 6 percent right now with interest rates where they are without some equity exposure. However, once I explain to those people the die in a down market clause of variable annuities, they often change their tune and agree to put some of their investment into equities through an annuity. Others agree to put a higher percentage of their investments into equities. Why is that a benefit? Because, despite the performance of the 2000–2002 bear market, dollars invested in stocks for periods of 10 years or longer historically have earned better returns than fixed-interest alternatives.

If the die in a down market clause gets an investor to accept some equity exposure or more equity exposure, they are likely, based on historical averages, to see enhanced long-term performance. Same investor. Same risk tolerance. Same time horizon. Same investment objectives. But because of the die in a down market clause, because of the guarantee that their survivor is not going to lose money, they are willing to invest more aggressively. So the real value of the death benefit is that it makes investors more comfortable with exposure to equities than they otherwise would be willing to accept.

What about the second criticism of the death benefit, that similar protection can be purchased more cheaply with a simple term life insurance policy. That is not an attractive option for many people. The time and effort required to jump through the hoops to obtain life insurance discourage many people from doing so. Not to mention the fact that some people are uninsurable because of health problems or at the very least are quoted higher rates owing to their health. And even those who could make the case that they could do it for less money, rarely do. Within the annuity, within one contract—it's simple, seamless, and painless—people do it and like it.

A variable annuity presents a clear option to investors. If they want liquidity, a mutual fund or brokerage wrap account makes the most sense. Do they prefer tax deferral on earnings and protection for a beneficiary against a down market? Then a variable annuity makes sense. There is no right or wrong answer. It will vary by individual, depending on needs, goals, investment objectives, risk tolerance, and time horizon. I believe the only misguided course of action is to dismiss variable annuities out of hand. It will come as no surprise to financial advisers who understand variable annuities, and take the time to explain them, that investors often find them very attractive. They see value where the critics of variable annuities see only cost.

### Variable Annuities and IRAs

Let's return for a moment to a discussion of variable annuities and IRAs. Remember that a variable annuity even outside an IRA accrues tax-deferred earnings, just like an IRA, and distribution prior to age 59½ may be subject not only to ordinary income taxes but also to a 10 percent premature distribution penalty. In other words, a variable annuity looks, smells, and acts like an IRA. Why, the critics would ask, would you then put a variable annuity inside an IRA? Putting something that's tax-deferred into an account that is already tax-deferred seems redundant and inefficient. This criticism is, in my view, one of the most alarming in our industry, in part because it has come from regulators as well as self-appointed personal finance gurus in the media.

It's a silly objection. Why? In part because an investor is not paying for the tax deferral. The tax deferral itself incurs no cost. The additional cost of a variable annuity compared to a mutual fund (remember that the cost is roughly equal to a more comparable brokerage wrap account) is for some of the other features, such as the die in a down market clause and access to various subaccounts or equity portfolio managers.

I believe that, because of surrender penalties, variable annuities may not be appropriate for many people *outside* of an IRA. An efficient financial plan should include a variety of assets, and some of those assets should be accessible and liquid. Having a tax-deferred IRA *and* a tax-deferred annuity increases potential liquidity problems.

But the idea that today we can have regulators and lawsuits opposing variable annuities just because we're using them inside of IRAs or other qualified plans is absolutely insane. Annuities were created in 1952 specifically for teachers' retirement accounts, known as 403(b) accounts. These were qualified plans that were endorsed by the government through the federal tax code. How could something created by the government now become inappropriate in the eyes of government regulators?

Later, the use of variable annuities was expanded by Congress to allow them to be a part of other qualified plans. Under current Employee Retirement Income Security Act statutes, variable annuities are required to be the primary investment for 403(b) plans. How does it follow, then, that variable annuities would be inappropriate for other qualified plans? It defies logic. Additionally, many 401(k) plans, by their own choice and under their own terms, restrict investments in their plans to variable annuities.

## What's Good for the Goose

Financial advisers who recommend variable annuities in some cases have been criticized for simply seeking the compensation we get for enrolling investors in variable annuities. But if that were the only reason I sell such accounts, if they had no value, I would not own them myself. I do—and for very good reason. If all I wanted was the highest possible compensation, believe me, there are other financial products, and other variable annuity brands than the ones I recommend, that would pay me more money. I believe in the value of variable annuities, despite the criticism they receive. And what's good for me, I should tell my clients about.

Of course, I tell my clients exactly the advantages and disadvantages I have laid out here. I give them the pros and cons, and the investment alternatives, and let them decide what is appropriate for them. They often decide, as I have, that the benefits of variable annuities—the value—justifies the cost. Cost is only an issue in the absence of value.

When I recommend a variable annuity, or any investment for that matter, my client should be able to look me in the eye and ask, "Do you do this yourself?" I can answer, "Yes." And I believe that any adviser should be forthright in telling you the reasons he or she does or does not take his or her own advice on financial products.

## Living Benefits

One relatively new feature of variable annuities needs to be mentioned, the Living Benefit. One criticism of variable annuities has been that somebody has to die to for the death benefit to take effect. In a sense, the annuity holder was at times worth more dead than alive. To address that issue the variable annuity companies have developed a Living Benefit that essentially guarantees a return of your principal while you're alive, regardless of the underlying performance of the market.

For example, let's say that you invested $100,000 into a variable annuity and you wanted to take an income stream of $500 a month, or $6,000 a year. What if that annuity assured that you would at least get back your

$100,000 or have your income stream for roughly 16.8 years minimum, regardless of the underlying performance of the portfolio? Or, let's say you wanted 7 percent a year. It would pay you an income stream for a little over 14 years, worst case, before the money ran out, regardless of how the underlying portfolio does. Of course, if the markets do well the income stream could last significantly longer, paying you income for as long as you live. It could even grow in value during that time. But in the worst case you get your principal back first, and it's guaranteed that, regardless of underlying market performance, you will at least get your money back.

Now, after the down markets in the first years of this century, this feature is attractive to a lot of investors. Even if you believe the markets will remain healthy, even if you're not worried about the losses you sustained in recent years being permanent, it is hard to quantify the peace of mind that investors feel knowing that the worst that can happen is they will get their money back—or their survivor will get at least a 4 percent return on principal.

Furthermore, many of these contracts allow the investor to "step up" or "raise the bar" periodically. Let's say an investor starts with $100,000 and begins immediately to spend 7 percent, or $7,000, per year. Further assume that after five years, the account value has grown to $125,000. In other words, the investor had robust hypothetical performance because he or she spent $35,000 ($7,000 x 5 years) and the account still appreciated by $25,000.

After five years, the investor may lock in his or her gains and begin taking 7 percent of $125,000, or $8,700, per year for slightly more than 14 years. Or, in other words, the worst possible outcome is now to receive another $125,000 in addition to the $35,000 already received. Therefore, even if the stock market started a nosedive after the fifth year and continued down for 14 consecutive years, our hypothetical investor receives no less than $160,000 cumulatively over about 19 years on the original $100,000 investment.

The authors who criticize variable annuities have probably never had to sit face-to-face with an heir, with a child whose parent has died in a down market. If the parent had purchased a variable annuity with a death benefit, instead of inheriting maybe half of what the parents had invested, the heir would receive the principal plus a 4 percent return. Walk a mile in my shoes, sit in my chair, and meet these people, and you will have a greater appreciation for the features of a variable annuity. I don't work in an ivory tower. I work with people and their hard-earned assets—assets they want their children to enjoy.

Do these benefits have a cost? Of course they do. And that cost will vary from one annuity product to another. Do we hide the costs from our clients when we propose the strategy? Of course not. We say to the client, "Here's the cost. Here's what you get for the cost. You make the decision as an investor. Is this feature or this benefit worth that extra cost to you?" Some investors decide that it is not. Many others, fully aware of the cost, say, "Yes, I want that peace of mind. I want that security. I want that sleep factor at night. I don't want to get an ulcer worrying about this. It's worth it." That's why I often suggest variable annuities. My clients see value in them.

## Don't Wear Blinders

Keep one thing in mind as you consider investment vehicles: Don't wear blinders. Consider all your options—even if someone with nice hair on TV tells you it's a bad idea. Don't just accept conventional wisdom and don't listen exclusively to any one "authority" on any of these vehicles— not even me. I encourage you to challenge my views. Test them and see if they make sense for you. I know what has worked for me and for my clients, and I'm happy to debate my positions with anyone. Ultimately your investment choices depend on your unique goals and strategy. Explore every possibility. You might find an investment avenue that offers you a better way to achieve your investing goals.

I cannot emphasize enough the importance of establishing clear goals and determining the balance of risk and reward you will need to meet them. If your strategy is clear, you will be able to sift through your many options with a greater understanding of the advantages and disadvantages of various options such as tax-deferred accounts, variable universal life, and variable annuities. Some may be inappropriate for your plan; others may help accomplish exactly what you want. You'll never know which options are right for you if you don't look at all the possibilities.

### TEN THINGS INVESTORS WORRY ABOUT TOO MUCH

1. **The Federal Reserve.** Will it lower interest rates? Is it focusing more on inflation or deflation? As Bill Murray said in the movie *Meatballs*, "It just doesn't matter."

2. **Talking heads.** Do yourself a favor. Stop watching CNBC. Don't listen to or read Suze Orman or Louis Rukeyser. Get an adviser you trust and listen to your adviser.

3. **What their friends are doing.** Their situation is different from yours—and when they brag about their great investments, they're probably embellishing. And, by the way, in addition to tuning out your friends, tune out prominent investors like Warren Buffett. I know people pay a lot of attention to him and he is arguably the greatest investor we've ever seen. I'm not dismissing Warren Buffett. But, to do what he does would make no sense for most of us. Warren Buffett is worth trillions. If he's out of the market during a recovery, it's not going to have any impact on his lifestyle. Believe me, his house is paid for. But those of us who need certain investment returns and rely on certain investment returns cannot afford to be out of the market if there's a recovery. It could definitely impact our lifestyle. So don't pay any attention to what others are doing, whether friends or a famous investor like Warren Buffett. You have to focus on your goals, your objectives, your time horizon, your risk tolerance, the rate of return you need, and what you're going to use the money for. Focus on yourself.

4. **The investment's cost.** Cost is only an issue in the absence of value. What features or benefits are provided by the extra cost? Are they worth it?

5. **The calendar.** Summer rally? January effect? October swoon? Again, who knows? Time—not timing.

6. **Every single investment they own.** Some will be up, some will be down. That's normal. Don't worry about it. If you do, ask yourself,

"Do I really trust my adviser to put me into these investments?" You have to look at the big picture. You cannot worry daily about each individual investment.

7. **Cost basis.** Gains or losses are what they are. So what! If you made a lot of money, you pay some tax; your net-net is still attractive and still desirable.

8. **Stocks they sold.** After you sell it and it continues to do well, do you kick yourself? Don't. If your investment strategy is sound and the sale was part of your strategy, forget about it. Even if you made the mistake of investing emotionally and were reacting to temporary market news or conditions, move on. Focus on your strategy—and promise yourself that your future actions will be based on strategy, not emotion.

9. **Stocks they never bought.** "Oh, man, I passed on ABC Widgets and the price tripled!" Same argument as before. We've all done it. Every day some stocks soar and others tumble. So what. Get over it! Mathematicians will tell you that over time any random series of numbers will regress to the mean. That means that if you flip a coin 10 times you could get "heads" on nine flips. If you called heads every time, you'd have a 90 percent success rate. Phenomenal! But if you continue for another 10,000 flips, you'll be very close to 50 percent. The corollary in the investment world is that over time, your performance will be roughly equal to broader market returns. And that's a good thing given what we know about historical returns on investments. Of course, investment performance is not purely random. How can you improve your likelihood of success? Not with stock picking but with asset allocation.

10. **Short-term performance.** Nothing—positive or negative—can be determined in the short term. Anything related to the stock market has got to be measured in long blocks of time—five years or more.

## INVESTING: A CONCISE SUMMARY

1. Develop an investment strategy tailored to your life and your goals.

2. Start now. Time is your greatest ally.

3. Allocate investments into a variety of asset classes according to your investment time horizon and risk tolerance. Negative correlation is desirable. If you hope to earn a return that beats the effects of inflation, your asset allocation should include some investment in stocks. Returns on stocks, measured by broad market averages, have been remarkably consistent over the past 70 years.

4. Continuously manage your investments and rebalance your portfolio at least once a year to maintain your desired asset allocation.

5. Do not rely solely on any single type of retirement portfolio vehicle. Tax-deferred retirement plans have a place in your plan, but not to the exclusion of other possibilities such as variable universal life insurance, variable annuities, or Roth IRAs. Do your homework and understand any product before investing.

6. Do not try to time the market. Let time work to your advantage. History demonstrates that it will.

7. Rely on your strategy, not your emotions. By following a strategic path you will not be sidetracked by fear or greed.

# 4

## Paying Taxes

■ ■ ■

Taxes can be a complex and an overlooked element of a financial plan. Yet, tax planning is critical to long-term financial success. Obviously, your goal is to pay as little tax as possible. But just as you never want to invest without considering tax implications, you never want to invest for *only* tax reasons. Tax reduction is one part of the potential total return that you must analyze. (See "Your Money Matrix"™ at the conclusion of this chapter for discussion on how to consider tax implications strategically when you invest.)

### Three File Cabinets

When exploring how investments may be treated for tax purposes I find it useful to think of a home office and individual filing cabinets:

- The first filing cabinet is for *taxable investments*: Earnings on these investments are fully taxed in the year earned.
- The second filing cabinet is for *tax-deferred investments*: Taxes on these investments are not paid when earned but are deferred until withdrawn, such as with 401(k)s and IRAs.
- The third filing cabinet is for *tax-advantaged investments*. This category includes deductions and credits that may reduce one's tax obligation, and investments such as Roth IRAs for which no taxes are due upon distributions, as well as when earnings are accrued.

## Taxable Investments

The first file cabinet would contain all of your taxable investments or savings. We won't distinguish here between investments that produce ordinary income and investments that produce capital gains. Taxable investments include money market accounts, CDs, mutual funds, stocks and bonds, and everything else where income or loss is fully taxed when earned. All of these types of investments give you almost immediate access to your money when you need it.

I recommend trying to have enough money in liquid accounts to cover living expenses for three to six months. When I say liquid accounts, I am not suggesting that you buy stock in Coca-Cola or Budweiser. Liquid assets are assets that can be converted into cash (liquidated) quickly at any time. A checking account is very liquid; a Stradivarius violin or a 1952 Mickey Mantle baseball card is not. The violin and the card may be worth far more than your checking account, but you couldn't just sell them on the street corner. You would have to find a qualified buyer, which could take some time, and the buyer would have to meet your price. If you were forced to unload your fiddle or Mickey quickly, you might have to sell at a substantial loss or at least at a price well below the current market value.

Occasionally you will hear someone talk about having a "liquidity" problem. That could mean the person is worth billions but those billions are all tied up in investments that can't be liquidated easily. It could also mean that a person is flat broke and is putting a dire situation in the best light. You can avoid the worst liquidity problems by maintaining some investments in the first file cabinet.

## Tax-Deferred Investments

The second file cabinet holds your tax-deferred investments. This category would include any nonqualified tax-deferred annuity, individual retirement account (IRA), simplified employee pension, 401(k), 403(b), Keogh, 457, or any other pretax retirement plan in which the amount of the contribution is deducted from your income for tax purposes in the year in which you make the contribution. Most investors put the lion's share of their investment dollars into this file cabinet. I have already indicated that overfunding these types of investments can actually be inefficient and counterproductive.

## Tax-Advantaged Investments

The third file cabinet is for tax-advantaged investments. An ideal financial plan has dollars in all three file cabinets. Unfortunately, most investors have an overflowing tax-deferred file cabinet and do not even have a third file cabinet. Tax-advantaged investments would include those that may be tax-free or tax-deductible or that give the investor a tax credit. The essential difference between this file cabinet and the second one is that tax-advantaged investments aren't just taxed at a later time; all or part of the earnings from a tax-advantaged investment may not be taxed at all. Obviously, all things being equal, tax-free is preferable to taxable or tax-deferred.

As I mentioned when discussing pretax retirement plans, most people put too high a percentage of their resources in the second file cabinet and ignore the third. Investments that are potentially tax-free include municipal bonds, some life insurance, and Roth IRAs. Your earnings on those investments are not subject to income taxes in many cases.

Don't wait for the target to stop moving, however, because it won't. Tax policy always has been and always will be tinkered with by presidents and Congress. It's impossible to predict what will happen with tax rates and tax policies, so create the best tax plan to account for present tax law and make adjustments to your plan as changes occur. Most important, I would recommend that you get the advice of professionals well before tax time comes.

## TAXES: A CONCISE SUMMARY

I think there are three lessons to be drawn from any close examination of tax policy and its impact on individuals.

One, the current tax system allows tax-reduction strategies that are not considered by many people who should be taking advantage of them. They are overlooked, in part, owing to an overreliance on tax-deferred retirement plans. Most people, with more careful and detailed tax planning as part of an integrated financial plan, could reduce their tax burden now and in the future, including taxes on their estates.

Two, the current tax system is extremely complex and eats up a lot of what could be otherwise productive time for CPAs and other financial professionals—not to mention our elected representatives. Wouldn't the world be a better place if that brilliance could be applied elsewhere?

Three, individuals who try to do their own financial planning cannot possibly keep up with all this stuff, which once again illustrates a constant theme in this book and everything I have ever written, every lecture I have ever given, every radio show I have ever done: People should not try to do this themselves. Seek the help and guidance of a qualified and trustworthy financial professional.

### APPLICATION: YOUR MONEY MATRIX

In the introduction to this section I wrote about your financial "pie" and how you slice it. All the ways you can use money are interrelated. A good example of that is "Your Money Matrix," a tool we developed at Wealth Enhancement Group to help guide investment considerations and the impact of taxes. Now that you have a basic understanding of primary investment considerations and the tax cabinets into which investments may be put, let's examine Your Money Matrix.

For each row, we add a column that indicates the estimated annual cash flow from all the assets in that row.

Your Money Matrix provides basic guidelines for approaching asset allocation in the broadest terms with the tax implications of investments clearly in mind. Obviously, your age and personal goals play a central role in the mixture of investments you would choose.

I have introduced Your Money Matrix here as a way to encourage you to consider your financial future and the efficient use of money in broader terms than perhaps you have until now. As I have noted, most people have too high a percentage of their assets in the taxable and tax-deferred columns, leaving the tax-advantaged column empty.

As an exercise, I would encourage you to plug your assets into each of the rows and columns to see if your investments truly meet your goals

**YOUR MONEY MATRIX™**

| Time Horizon | Taxable | Tax-Deferred | Tax-Advantaged | Estimated Annual Cash Flow |
|---|---|---|---|---|
| Short-term income (0–7 years) | Money market<br>Bank deposits<br>CDs<br>Treasury notes | IRA (conservative)<br>Corporate retirement plan (conservative)<br>Fixed annuities | Roth IRA (conservative)<br>Municipal bonds (short term)<br>Fixed % life insurance | |
| Medium-term growth and income (7–15 years) | Money market<br>Bank deposits<br>CDs<br>Stocks<br>Real estate<br>Investment trusts<br>Treasury bills<br>Intermediate Corporate bonds | IRA (moderate)<br>Corporate retirement plan (moderate)<br>Variable annuities (balanced, moderate) | Roth IRA (balanced, moderate)<br>Municipal bonds<br>Variable life (balanced) | |
| Long-term growth (15+ years) | Stocks<br>Long-term CDs<br>Real estate<br>Investment trusts<br>Long-term corporate bonds<br>Treasury bonds | IRA (aggressive)<br>Corporate retirement plan (aggressive)<br>Variable annuity (aggressive) | Roth IRA (aggressive)<br>Tax credit investments<br>Tax-deductible investments<br>Variable life (aggressive)<br>Municipal bonds | |
| Total Investments | $ | $ | $ | $ |

and time horizon. Are all of your assets crammed into one box? Is it realistic for you to spread those assets more evenly among the boxes?

Your individual objectives will make this a very personal tool to use in planning your financial future. Few people complete this matrix in identical ways, because their lives and aspirations are not identical. Some place a priority on retirement investing; others add investing to pay college tuition; still others focus primarily on creating an inheritance for their families. The Money Matrix exercise will help you focus more clearly on your goals and see the actions you may need to take to accomplish those goals. It is a very useful second step—once you understand the fundamentals of money and your personal approach to money.

# 5

## Sharing Your Wealth

■ ■ ■

For so many people in these affluent times, giving money to a faith community, charity, community or arts organization, an educational institution, or hurricane victims is a primary motivation for financial planning. Even for many of my clients who don't have large net worths, giving some money to others is very important, either during their lives or upon their deaths.

I believe strongly in the importance of making charitable donations, and I have been pleased to be able to work with many clients who have made very generous contributions to their favorite nonprofit organizations. They have been delighted to make those gifts—and to discover that they received very significant economic benefits from their generosity.

Giving can be a rewarding part of your financial strategy, and you can do it in ways that benefit yourself as well as your favorite organizations or causes.

### Why Give?

I have encountered nearly every reason imaginable for making contributions to charitable organizations. The most common, however, are the following:

- Compassion for those in need;
- Religious and spiritual commitment;
- Desire to perpetuate one's beliefs, values, and ideals;

- Support for the arts, sciences, and education; and
- A desire to share "good fortune" with others.

The tax laws of the United States encourage these gifts by granting tax deductions for them in many cases. If individual citizens voluntarily help meet our country's needs, their contributions reduce the responsibility of the government. Many would also argue that private support of charitable activities is more efficient than public support.

Due to the tax treatment of charitable contributions, individuals may realize not only immediate tax benefits but also advantages in terms of after-tax cash flow and the size of the estate they may pass on to their heirs. Gifts to charity during one's lifetime or at death, if structured properly, will reduce the estate tax liability. An additional benefit of lifetime gifts is that an income tax deduction is available within certain percentage limitations.

## A FARM, A CHURCH, AND A FAMILY

How can giving money away provide economic benefits beyond the tax deduction? Let's consider the case of Howard and Betty.

They were in their early 60s when they came to me. They had owned and operated a family farm for 40 years, but they were preparing to sell their farm for $1.2 million to a real estate developer. Their cost in the property, or basis, was about $200,000, so they would have a gain of $1 million. That gain would be taxed as a long-term capital gain at a federal rate of 20 percent, for a liability of $200,000. This was a big tax liability, but they would still net $1 million after taxes. Assuming a fairly conservative hypothetical investment rate of return of 8 percent on a portfolio, the proceeds from the farm sale would generate $80,000 in income per year without invading the principal.

During an introductory meeting with Howard and Betty, I discovered two important things. First, they were very spiritual people who gave a lot to their church and wanted to do even more for it. Second, even though they felt blessed to have a $1,000,000 gain on their land, net of tax, they were unhappy about having to pay $200,000 in taxes, but they felt there was nothing they could do about it.

I advised Howard and Betty to create a charitable remainder trust (CRT) and fund the trust with the property. Then the CRT would sell the land to the developer. Because the asset would be sold through the CRT, there would be no capital gains tax liability for Howard and Betty. The CRT would provide them with an income stream of $96,000 per year (8% x $1.2 million) instead of $80,000. They would also receive a tax deduction now for the future gift to their church, because when they passed away, the remainder of the trust would go to the church. The gift they could make to their church was the primary motivating factor for Howard and Betty to pursue this strategy, but it also gave them an extra $16,000 of income each year that they could have obtained no other way.

The one flaw that Betty and Howard saw in the plan was that they would be disinheriting their children. Although they wanted to give a lot to their church, they also wanted to leave something for their children. We solved the problem by using the tax deduction over five years and fully paying for a $1 million last survivor or second-to-die life insurance policy, so their children would have $1 million tax-free to split after Betty and Howard passed away. This strategy would allow Howard and Betty not only to provide for their children but also to increase the money their children would divide by $400,000, because the $1 million life insurance benefit would not be calculated as part of their taxable estate.

The result of this strategy was to:

- Make a profound gift to their church;
- Increase Howard and Betty's annual income;
- Generate a significant tax deduction they could spread over five years; and
- Protect their children's inheritance by using the tax savings created by the deduction to purchase life insurance at essentially no out-of-pocket cost.

Howard and Betty felt very good about their gift, which certainly did a lot of good for their church, and they also increased their income and the money they left to their children.

You may find, as Howard and Betty did, that a gift to your favorite charity, if structured properly, actually increases your after-tax cash flow during your lifetime. Moreover, your charitable contributions enable you to decide how your money is used, rather than letting the government decide.

Your charitable gift may provide economic benefits to you and your heirs. Although that may not be your primary motivation for giving, it can be a very attractive fringe benefit—one that is readily available and could be used by many more people if they planned carefully.

## GIVING SOONER OR LATER:
## DIFFERENT TYPES OF CHARITABLE GIFTS

Tax laws pertaining to charitable contributions can be very complex—and allow for many types of gifts.

- **Cash gifts.** The simplest form of donation in terms of tax treatment is an outright gift of cash or other valuable assets. Within certain limitations, such gifts generate income tax deductions at the time the gift is made and reduce the estate tax liability.
- **Wills.** Individuals who might depend on income from their assets to meet their needs often designate a portion of their estate to go to a charity upon their death. Such a bequest, if properly structured, will reduce the estate tax liability.
- **Split-interest gifts.** Split-interest gifts are a method of widely used charitable giving that is much more complicated and can take many forms. In the interest of simplicity, I will provide a very general description of this type of gift. Please consult professionals to determine the various forms these gifts may take.

A split-interest gift operates on the principle that any sum of money or property is valued in two ways: as the value of the thing itself, or the principal, and as the value of the income stream or earning power of that asset. For instance, if you have $10,000, you have not only the money but also the potential to earn a return on that money. With a split-interest gift, you either donate the principal, but retain the income stream from that gift for your life, or donate the earning power of that asset, which reverts to your estate upon your death.

Most plans under which you make a gift but retain the income from that gift are called charitable *remainder* trusts. You receive income from the gift, but the remainder, the underlying asset, goes to the charitable organization when you die or after a predetermined period of time. One of the tax advantages of this type of gift is that, in many cases, the tax deduction for the remainder gift may be taken when the gift is made.

Remainder trusts are especially attractive when donating highly appreciated assets, such as stocks that have been owned for a long period of time. In most cases, the donor does not have to pay capital gains taxes on the appreciation of the asset, yet can take a tax deduction, within IRS limitations, for the gift.

The other type of split-interest gift is usually called a *charitable lead trust*. In that case, you donate income earned by an asset, but the asset reverts to your estate upon your death.

Your individual situation will determine which of several methods will be most advantageous for you and the organization to which you are making a donation. Each approach generates different income tax and estate tax consequences. Each of them may also have different gift tax consequences, if you designate others, such as your children or grandchildren, as the beneficiaries of your interest in the trust.

## Don't Try This at Home

These giving strategies are not do-it-yourself undertakings. You will need assistance from professionals to do it properly, so that you and the organization to which you are contributing obtain the maximum benefit from your gift. The last thing you want is for neither you nor your heirs, nor your favorite charitable organization, to receive the full benefit of your generosity. The IRS has strict rules on what is permissible if you are doing anything more complicated than making a straight cash gift.

Many charitable, religious, and educational organizations will provide considerable assistance to you in handling the legal and accounting aspects of making a gift to them. It makes sense to discuss your desires and plans with the organization as early as possible to make the most of their assistance and expertise.

What those organizations may not be able to provide, however, is advice on where your gift fits in your overall plan. Will your gift create unanticipated hardship for you at some point? Is your gift actually much smaller than you would like to give and could comfortably afford to give if your money were working more efficiently? These questions can be answered only in the context of a complete financial plan that takes into account your needs and your investment strategy.

It may seem like a lot of hassle to go through just to give your money away, but it would be inefficient for you and your favorite charity *not* to take advantage of the tax breaks available by doing it the IRS's way.

# 6

## PLANNING

■ ■ ■

Planning is the only way to make sense of the five things you can do with money. If you don't plan, you will likely spend more, save less, invest less, and do nothing to reduce your taxes.

Don't sell yourself short by planning your retirement based on some arbitrary percentage of your income. "Needs planning" is a good start for someone who has given no thought to retirement savings. It's a way to convince people that they should save something, but it's not good for people who want to do better than get by. Don't settle for mediocrity in your investment planning. Try to excel. It's fine to set a floor for what you will need, but then aim higher—and plan to get there! Become a "wants" planner, instead of a "needs" planner. Only when you determine what you want from life can you determine the role money will play in helping you achieve your dreams.

### THE GREAT UNKNOWN

Will you live to be 100 or will you die earlier, perhaps much earlier? The greatest fear of many people, especially as they approach their golden years, is that they will run out of money before they run out of breath.

Of course, none of us has a crystal ball, so we can't say for certain when that will be. We do know, however, that we are living longer than ever before. It was statistically unlikely that people born in 1900 would live until age 50. Today, just over a century later, your life expectancy is between 75 and 80.

An efficient financial plan acknowledges and prepares for a premature death before statistical life expectancy by using life insurance efficiently. But you should also acknowledge and prepare for the possibility that you will live beyond age 100. You don't plan to spend your last dollar on the day you think you'll die. What if you exceed the statistical average and live a lot longer?

## THREE PLANNING PHASES

In the face of that great unknown, efficient financial planning requires you to consider three phases of your financial life: accumulation, distribution, and legacy or transfer of wealth. Nearly everyone focuses on the first of those phases, accumulation, and ignores the others until they are near or in retirement. In effect, a simple focus on accumulation of assets is not much better than not planning at all. It's a bit like jumping in your car to start your vacation, your money tucked in your pocket, without any idea where you are going.

*Accumulation* concentrates on gathering and growing assets. There are many ways to accumulate wealth: saving what you earn, being the beneficiary of life insurance, inheriting wealth, investing in securities that grow in value, building up a business to increase its value, earning interest on a savings account (although this will not likely outpace inflation). All financial service organizations and their representatives— stockbrokers, insurance agents, financial planners, CPAs, or other types of advisers—are interested in helping you in the accumulation phase of planning.

We all want to see our portfolios grow without any losses. Most people tend to think of financial planning as a process of accumulation coupled with tax deferment through pretax plans such as 401(k)s or pension funds. This simplistic approach focuses mostly on the accumulation phase.

*Distribution* focuses on how you spend your assets when the time comes that you no longer live off your wages, or you choose to live off the value of accumulated assets. There are several keys to good distribution strategies, including an estimated cost of living adjusted for inflation and lifestyle, the order in which you spend your assets, tax-deferred investments, legal tax avoidance tactics, and certain types of insurance products. This phase of financial planning takes much training and continuing education on the part of the financial adviser and focused effort by both the adviser and the client. Although many stockbrokers, insurance agents, and bankers are able to provide some of these products, it is usually CPAs and financial planners who assist in creating distribution strategies that best suit individual needs.

*Legacy or transfer* addresses what you ultimately wish to do with your assets. Some of these strategies include family limited partnerships, charitable and other foundations, risk-based products (life and disability insurance), tax-reduction strategies, formal estate planning, and trusts. Usually lawyers, CPAs, banks, insurance agents, and high-level financial advisers provide these services.

### WHO CAN HELP? THE FOCUS OF FINANCIAL PROFESSIONALS

Together, accumulation, distribution, and legacy/transfer demand a high level of training in many disciplines. The tax code alone is so large that no single tax specialist can possibly know all of it. As a result, the average person faces a great challenge in building a comprehensive strategy. Intelligently addressing these three issues is daunting. Many top financial advisers tend to focus on the accumulation and distribution needs of their clients. A few of them have some background or training in legacy/ transfer, but they tend to concentrate their efforts on the very wealthy.

In today's world, many financial institutions offer a wide range of financial services to clients. Since the regulatory wall between banks and brokers was knocked down, the distinctions have been blurred, with many banks offering brokerage services, and vice versa. Still, I believe it remains true that most professionals tend to focus their efforts more narrowly.

**Stockbrokers.** Most stockbrokers help primarily with the accumulation phase. They still usually earn commissions on trades and focus on the success of your portfolio. In my experience, they have a shorter-term approach to investing, concentrating on the best possible returns at any given time, rather than a longer-term view that helps you get to where you want to be.

**CPAs.** Certified public accountants are primarily tax specialists, not investment specialists. Although many that I know try to help their clients reduce tax liability through investments, and many even broker specific investments, their focus is usually on the tax implications of an investment and not where the investment fits in an overall financial strategy.

**Private bankers.** Banks tend to focus on trusts, so they offer legacy/transfer services but usually not broad-based planning.

**Insurance agents.** Insurance agents focus on risk or the legacy/transfer phase of planning. They are often also well versed in certain types of tax-deferral or tax-avoidance products that are insurance related. Most do not, however, offer well-rounded financial strategies. Many insurance companies have now established financial planning services that are available not through the agent but through the parent company. Owing to their captive nature, they tend to offer only products created by the parent company.

**Attorneys.** Lawyers work primarily on estate planning, a legacy/transfer niche. While estate planning is useful for many people, and I would strongly advise it, in the absence of an integrated financial plan it can play only a limited role in an efficient financial strategy.

**Financial advisers.** Okay, I'm biased. At the risk of sounding self-serving, I believe that only professional financial advisers who are not tied to a specific company's products or range of investments can offer effective assistance on all three phases of a financial plan. Financial advisers can take your financial plan beyond accumulation strategies to address distribution and legacy/transfer issues as part of a comprehensive plan. I'm proud of what I do, and I believe independent companies like mine, by bringing together experts in all of the planning phases, offer the most comprehensive service.

I know it's not easy to choose someone to guide your financial plan. That is why I have devoted several pages in Chapter 22 to helping you select a financial adviser. Can you create your own financial plan? If you have the time and aptitude, you probably can do much of the work yourself, with the exception of tax planning. The tax code is so complex that few people have the stomach or the stamina to master it on their own. I know I don't. That's why my company employs tax professionals.

The problem with creating your own plan is that, as in most fields, you probably don't know what you don't know. I hope this book helps give you a foundation in some basic principles, but what it cannot do (no book can) is guide you through all the variations and considerations that are appropriate to your circumstances, your life, your dreams.

## No More Excuses

I have heard all the excuses for not planning. Whether you intend to hire someone to help you or decide to go it alone, start your financial plan now. It is very difficult to make up for lost time, whether years or decades, in making your money work efficiently to help you achieve the future you want for yourself and for the ones you love.

Of course, the challenges and the rewards of financial planning are compounded when your financial life involves others. In the next section I will address some of the details of personal finance as they relate to your family. Most of that advice revolves around the fundamentals of money that I have addressed in this section. If you have questions as you read subsequent chapters, please turn back to these pages to review what I consider the basics of using money efficiently.

As you read the subsequent chapters that pertain to your situation, please write down your thoughts or questions. Perhaps they will be answered elsewhere in this book or they will lead you to do more of your own research. In fact, they may form the foundation of a discussion with a financial planner.

Most important, reflect on and make a list of your goals. That's how we often begin our consultations with our clients: We ask them to write down their goals in life, not just their financial goals, and to be as precise as they can be. If you are not clear about your goals, it is impossible to achieve them. If you don't have dreams or aspirations, if you think only about everyday life, you'll remain stuck in the rut of the mundane. Yes, of course, you have to take time to smell the roses, to play with your kids, but even that will be more enjoyable for you if you believe you are focused clearly on the future you desire. Someone a whole lot smarter than I am once said that if you don't think about the future, you won't have one.

The best way to predict the future is to *create* the future. The journey of a thousand miles begins with a single step. Begin now. Once you get started, once you set a plan in motion, momentum takes over. Think of it as a buffet line. The line may be long and slow, but at least you're moving. You're going to get your meal faster than if you wait for the line to get shorter.

## GET AND STAY HEALTHY

Finally, no matter how efficiently you use money to pursue your goals, good health will help you enjoy the journey. For that reason, indulge me as I pause for a moment to think about health. With good health, a financial plan can be a tremendous asset in living life to the fullest. Without good health, a financial plan is a *must* to provide for loved ones when you cannot.

In my profession, I'm required to spend a good bit of time with my clients anticipating worst-case scenarios to ensure that loved ones are provided for in the event of disability or death. But it's much more fun for me to help people plan the rest of their lives, instead of the life of their family without them. Pay attention to your health. The love you can give your family during a long life is far more valuable than any financial provisions you can make for them after you die. Plan to stay with them for a very long time.

One of my primary objectives as a financial planner is (and always has been) to enhance the lives of our company's clients, employees, stakeholders, and families. The goal of enhancing wealth is not to generate money you can clutch tightly until you die. Improving our personal financial situations gives us more freedom to choose our lifestyle and enhance our quality of life. We want to see people walk, golf, fish, play tennis, ski, bowl, travel, and enjoy life into their 70s, 80s, and 90s. However, all the financial success in the world can't help you enjoy life if you are physically unable to live fully.

I was a pretty decent high school and college athlete, and for most of my life I have thought of myself as physically fit. In recent years, however, I had become more and more complacent about finding time to exercise. Work and family commitments seemed to dominate my waking hours. I fooled myself into thinking I was still in pretty good shape for a guy in my 40s. Then, a few years ago, reality reared its ugly head. After months, maybe even a year, of avoiding it, I stepped on my bathroom scale. Now, just to put things into perspective, I am six feet, three inches tall. Upon high school graduation I weighed about 200 pounds. Even in college, my football playing weight was only 215. After college, I took up distance running and dropped to about 190 pounds. Well, imagine my shock when I tipped the scales at 280!

As a former athlete, I always felt I knew how to maintain health and fitness. I didn't think that I needed professional help. But on that day, I realized that I didn't have all the answers.

The parallel between my quest for better health and the public's attitude toward personal finance was not lost on me. I was as guilty in my attitude toward fitness as the people I disagree with who are "do-it-yourselfers" in finance. (I suspect financial do-it-yourselfers are also fitness do-it-yourselfers.)

The decision to retain a personal trainer was one of the best I have ever made. He taught me that a lot of my thinking regarding fitness was off base. Much of the prevailing wisdom is wrong and may, in fact, be not only inefficient but dangerous. Steve also taught me to make my body a priority. The way he talks about fitness and personal health reminds me of how I talk about personal financial success.

In both physical and financial fitness, people don't know what they don't know. In both areas of life, mainstream thinking is wrong and misguided. Success for a healthy body or healthy portfolio requires an efficient strategy, methodology, technique, patience, persistence, and discipline. In my case, not only did I have flawed ideas about fitness, I also lacked discipline and needed help to do the things I should do. The same can often be said of most people's financial situation.

Professionally, I believe I can help you acquire the means to enjoy life into your 90s. But all the money in the world can't protect either of us from a fatal heart attack before age 50, or just plain poor health dictating a sit-on-the-porch-and-watch-the-cars-go-by lifestyle.

Today my weight is down to 250 and I'm wearing pants a couple of sizes smaller. I know you can't measure physical fitness just by the scale. But I also know that I'm doing the right things and that my patience and persistence will pay dividends. I have dreams of watching my son hit his first home run and my daughter win her first swimming event, and taking them out to dinner with *their* families to celebrate new jobs, promotions, and birthdays. My chances are better now that I have changed course. If you are not enjoying the health you want, I urge you to seek professional help. And you too will likely lead a happy, healthy, financially successful lifestyle well into your 90s.

### 10 ESSENTIAL HEALTH TIPS

1. **Move more.** Make it a daily challenge to find ways to move your body. Climb the stairs instead of taking the escalator or the elevator. Walk your dog. Play with your kids. Toss a ball. Mow the lawn. Anything that moves your limbs is not only a fitness tool, it's also a stress reliever.

2. **Eat in moderation.** Avoid foods that are obviously high in fat—fried foods, burgers, and so forth. Try to include all the food groups in your daily intake. It's okay to eat anything you want as long as you do so in moderation. Despite all the fad diets out there and all the debate that rages about the best way to lose weight, what it all boils down to is really quite simple. You have to take in fewer calories than you expend each day. So if you're gaining weight and you want to lose or stabilize, you either need to be more active (burn more calories), or you have to eat less. It's that simple.

3. **No smoking.** If you smoke now, quit. If you don't smoke, don't start.

4. **Reduce stress.** Spend 30 minutes a day doing something you like to do. Soak in a hot tub. Take a walk in the park. Read a book. Visit a friend. You need these little breaks from the day-to-day stress in your life. Count to 10 before you lose your temper or get aggravated. Avoid difficult people if you can. As much as you love your family and as much as you love to spend time with them, take 30 minutes a day for yourself. Go off somewhere to a quiet place.

5. **Protect yourself from pollution.** Avoid smoke-filled rooms and dangerous secondhand smoke. Wear sunscreen if you have to be outside to protect yourself from the potential damaging rays of the sun.

6. **Wear your seatbelt.** Statistics show that buckling up adds to longevity and helps alleviate potential injuries in car crashes.

7. **Floss.** Recent studies make a direct connection between longevity and teeth flossing.

8. **Avoid excessive drinking.** The consumption of alcohol can cause health problems such as liver and kidney disease and cancer. Again, moderation is okay. A beer here and there, a glass a wine with dinner, a cocktail after a stressful day or before an elegant meal—fine. Just don't overdo it.

9. **Keep a positive mental outlook.** There's a definite connection between living well and healthfully and having a cheerful outlook on life. Smile. When you pick up the phone to make a call, smile. It's amazing. People can hear a smile in your voice. Hug your family. Shake hands with friends. Greet colleagues. Be positive. It becomes self-perpetuating. It becomes contagious to others. It will prolong your life and enhance your attitude toward life.

10. **Get professional help.** Many people are overweight and they think, "Well, there's nothing I can do about it. It's genetic. I'm trying. I can do it myself." I used to think I could control my own health. Intellectually I knew everything, and how could a professional help me? One of the best decisions I ever made was to engage a personal trainer who happens to have a master's degree in exercise physiology and kinesiology, and who also counsels me on nutrition. You just don't know what you don't know. It's like financial planning. You may think you're leading a healthy lifestyle and you'd be amazed to find out you're not doing things as efficiently as you could. Seek professional guidance.

# PART II

# Money and Spouses

The love of your life. The power of two. Common dreams and vision. A partner. Shared responsibilities. There are many great reasons to have a soulmate and spouse. You could add another item to the list of advantages of marriage: pooled resources. But pooled resources are only an advantage if you avoid the common pitfalls that trap the unsuspecting or unprepared. Along with the benefit of jointly held assets come what can develop into an enormous headache: shared obligations and the doubling of an inclination to consume and spend.

Love does not conquer all. It takes two to meet financial goals, but only one to torpedo a plan. Financial planning with a spouse takes extra care and forethought to reach clear agreement on your financial goals and to pursue your dreams. As a financial adviser, I don't always know the causes of marital problems, but I often see the symptoms. Financial problems or differences are often cited as a primary cause of divorces. And, about 50 percent of marriages end in divorce.

The greatest challenge for couples is the tendency to increase spending beyond what either person would spend on his or her own. If you're married, you know how it works: Your husband craves a glass of wine with dinner, a small thing, so you buy a nice bottle of wine even though it really is not important to you. You're already splurging, so you buy a chocolate torte for dessert, a delicacy you daydream about, but one that doesn't matter much to him. You both enjoy your respective treats, but neither of you would have purchased for yourself what the other wanted. You not only spend more money than you anticipated, you also consume more calories. Sometimes the checking account balance shrinks even as your waist expands.

It's a silly example perhaps, inconsequential to many people, but it gets to the root of money problems that many couples have. You can't negotiate the financial implications of every craving each of you has, so you indulge each other. Maybe it goes beyond a craving for sweets. She hates the rug that you kind of like, so she talks you into getting a different one. While you're rearranging your living room, you decide it's time to replace the light fixture that has always seemed just wrong for the room. It makes sense to make all the improvements at once. You hadn't really budgeted for either item, but both can go on the credit card and you'll pay off the bill next month. But next month something else comes up, and the balance on your credit card grows.

Or your wife really needs to see her mom in Boston. She sounded lonely and upset on the phone, and you haven't visited in almost a year. You hadn't budgeted for the trip, but it's important. Does that mean you cancel the family vacation you had planned for later in the summer? Maybe you can squeeze them both in.

Before long you are asking yourself—and your spouse—"What happened?" What happened is that your financial life is out of control. As in much else in marriage, you and your spouse react to many subtle clues or behaviors you see in each other—or *think* you see. For example, despite your talk about sticking to a budget, he buys a new putter, a great deal he couldn't pass up. So you think maybe money isn't as tight as he said it was, and you buy the purse you see on sale.

Expenditures can soar even when you work closely together to manage your money. Imagine how bad it can be when couples don't co-operate on spending or, worse, if they spend spitefully. "If you're going golfing in Arizona with your friends, then I'm going with mine to Los Cabos." Will you tell your friends you can't go golfing with them? Or will you take it to another level? "Will I still drive the old Honda when you get a new Lexus? Let's lease two new cars." Can you afford both? Will you pass on the Lexus you had your heart set on because you can't afford two new cars? Probably not. Even if you don't get two new cars, you might get the Lexus, but then your wife goes to Los Cabos.

It can get worse, much worse. Every person has a spending comfort level that can be exceeded when part of a twosome, often without recognition or understanding by his or her partner. Throw in the unexpected expenses that come with children and you can really have a financial mess.

Now let's complicate the challenge even more. Let's assume that one of you accepts most of the responsibility for managing your money. Rarely do I encounter in my practice a couple that divides money management equally, regardless of whether they have roughly equal incomes or one of them earns considerably more than the other. It's often a matter of affinity or interest in financial affairs. In my experience, men are more likely to manage a couple's finances. I mean the big picture: savings, investments, retirement accounts. Spending for the household is still often managed by women, but men are more likely to look after "future" money.

This system works well for many couples as long as both know—and agree on—the goals, status, and progress toward meeting them. That's one of the enormous advantages of working with a professional financial adviser. Periodic meetings with an adviser—quarterly, semiannually, or yearly—give both partners a chance to get up to speed on the details, direction, and progress of their financial plans. (We will return to this topic.)

When one partner manages the finances, without regular updating, what happens if there is an illness or death? You not only probably have bills associated with that tragedy, but you may have the surviving or healthy spouse left in the dark about finances. Too often that is exactly what happens. Men usually manage the money—and they usually die first. Women's life expectancy is 79 versus 72 for men.

Consider the following sobering statistics:

- Among the elderly poor, 75 percent are women and 80 percent were *not* poor before they were widowed (U.S. Census Bureau).
- Eighty percent of men die married, but 80 percent of women die single (Women's Institute for Secure Retirement).
- Only 21 percent of women receive survivor benefits income based on their husbands' pensions. The average elderly widow receives only 40 percent of the Social Security benefits for a married couple. Older divorced women or widows without

personal savings find their income drastically slashed by the loss of a spouse (Women's Institute for Secure Retirement).

- Almost 90 percent of women will be responsible for their own finances at some point in their lives (Women's Institute for Secure Retirement).
- Eighty percent of retired women have no pension benefits (U.S. Census Bureau).
- Women change jobs more often than men. They also spend an average of 15 percent of their careers out of the paid workforce caring for children or parents. This interruption of their careers can have a significant impact on such long-term financial planning factors as salary base, Social Security benefits, 401(k) contributions, and pension plans (Women's Institute for Secure Retirement).

Because women outlive men by an average of seven years, their financial planning strategies need to take into account a longer life and the additional health care needs that may be associated with it. For many stay-at-home caregivers, divorce or the death of a spouse leaves them financially strapped.

These statistics make it clear why both spouses need to be involved in financial planning. At some point one of them, usually the woman, will be left to manage the finances alone—and will suffer alone the consequences of poor financial planning.

The tremendous potential financial benefit of marriage often dissipates between lack of control over spending and lack of communication on financial planning issues. In this section I will discuss the four most important financial planning issues spouses face together:

- Money management;
- Planning for emergencies;
- Planning to improve life; and
- Planning for retirement.

Before we dive into the challenges of managing money with your spouse, let me address briefly one other challenge that is increasingly common: couples who work together in a family business. If you think typical marital finances can get complicated, you should see what happens when you add joint responsibility for business decisions on top of that. Joint ownership or management of a business places unique strains on a marriage. To those who decide to work together, I strongly recommend that you seek the advice of a good accountant and perhaps an informal "board of directors" that can help you make important financial decisions. You will have to plan personal finances with special care because both of your incomes are tied to the same enterprise, which can be tricky, especially in start-up companies where revenues are unpredictable. Establish realistic personal financial plans for each of the basic areas I address in this section. Careful personal financial planning is as important as careful business planning, but it can be forgotten amid the day-to-day stresses of running a business.

# 7

## MONEY MANAGEMENT

■ ■ ■

The tendency of most couples is to divide money issues into two categories: periodic or regular expenses and savings or investments to finance future goals and plans. As I have noted, women are often responsible for the first, men for the second. Successful money management requires that those lines be erased. We discussed in the first section of this book the interdependence of the five things we can do with money. Spending and saving or investing draw from the same stream of income. If one is larger, the other is smaller, which should make them of equal interest and importance to both spouses.

The result is that all money in your household should be managed jointly and with agreement on your financial priorities. It doesn't matter if $100 is mere pocket change to you or if it is your monthly savings. The same principles apply.

In light of the statistics quoted in the introduction to this section I urge women especially to become more involved in the longer-term aspects of financial planning. It is very likely that you will be the one who lives with the success or failure of your and your husband's financial plan.

Let me offer a word of encouragement. I have worked with many married women and widows who were at first overwhelmed by the terminology and concepts of financial planning. Perhaps they have been of a generation of women who did not perceive their role in the family to include being knowledgeable on financial matters. They have often expressed a lack of interest or confidence in their ability to understand, let alone master, the intricacies of personal finance. Almost without exception I have seen them rise to the task and become astute overseers of their finances. Their disinterest in finance was not innate but learned. When they decided to come to terms with the concepts of personal finance or when they needed to, they did.

If you are a woman who has deferred to her husband on financial matters, it's time to get involved while you can still have an impact on your financial future. If you are a man who has made all the longer-term financial decisions, it's time to bring your wife up to speed. Don't make her learn while she is grieving your death. That's not a morbid thought, it's just a statistical likelihood. Become a team now, regardless of your age or health. You are not shielding your wife from any unpleasantness by not including her in the details of your finances. You may, in fact, think you are doing what's best for her, but if she's not in on it, if she's not playing a role, you are not doing what's best for her, which is for her to participate in your financial planning and to know the details of your financial affairs and plans.

Fortunately, in the younger women I see, that pattern of dependent behavior is not as pronounced. Women are taking a more active, sometimes a lead role in family finances. That is as it should be.

The following topics suggest areas in which coordinated money management is required for you and your spouse to have the best possible financial future.

## BUDGETS

Agree on goals, divide responsibilities, share information. Find out from your spouse what a realistic budget is to meet his or her needs. For instance, men often don't realize what their wives spend on lipstick, moisturizer, or hairstylings, let alone a pair of shoes. A woman might not realize that when her husband says he's going to an NBA game with some buddies, he may have to lay out close to $100 for a decent seat. The key is not just how much you spend, but whether your spending is consistent with your priorities and plans.

Computer software programs, such as Quicken, can make it easier to see how much you are spending on what and to review periodically how you are doing against any budgets you set up. Periodic reviews are essential—either just with your spouse or together with your financial adviser. Most of all, avoid surprises. If you spend a few extra bucks on a circular saw or a bracelet, share your joy before the credit card bill arrives. It should go without saying, but many still need to hear it: If you have to hide expenditures, don't make them. Budget-busting spending on discretionary items tends to snowball. Just ask Congress.

## BANK ACCOUNTS

Maintain separate checking accounts. In my experience, professional and personal, this separation of accounts alleviates stress in a relationship. Neither spouse, regardless of their income, should have to be looking over their shoulder every time they write a check. Separate accounts give each partner some small sense of freedom. Even if one spouse doesn't earn income, he or she should have a separate account for day-to-day expenses.

## CREDIT RATINGS

As dangerous as credit cards are, using them regularly—and paying off the balance each month—establishes a payment history and credit rating. One problem for older couples in particular is that credit has always been in the name of the husband. That's fine except if he should die. His widow may have no credit history of her own, which could make it more difficult for her to obtain credit in her own name. Ensure that each of you has a good credit history in your own name.

## BENEFITS

Coordinate job benefits if you both earn income outside the home. I find that most people get excellent help from their employers' human resource departments in determining the best way to coordinate benefits. Most couples understand where they will get the most bang from the benefit buck. The one exception is life insurance. Employer-sponsored life insurance policies vary greatly and can be difficult to compare without experience. Don't assume that your life insurance policy through your employer is cheaper than one you could acquire independently. That's not always true because employer-sponsored plans often group the un-healthy with the healthy. Especially if you have no health problems, you may find a better deal on life insurance on your own. Special attention to financial efficiency is required if neither spouse is covered by employee benefits, a situation that has increased as more people have chosen self-employment in recent years.

## PRETAX RETIREMENT PLANS AND PENSIONS

I am going to repeat some controversial advice: Don't rely too heavily on pretax plans for retirement investing. You should diversify your retire-ment planning beyond a 401(k), IRA, or SEP account. I'll get into this in more depth in Chapter 10, "Planning for Retirement." For now, just focus on the need to coordinate your contributions to those plans.

Look closely at the asset allocation across both of your employer-sponsored or employer-matched plans as part of your annual or semi-annual review of your investments. Too often we see duplication or im-balance in assets in two separate pension plans. Your asset allocation should include all assets. When you periodically rebalance your port-folio, be sure to look at both of your pension plans as if they were one, to determine appropriate and balanced allocation. If you cannot achieve the asset allocation you desire between your two pension plans, investi-gate your options for diversifying your retirement investments beyond pretax plans, especially for any portion of your contributions that is not matched by your employers.

## TAXES

Taxes are likely to be somewhat more complex for couples. That could be a good thing. With two incomes, in many cases, you may have the means to participate in tax-reduction strategies that many people aren't familiar with. You could be shortchanging yourself if you do not investigate tax-reduction strategies that may be more affordable than you realize. Strate-gies that reduce taxes are not just for the superrich. Many of you could take advantage of them, but because the tax code can be so complex, you may not be aware of them. You should also begin to pay attention—the earlier, the better—to the tax implications of eventual distribution strate-gies. You probably are well aware of taxes on your current income, but most people overlook the potentially significant impact of taxes on the distribution of retirement savings or estates. Accumulating assets is the narrow focus of most people, but a plan to distribute those assets requires attention long before retirement comes. Don't wait until it's too late. And don't forget to consider the implications for your distribution strategy, including taxes, of the wife outliving the husband.

## USE A MODERATOR OR MEDIATOR

Financial issues can be a wedge between couples. Some of the preced-ing issues may be contentious. I know few couples who are in complete agreement on how they manage money.

One of the overlooked advantages of working with a professional fi-nancial adviser is that he or she can serve as a moderator or mediator for financial discussions between a couple. For couples who are having a hard time agreeing on priorities or sticking to plans, an adviser can provide an impartial perspective and a calming voice.

For couples who have never worked together on financial plans be-fore, an adviser can help bridge the gap in knowledge or interest. For instance, maybe it's not so easy for a husband of a certain age to bring his wife into discussions of finances when she has participated little, if at all, in the past. Maybe it's frustrating for him to explain some of the financial principles he has learned. Maybe she wants to be included but lacks the knowledge or the confidence to have her say—or to disagree. (This description is not sexist in the least. Such relationships are a fact. I have seen them many times. As is true with so much of the information I am relating here, these considerations are based on my experiences with real people who are struggling with real issues.)

I believe a good financial adviser can help husbands and wives learn to communicate financial information and evaluate possibilities without the emotional baggage couples sometimes bring to the subject. A finan-cial adviser can initiate talk about the elephant in the living room that everyone has always tried to ignore.

Beyond that, successful financial plans can often help remove a huge source of conflict, sometimes unspoken, in a marriage. Financial stress can exact an enormous toll on a marriage, once again without regard to net worth. Couples with significant assets can have as much money tension in their lives as those scraping to pay their mortgage each month. Having a good plan in place to address the issues, whatever they may be, removes a tremendous burden from a relationship. I have seen the mere creation and agreement on a financial plan lift a crushing weight off a couple's shoulders.

# 8

## Planning for Emergencies

. . .

### The Rainy Day Account

At the top of the list in being prepared for emergencies is to have access to immediate cash to meet your obligations in the short term. Once again, I part company with conventional wisdom on the approach to money for emergencies such as sickness, injury, unemployment, or some unforeseen catastrophe.

Many advisers will tell you to keep three months worth of living expenses in savings or some liquid investment. (By "liquid," I mean money that you could withdraw tomorrow if you needed it.) In many respects, I am more aggressive than others in financial matters, but when it comes to emergencies, I am more conservative. I recommend maintaining six months worth of living expenses in a reserve fund. Jobs are less secure these days, new ones take longer to find, and medical costs are in the stratosphere. All of these factors are sound reasons to provide yourself and your family with a bigger cushion.

Perhaps my approach to a rainy-day account is conditioned by the innate conservative nature of the farming heartland where I grew up and which remains arguably the foundation of the economy in this part of the world. Even if our economy is no longer farm-based, many of our social practices and customs are. Not too many of us in the Midwest are more than a generation or two removed from a farm economy. Why do farming areas tend to be conservative? Farmers can't take too many risks, because the price of failure is too high. They get one shot each year at a decent crop. There is no fallback position if what you plant doesn't grow or yields too little. Change is measured in years, not weeks.

## PROTECTING THE FUTURE:
## AN INTRODUCTION TO INSURANCE

The ideal financial plan has contingencies for complications that may arise. What if the primary wage earner loses his or her job? What if someone dies suddenly? What if you become disabled? Ask yourself whether your financial plan will still succeed if an unforeseen emergency strikes your family. Will you still be able to save and invest and to have a secure financial future?

Many of the financial plans that I review, whether devised by another professional or by an individual, will break down and fail under the worst of circumstances. A plan may look great if life stays rosy, but, unfortunately, life can turn bleak. The ideal plan succeeds in the best and the worst cases.

### Property and Casualty Insurance

An important component of worst-case planning is property and casualty insurance. The term "property and casualty insurance" generally refers to auto and homeowner's insurance. Most Americans have deductibles that are too low and do not carry enough liability protection.

The lower the insurance deductible (i.e., what you must pay out of pocket before your insurance company will reimburse you), the higher the premium. Let's assume that our auto insurance has a deductible of $250. If we raise the deductible to $500, it saves $50 in premium. If we go only five years without a claim, we can self-insure and be ahead. Even in a worst-case scenario of having an accident and filing a claim every year, it still costs only an extra $250 per year, which has a minimal financial impact on most of us. Deductibles should always be at least $500, if not $1,000.

Let's look at another problem most Americans face but do not realize it. Consider the following scenario. Your husband is 35, earns $50,000 per year, and plans to work at least 20 more years. That means he would earn $1,000,000 in those 20 years. But your husband dies in an auto accident caused by a drunk driver who has only $100,000 of liability coverage on his auto policy—not atypical for Americans. That person's insurance carrier sends you a check for $100,000. How do you feel? What would you do? Would you consult an attorney and file a lawsuit against the drunken driver? Of course you would, because $100,000 is only a small fraction of the economic value of your deceased spouse.

Now, reverse the situation. What if you make a driving error and someone is seriously hurt or killed. Do you think you are likely to be sued? Of course you are! Protecting yourself from this potential financial devastation costs roughly the same as carrying the lower deductibles you had. The liability limits should be increased on auto and homeowner insurance and an umbrella or personal liability policy should be placed over that. Liability coverage is one of the most important, necessary, and affordable things you can ever buy. No matter how much money you make, how much net worth you have, or how great a return you get from your investment portfolio, without proper liability protection you are only a slip on a banana peel away from financial devastation.

Life changes quickly. Many people commit to investment strategies that they cannot reverse when their life situation changes. It's virtually impossible to anticipate all of our future needs today. Advances in technology, tax law changes, planned obsolescence, and a propensity to consume will complicate and cause changes in our lives. We must have a plan that is adaptable.

## The Worst, Worst Case: Life Insurance

What would happen if you died? What would happen if your spouse died? Every couple should ask these questions, whether they have children or not. For most couples, the death of one of them will have a significant financial impact on the other. It could affect their ability to maintain their lifestyle and home. It could affect their ability to save and invest. The answer for most couples is life insurance—on one or both spouses, depending on their circumstances.

In past generations, when many households had only one income earner, protection for the nonearning spouse was more important. In today's two-income households, where the incomes are often roughly equal, the need for insurance for a spouse is less compelling, but for many couples it still exists.

Furthermore, I encourage all couples to look closely at life insurance before they have children, because the death benefit is more affordable the younger and healthier you are. Even if you don't have children now, you establish your policy at a lower cost than if you wait until you have children.

So let's take an "in detail" look at life insurance now. The other reason for doing this here is that life insurance could play an important role in your plans for later life as an investment and as an estate-planning tool. Surprised? I thought you would be.

## LIFE INSURANCE IN DETAIL

The value of life insurance is, first of all, pure protection for your loved ones. Your spouse (and perhaps children) receives some benefit if you die. It simply enables him or her to carry on living without your income.

Second, life insurance can provide value as an excellent investment—even if you don't die for a very long time. As I write this I can already imagine the blood pressure rising in a lot of financial gurus as they leap to their feet to object. "Life insurance as an investment vehicle? Are you kidding me?" Keep an open mind and read on.

Third, life insurance can be a valuable tool in estate planning and charitable giving. Many people buy life insurance as part of their estate planning because life insurance benefits are usually received tax free by beneficiaries. Life insurance can also be an excellent vehicle for your heirs to pay estate taxes.

Let's begin at the point where most people get stuck when it comes to considering life insurance. They ask, "How much do I need?" Uh-oh. Bad start! They've already turned down the wrong road—and they won't get far.

## Do You Need It or Want It?

When people ask me how much life insurance they need, I tell them that life insurance is not a need product, it's a *want* product, a love product. If I die before my wife and kids, I want them to have as much money as possible in my absence.

Why do people get hung up on looking at life insurance as a need?

First, most people aren't willing to face death, so it's hard to convince them that they really do *need* life insurance. None of us wants to consider the prospect that we will die soon; if we do consider the possibility, we dismiss it as very remote. Chances are, however, that you currently have auto and homeowner's insurance. You may also be insured for health care, disability income, and liability risks. But you may never even file a claim on any of these policies. You may never sustain damage to your home, for example, but you cannot afford not to cover that risk. However, we all die someday. Death is inevitable. Why do we insure assets with less value than our lives against risks that may never occur and yet we choose not to insure a risk that is certain—death?

Second, when people try to figure out how much life insurance they need, they tend to become immobilized and do nothing.

How do you calculate your life insurance needs anyway? How do you know what your family's needs will be in an indefinite future? DVD players, cellular phones, home computers, and the Internet are just some of the things that did not exist a few short years ago. How could you have planned for needs that did not exist in even the recent past?

Is homeowner's insurance a need product? Let's think about that. Assume you own a home worth $200,000. Does your policy cover the entire $200,000 value? Consider the following scenarios:

- You have $50,000 cash in the bank, which you could access if your house were destroyed and you needed to rebuild. So, would you insure your home for only $150,000?
- You *want* that $200,000 home but really only *need* a home that costs about $125,000. Would you insure your home for only $125,000?

- You have a lake cabin worth $75,000. Nobody *needs* a lake cabin. So, since it's something you only *want* but don't *need,* you probably wouldn't insure your cabin at all, right?

Don't these examples sound silly? Obviously, you would insure these assets for what they are worth. That's why we have insurance: to replace things of value. Would it not then follow that you would also insure your life for what it's worth to your family? Most Americans don't. They have been told by nearly everyone that life insurance beyond some minimal level is a waste of money.

The third problem with a focus on need is that most of us are motivated more by what we want than by what we need—especially when that need does not seem urgent. Instead, we spend our money on what we want today.

Sometimes people don't do what's good for them even as they acknowledge that it would be good for them. Consider the case of my clients Jan and Gary. I advised Jan and Gary to buy variable universal life (VUL) insurance contracts on themselves. There were two very good reasons for them to be motivated to follow my advice. First, they had small children and a mortgage, so if either of them died, the survivor would face severe financial hardship. Second, Jan and Gary were in their early 30s; since the cost would be relatively low, the VULs would be an excellent long-term investment strategy.

They agreed that the VULs made sense. However, here we are, years later, and they still haven't taken any action on the VUL policies. Every time I remind them, they tell me they like the idea but just don't have the cash flow right now, but they soon will. At that point, they'll buy the VUL contracts.

Their reasoning doesn't work for me, however, because I know that both Jan and Gary participate in their company 401(k) plans. I consider the VULs a better alternative for them at this point than the 401(k)s. Furthermore, they have bought many consumer toys and taken costly vacations. Obviously, I would consider the VULs to be more important than a boat.

Why haven't Jan and Gary invested in VULs? My guess is that they see the policies as something they need as opposed to something they really want. We are all more motivated by our wants than by our needs. Sound silly? Would you rather spend your money on medicine or a nice juicy steak? A lawnmower or a snowmobile? Sensible shoes or a new dress?

Even though Jan and Gary feel they ought to have the VULs, the policies have not been a priority, because they don't truly want them. Don't misunderstand my point: I'm not against enjoying life. Maybe it's my fault for not demonstrating effectively enough why they should really *want* the VULs.

As long as they treat it as a need product, people tend to view life insurance as something they'll get tomorrow or they view it as a need to meet at a minimum and then move on.

Those people are missing an important financial opportunity. This is where I begin to get frustrated. Life insurance is so misunderstood, even by the financial masters, that it's no wonder people raise their eyebrows when I recommend it.

Why do I recommend it? Because it's the most efficient way to ensure the financial security of your family. Is it a waste of money? Only if you do it the way people in the financial industry—even the insurance companies—recommend. But if you do it the right way, life insurance provides protection for your family, very attractive appreciation potential, significant tax benefits, and financial flexibility like no other financial products. For those reasons, nearly everyone should *want* life insurance even if they plan to defy mortality.

But it's tough to convince people of those advantages. So, before we get into the reasons why you would want life insurance in your investment universe, let's back up a minute and look at how we got to the point where life insurance as an investment is so reviled.

## Giving Money to Insurance Companies: Term versus Perm

For years the debate has raged: Which is more efficient, buying permanent life insurance, or buying term insurance and investing the cost difference?

A term insurance policy provides a fixed sum of death benefit for a fixed length of time, usually 20–30 years. The policy is priced according to the statistical likelihood of the death of the person insured. If you're young and healthy, you can buy term insurance very cheaply, because the odds are against your dying during the term the insurance is in force. If you're old and sick, the cost is very, very high, because it's much more likely that the insurance company will have to pay.

Permanent life insurance (or "perm") is a policy that pays a predetermined death benefit for which you pay a set premium for your life. It covers your life, not for a set period of time, or term, but until you actually die. Because the permanent policy will almost certainly pay a death benefit at some time—we all die!—it's naturally more expensive. The payments for that insurance are spread out over your expected life.

The higher premiums are the cause for the debate about whether to buy perm or settle for term and invest the difference in premiums in other assets.

A lot of powerful interests have a stake in whether you buy term or perm, and all of them—including the life insurance companies themselves!—prefer that you buy term insurance.

It's easy to see why the broker-dealers, mutual fund companies, and banks prefer that you buy term. If you buy term and invest the difference, where will you put that money? Of course, you'll avail yourself of the services of these institutions. You'll invest your money with them, probably for a very long time. They get the money, not the insurance companies. (One of the catches to the term versus perm debate, however, is that many people do not actually invest the difference in premiums; they spend it. But enough invest it that it's in the interests of Wall Street to advocate for term insurance and hope to get your money.)

But why would insurance companies prefer to sell term insurance if they get more money up front by selling perm? The answer can be found in a study done at Pennsylvania State University, which concluded that fewer than one term policy in six survives to the end of the term for which it was written and less than 1 percent of all term insurance policies *ever* pay a death claim.[6] As a result, most people who buy term insurance quit paying

---

[6] Arthur L. Williams, "Some Empirical Observations on Term Life Insurance: Revisited," *Journal of Insurance Issues and Practices*, 7, no. 1 (1984): 52–62.

the premiums before the term ends, and a very low percentage of policies results in claims paid. Since they seldom pay a death claim, one can reasonably assume that insurance companies love to issue term insurance. The money goes only one way, into the insurance companies' coffers.

Life insurance companies are aware of this fact, but most people who buy term life insurance don't consider it. But this discrepancy is one big reason why term insurance is a very inefficient use of your money—even apart from the other advantages of perm insurance, which I'll discuss in a minute.

But now let's also throw in another concept: opportunity cost. Whenever there's a cost in our financial world, we have not only that cost but also the cost of not being able to use that money to earn a return. When you add the cost of lost opportunity to the cost of premiums, term insurance is not nearly as cheap as you might think.

Assume that a 35-year-old male pays $360 per year for $250,000 in term death benefit coverage for 30 years. That $360 earns nothing. If we assume he earns a hypothetical 10 percent annual return on that money if he invests it, the actual cost of his insurance over 30 years, if premiums *never* go up, is not just $10,800 ($360 x 30 years), but $65,140 ($360 x 30 years compounding at 10 percent). Furthermore, if he then drops the coverage at age 65, because it's become cost-prohibitive and he doesn't really need it anymore, the opportunity cost still continues through the rest of his life (14 more years, statistically). Therefore, the total cost is $247,369 ($65,140 x 14 years compounding at 10 percent)! In the final analysis, $250,000 of death benefit costs nearly $250,000, but he drops the coverage before he can collect—at an age when statistically he is more likely to die. Of course, this entire scenario is extremely improbable because, according to the Penn State study, it is unlikely that this person would actually pay the premium for 30 years.

So you are very unlikely to get any benefit from buying term insurance—ever! But is perm any better?

## Renting versus Owning

You probably make mortgage payments. If you're renting instead, you perhaps plan to buy a home someday. In most cases you can rent for a lower monthly cost than a mortgage payment. So why not continue to rent? There are no doubt many reasons why you are willing to pay more to buy a home (remember: cost is an issue only in the absence of value), but one primary reason is because you will *own* the home. You build equity with your mortgage payment. With rent, the money all goes down the drain. You ultimately move and get nothing back from all your rent payments.

Term life insurance is comparable to renting, whereas permanent life insurance is comparable to owning. Your payments for perm give you something with tangible value, just like owning real estate. Perm is an asset. It has cash value and a death benefit for life. With term there is a greater than 99 percent chance you won't even make your rent payments to the end of the lease, and you won't get any money back anyway.

### Permanent Changes for the Better

The problem with permanent life insurance, if you go back a couple of decades to the time when many of us learned about finances from our parents, was that the returns you could earn on the money invested in perm insurance, above the cost of the death benefit, were very conservative. You probably could do better investing the difference in premiums yourself, because the cash value of the life insurance was invested in fixed-interest investments that provided a low return.

The returns on permanent life insurance changed dramatically, however, when a new type of permanent life insurance was created in the late 1970s—variable universal life insurance.

With a VUL policy, the cash value of life insurance is invested in equity portfolios wrapped inside the life insurance. The internal mutual fund–like accounts are called subaccounts, and they can be compared to retail mutual funds. Insurance subaccounts, in fact, are often managed by the same people who manage retail mutual funds. The performance is likely to be comparable, except for two major differences:

- The earnings of a retail mutual fund are taxable (unless owned inside some type of pretax retirement plan), while earnings in a VUL are not; and
- The VUL deducts life insurance costs.

The performance of VUL subaccounts often exceeds that of retail funds, however, because the managers don't have to be concerned about tax liabilities for shareholders. That improved performance often makes up for some of the insurance cost. With access to typical market returns on investment, the VUL offers the potential of significantly better performance than earlier life insurance investments provided. This innovation eliminated one of the major objections to permanent life insurance—that it was a bad investment. For investors who are middle-aged or younger, and in a moderate tax bracket, it is possible that a VUL policy will *outperform* retail mutual funds. (Note: Both mutual funds and VUL investment subaccounts involve market risk, including fluctuating returns and possible loss of principal. In addition, early withdrawals from and loans taken against VULs may involve additional fees and tax penalties and may negatively affect death benefits.)

With the advent of the VUL, you could buy life insurance that would almost certainly pay a benefit someday (unlike term insurance) and has the potential to earn competitive returns. But the advantages don't end there. You will understand why you should truly *want* life insurance as an investment vehicle, however, when we look at the strategic applications of life insurance.

### Strategic Applications of Permanent Life Insurance

The current tax advantages of life insurance can make it an attractive investment strategy even if you have no desire (or need) for the death benefit. There is a drag on the internal rate of return for the costs unique to life insurance, primarily for the death benefit. However, depending on your age, gender, health, and tax bracket, the tax advantages of life insurance may more than offset the internal costs.

The higher the tax bracket, the greater the advantages. The greatest advantages also will be enjoyed by people who are young and healthy, because the mortality cost of the insurance (the amount you pay for the death benefit) is lower for those who are not likely to die for a long time. Women also enjoy some advantages in the cost of life insurance, because statistically they live longer.

In my experience, permanent life insurance is almost certain to be advantageous for healthy people up to the age of 50. After that age, health becomes a critical factor in determining the potential benefits. Even more important is how long one plans to fund the contract. We advise at least 10 years, preferably longer.

The often-overlooked strategic advantage of permanent life insurance in a financial plan is that it can be used as a conduit to other investment strategies. New money goes into perm, which then serves as a "holding tank." We can take distributions from our holding tank for personal use (such as to pay for college or start a new business) or invest in assets not available through the insurance subaccounts (such as a stock opportunity or real estate). We can even take distributions and reinvest them in pretax plans or a Roth IRA if we want to.

If we have taxable earnings on our new investment, those earnings can then be directed back into the insurance policy and not allowed to compound. Using perm insurance as the conduit to other investments is an effective way to potentially increase benefits and earnings, because no new money is wasted by first going into assets that don't produce benefits. Perm insurance does not replace other investments and is not necessarily better than other investments. But, it enhances those other investments by making them more efficient.

Let's assume you contribute $5,000 a year to a permanent life insurance policy for 10 years. Therefore, you have a basis of $50,000. However, there is $100,000 of equity (cash value) in the contract. Because the policy has the unique accounting treatment of first-in, first-out, you could withdraw $50,000 and not trigger a tax liability because the withdrawal is treated as a return of basis. However, if you withdrew the entire $100,000, you would receive a 1099 for the $50,000 gain and that gain would be taxed at ordinary income tax rates. The way to avoid the income tax, if you desire a distribution that exceeds your basis, is to take out a loan from the insurance company, with your policy as collateral.

Most permanent life insurance contracts offer a very low net cost to borrow money against the cash value of your policy. Unlike a withdrawal, a policy loan does not disturb the contract's equity: The company actually lends you money, and the equity in the contract serves as collateral. An amount equal to the loan is set aside and credited with an interest rate generally in a range from 2 percent to 4 percent below to the same interest rate you are being charged to borrow. In other words, generally the worst case is a 4 percent net cost, but some contracts even allow for zero-cost loans.

Now, here's where things get interesting. Assume you are able to have a zero-cost loan: The insurance company charges you 6 percent and internally credits back the same 6 percent on the same dollar value as the loan. You would still have a statement showing the interest cost, which is effectively a phantom number because you earned the same interest within the contract equity.

Further assume you get the loan in order to reinvest. If you borrow $10,000 at 6 percent, you get a statement showing $600 in interest cost after a year. (You also simultaneously earned $600 in the contract.) You reinvest the $10,000 somewhere that earns a hypothetical 12 percent, generating a 1099 showing $1,200 in taxable earnings. It would be a good idea for you to put the $1,200 of earnings back into the insurance contract so that your tax liability does not compound. Under current tax laws, the $600 interest cost is deductible against the $1,200 of investment income, thus creating yet another tax advantage.

So, not only did the contract allow for a tax-free distribution, it also allowed for a deduction against portfolio earnings. If you use the proceeds of a policy loan for investment or business purposes, and you can prove that use, the interest on the loan is usually deductible. You can do this not just once but as often as you would like. Dollars go into the insurance account, then are repositioned to other investments, then back into insurance repeatedly, thus increasing the acceleration of money.

Moreover, the earnings in your insurance contract are in most cases income tax free, and unlike a traditional IRA those earnings may be income tax free to your heirs, an enormous advantage over investing the money yourself, even if the taxes are deferred.

## THE THREE LITTLE PIGS: INVESTMENT STRATEGIES

Most of us know the story of the three little pigs. But, you probably don't know what happened to them after they escaped the wolf by taking refuge in the third pig's house of bricks.

The three little pigs continued to live and work together. They all became independent corn tasters at corn canning and processing plants.

They greatly enjoyed their jobs and prospered equally. Each of the three pigs earned about $60,000 per year, which put them all in a combined state and federal tax bracket of 35 percent. Also, they all determined to invest about 10 percent of their annual incomes.

The first little pig, the genius who built the straw house, started to save $500 dollars per month at age 45 (in pig years). Each month, he put his $500 into a nice portfolio of taxable mutual funds that earned 10 percent per year. By age 60, when he retired, he had accumulated $150,127 in his portfolio after taxes.

The second little pig, the one who had lived in the stick house, also started saving at age 45; he put $500 per month into a tax-deferred portfolio that earned 9 percent per year. By age 60 he had accumulated $184,641. Of course, upon beginning any distributions he would have to pay the taxes that he had been deferring while accumulating the money.

The third little pig, he of brick house fame, like his brothers began saving $500 per month at age 45. He invested in a tax-advantaged plan that earned 9 percent. By age 60 he had accumulated $162,207.

You're probably wondering how pig 2 invested the same amount, over the same 15 years, and earned the same 9 percent but by age 60 had accumulated an additional $22,434. That's because the third little pig's tax-advantaged investment strategy was a variable universal life insurance policy. His return was lower due to his insurance cost. Ouch! Seems like a bad deal so far—but let's look at the impact on their retirement years.

At age 60, each of the three pigs decided he needed $1,000 per month in his 35 percent tax bracket to support his lifestyle in retirement. The first little pig needed to withdraw $16,671 per year to net that $12,000. The second little pig needed to withdraw $18,462 from his tax-deferred account per year to net $12,000. (Because the first little pig had invested after-tax dollars, some of the value of his account was his basis, which could not be taxed again. Since he owed less tax on what he withdrew than the second pig, he did not need to withdraw as much to net $12,000.) The third little pig was able to take $12,000 per year in distributions with no tax liability.

Unfortunately, the first pig ran out of money at age 82. Even though he continued to earn 10 percent on his investments, the annual distribution of $16,671 wore the account down to nothing in 22 years. The second little pig had only $9,201 left at age 82, so he would run out of money six months later. However, the third little pig still had $219,271 in his account. Not only had he not run out of money like pigs 1 and 2, but his account had actually grown by more than $57,000. In fact, when he died at age 95, the third little pig's *tax-advantaged* account was worth $231,889: It had kept him living comfortably—and grown another $12,618 after he turned 82.

Table 8.1 summarizes the experiences of the three little pigs. Each started saving $500 a month at age 45 and retired at age 60. The first little pig earned 10 percent a year on his savings in a taxable account. The second little pig earned 9 percent a year in a tax-deferred account. The third little pig earned 9 percent a year in a tax-advantaged account—a variable universal life insurance policy. Each little pig was in a combined federal and state tax bracket of 35 percent.

### TABLE 8.1. WHICH INVESTMENT STRATEGY WOULD YOU COPY?

|  | Pig 1 | Pig 2 | Pig 3 |
| --- | --- | --- | --- |
| Account at age 60 | $150,127 | $184,641 | $162,207 |
| Annual withdrawal to net $12,000 | 16,671 | 18,462 | 12,000 |
| Account at age 80 | 12,810 | 32,243 | 212,481 |
| Account at age 82 | 0 | 9,201 | 219,271 |
| Account at age 95 | 0 | 0 | 231,889 |

Let's take a closer look at the results of the third little pig's investment strategy. He invested $6,000 per year for 15 years for a total investment of $90,000. He received distributions of $12,000 per year for 35 years, totaling $420,000. When he died he still had $231,889 in his account. Think about this a moment. He invested $90,000 and received $420,000 in his golden years and then left another $231,889 income tax-free to his heirs! Are you impressed by this investment strategy? I think you should be.

Whose investment strategy would you copy? We knew that third little pig was smart from the time we first met him in his encounter with the wolf. Just as his investment in a brick house kept him safe from the wolf at his door, his investment of $500 per month in a variable universal life insurance policy put him far ahead in his later years. (Oh, by the way, the third little pig did not *need* the life insurance. He *wanted* it.)

You can see that the beauty of life insurance is that it does provide for the greatest emergency of all, a death, but at its best it is also a springboard into planning for the rest of your life and even your legacy if you live to a ripe old age.

## INJURED WITH NO INCOME:
## DISABILITY INSURANCE IN DETAIL

After death, the most serious emergency for your spouse (and children) is a disability that prevents you from working. In some cases, disability can impose a greater financial hardship on your family than your death, because along with the loss of income may come serious expenses to care for you.

Disability insurance is one of the most important types of insurance, yet only about 40 percent of workers in the United States are estimated to have it. Why do you need it? Your most significant asset is probably your ability to produce income. Statistically, you are more likely to suffer a disability than a serious loss on your home, but nearly everyone has homeowner's insurance. Most of us roll the dice, however, when it comes to disability income coverage. One reason why people avoid it is the cost. But in spite of the cost, most people should have disability insurance. The risk of not having it and suffering a disability is too great.

If we think of a financial plan as a roadmap to a destination, the fuel or the gas of the financial plan is income. Without income, the plan stops in its tracks. It's the equivalent of running out of gas in your car. You can't go anywhere. If you are unable to earn income, how can you have a successful financial plan? How can you reach your financial goals—retire at age 59, pay for your kids' college, travel—if you don't have income? Disability insurance protects you against the loss of income, against running out of gas. It keeps you on the road.

I believe that you should protect as much of your income as you can. Even if you choose not to fully protect your income, you can at least partially protect it. The fact is, no one ever has enough money when they are sick or hurt or unable to work. Money does not solve all the problems, but it sure helps. And not having money certainly accentuates the problem.

Disability income will protect your financial plan and ensure that you have resources to achieve your goals and fulfill your role as provider for your children. Some people leave their financial futures to chance. Here are some statistics that might inspire you to take some action and create an efficient financial plan that includes disability insurance:

- One out of every 106 people in this country dies every day.
- One out of every 88 homes will have a fire.
- One out of every 70 cars on the road will be involved in a serious car accident.
- One out of every eight people will suffer some form of disability.

Based on those numbers, you would expect disability insurance to be the most popular form of insurance. We all have insurance on our home and car, and many of us have life insurance, but relatively few of us have disability income insurance. Still not convinced? I can give you even scarier numbers:

- A disability is 16 times more likely than a death to cause fore-closure on a mortgage.
- If you're 25 years old there's almost a 50/50 chance that you will suffer at least a 90-day disability at some point in your life before you reach age 65. If you're 45 years old, the chances are about 40 percent.[7]

As if those figures are not at least sobering, consider your sources of assistance if you are disabled. If you think the government will take care

---

[7] Sources: The National Safety Council, the American Society of Actuaries, the Commissioner's Disability Table, and the National Center for Health Statistics.

of you if you suffer a disability, here is the Social Security Administration's definition of disability:

> The inability to engage in any substantial gainful activity by reason of any medically determinable physical or mental impairment which has lasted or could be expected to last for a continuous period of 12 months or result in death. Impairment must be so severe that the individual is unable to engage in substantial, gainful work that exists in the immediate area in which the applicant lives.

If you think you will be able to maintain your income and your lifestyle, if you think you can provide for your spouse or even avoid becoming a financial burden by that definition, you are most likely mistaken.

Even if you have disability coverage through your employer, you may need to supplement that coverage. You might suspect that many people are beginning to view favorably the advantages of supplemental disability insurance given the ubiquitous AFLAC duck on television commercials. I doubt that AFLAC would continue to run those commercials so often if people weren't getting the duck's message. More people should pay attention and investigate their disability insurance options.

Disability insurance is not cheap, however, which is probably the primary reason why way too few people have it. The cost of a disability policy will vary based on your age, gender, current health, and occupation. Annual premiums typically range from 2 percent to 3 percent of salary. Based on a 2003 sampling of rates, a 45-year-old male executive might pay somewhere in the neighborhood of $230 a month for a policy that provides benefits or coverage of about $5,000 a month. A female surgeon might pay $425 a month, or almost twice as much, for a similar policy with similar benefits.

One way to look at the cost of disability insurance, as with many other types of insurance, is as a mistake. Just assume that whether you buy it or you don't, you are making a financial error. Now calculate the potential cost of that mistake two ways.

If you are a potential candidate for disability income looking at a monthly benefit of $5,000, that amounts to an annual benefit of $60,000.

If you take out the policy at age 40 and receive benefits until age 65, you're looking at a total benefit of $1.5 million for a monthly cost of roughly $185. So, if you don't buy a policy, you lose $1.5 million or more. That's what a disability could cost you. There goes your family's financial future along with your own goals and objectives. One and a half million dollars! That's a big mistake.

On the other hand, if the worst thing that happens is that you never collect benefits, you have made a much less costly mistake. A policy that costs $185 a month, or about $2,220 a year, will cost $55,500 over 25 years. Compared to $1.5 million, that's a little mistake. The question is, would you rather make a little mistake or a big mistake?

As with all insurance, disability policies come in all shapes, colors, and sizes. Picking the right policy for yourself will require some research and, perhaps, some guidance from professionals who are familiar with the range of products offered. If you want to research policy possibilities, consider the following key variables:

**The definition of disability.** A few policies require total disability before payments begin. So-called residual benefits will make up for lost income if you can work, but not at your normal job. By contrast, *own-occupation* coverage will pay if you cannot hold down your job even if you can do something else. This coverage may run 20 percent more than a residual policy and may be difficult to obtain. The own-occupation definition of disability may not be available for all professions or all occupations. Some policies also define disability differently after a specified period of time. Your education, experience, and past earnings are taken into account to determine whether you are qualified to resume work. Partial or residual benefits may be paid on some policies when the impairment allows you to perform only a portion of your duties. This provision may also pay benefits in the event the disability reduces your income by a certain amount.

**Waiting period.** Benefits typically kick in after 90 days. You may be able to reduce your premium by selecting a longer waiting period before the policy pays benefits. Commonly available periods are 30, 60, 90, 180, or 360 days. Naturally, the longer the elimination or waiting period you select, the lower the premium. The key question is whether the waiting period, sometimes called an elimination period, is proper for your circumstances? Your needs, cash reserves, and other income sources, such as investments or spouse's income, should be the deciding factors in selecting a proper elimination period.

**Benefit period.** What benefit period should be selected? How long do you want to receive benefits? Since a long-term medical disability can be financially devastating, you should elect a long-term benefit if possible. Some companies offer lifetime benefit periods, but periods as short as 24 to 60 months are also available.

**Cost-of-living adjustment.** Is there a cost-of-living adjustment, which would increase benefit payments after disability occurs?

**Income caps.** Most policies pay up to 60 percent of your salary. In group policies, Social Security payments are counted against that cap and reduce your benefits. Even if you buy a supplemental policy, benefits from all sources generally cannot exceed about 70 percent of your pay.

**Premium structure.** Premiums are either level for the life of the policy or increase as you age. For a long-term need, a level term is best. Bear in mind that if *you* pay the premiums, the benefits received are not taxable as income. If your *employer* pays the premium, that payment is considered part of your income by the IRS and it will be taxed that way. Any benefits you receive would then also be taxable.

**Cancelability and renewability of policy.** Except for non-payment of premiums, a noncancelable or guaranteed-renewable policy cannot be canceled by the insurance company. Non-cancelable generally means that the insurance company cannot cancel the policy, change the policy provisions, or increase policy premiums as long as premiums are paid on time. Guaranteed-renewable is similar, but it does allow the insurance companies to increase the premium.

The bottom line in disability income insurance is this: Most Americans do not have adequate disability income coverage. If you are among them, investigate how you can acquire adequate coverage.

## Long-Term Care Insurance

Planning for emergencies must also take into account the potential need in your later years for long-term care. Long-term care insurance can provide for that contingency, but it is not a product that will be attractive to as many people as life insurance. How should you address the possibility that you will require long-term care?

Long-term care insurance is most attractive for those in the middle class. If your assets provide earnings more than the annual cost of nursing home care, then the cost probably will not deplete your assets and it may not be a financial concern for you. On the flip side, if you have few assets to protect, you probably do not need long-term care insurance—and cannot afford it anyway. People with lower incomes are eligible for Medicaid. It's the people in the middle who should consider long-term care insurance. The primary advantage of long-term care insurance is that it is the most effective way to protect your estate from being depleted by health care costs. If protecting your estate is not a concern, you may not want it.

The bottom line is this: If you can afford the cost of a long-term care policy without any detraction from your lifestyle, you should buy it. If, however, the premium cost is such that it changes the way you are able to live and makes you "insurance poor," you may have to alter the structure of the policy or take your chances without long-term care coverage.

The most efficient time to purchase long-term care insurance is when you are in your 50s. Although it's unlikely that you will need it for some time, it's much cheaper than if you wait until you are over 60. Also, from a health standpoint, you're far more likely to qualify for coverage while in your 50s. If you're over 70, it's probably too late because the cost likely will be prohibitive. If you are considering long-term care policies, look for several key features, including:

- Coverage of at least $100 per day;
- Inflation protection;
- Coverage not limited to skilled nursing homes;
- No prior hospitalization required;
- The ability to stop paying premiums once you've received benefits for 90 days; and
- Coverage for home health care.

## PART OF A PLAN

In this discussion of insurance, we have treated each type of insurance as a separate entity. In truth, they must be looked at in terms of your overall financial plan in combination with all other components. I recommend life insurance and disability insurance for most people, but your life situation and your goals will dictate whether they should be a part of your plan. As in all other aspects of financial planning, you cannot examine one variable in isolation. Planning for emergencies is but one consideration. You cannot spend your life and all your money waiting for catastrophe. You have to live for today and for tomorrow, too. So, in the next chapter we'll take a look at a much happier topic, planning to improve your life. Your love for others, your spouse and perhaps children, will be expressed by your plans to help them live full lives even if you do not. But your love for others will also be expressed in sharing the joys of living and the unique contributions you make to their lives every day by being who you are. Do we need to look the worst case in the face and plan for it? Yes. Do we need to be consumed by it? Never. Expect the best and plan for that, as well.

# 9

## Planning to Improve Your Life

■ ■ ■

Financial planning is not a drab endeavor that requires you to live a spartan lifestyle for the next 30 years so that you won't end up living on the streets with all your possessions in a shopping bag when you are 70. There is more to life than waiting for a disaster or retirement.

Quality-of-life issues require planning, too. Expand your horizons, have fun, acquire new skills. There is a lot of life to be lived between now and when you walk away from your job for the last time. People forget to plan for their lives in the short term. Maybe you want to see Paris before you need a walker. Maybe you want to cliff-dive in Acapulco, which may be inadvisable if you've already reached retirement age. Or maybe you want to take a cooking class now with Chef Luigi that will give you hours of pleasure for the rest of your life, instead of later when you might be on a restricted diet. Your goals for saving and investing don't have to be limited to three or four decades down the road.

A good plan takes into account how you want to live now as well as later in life. It strikes a balance between now and then. Are you living a humdrum life now so that you won't have to when you're older? That depends on your goals. Maybe sacrificing now, living a no-frills lifestyle, will enable you to do things you want to do when you're 65 or 45. On the other hand, you might be less healthy then.

I have a friend in his late 50s who spends as much time as possible with his year-old grandchild, often devoting entire days to her. He lights up when he talks about her. In a quiet moment he admitted that one reason he treasured the hours with her was that he missed his own daughters growing up when he was young, because he was so busy establishing himself in a career that required constant travel. He got a second chance to experience the joys of watching a child grow minute by minute. Some who miss out on that unique thrill when they are young don't get another opportunity.

You should not infer from my negative comments earlier regarding our propensity to consume that I think you should pinch pennies for some distant day. A good plan takes into account how you want to live now and later, and strikes a balance between being prudent and living poor now so you don't have to later. By curtailing frivolous spending now you may reap the benefits in one or two years instead of 25.

Often the best investments we can make are in ourselves. We can improve our quality of life by pursuing a passion or hobby. We can improve our earning potential by investing in education or professional credentials. We can sometimes do both by investing in our own business.

I can't be at all specific in telling you how to plan to enjoy life more, because your enjoyment and mine or another guy's are likely to be so vastly different. I can only urge you to dream a little and balance the future with the present. I am reminded of something a preschool teacher I know had her students say every morning when they arrived in class: "This is the day we have. We can use this day or throw it away, but this is the day we have." What a wonderful way to ingrain in children the notion that they can make of each day what they want. They are each responsible for how their day turns out. We adults are, too.

Remember John Lennon's famous line: "Life is what happens while we're making other plans." Don't let that happen to you while you're making your financial plan. Include the present in your plan so that it doesn't pass you by.

# 10

## PLANNING FOR RETIREMENT

■ ■ ■

When the topic is money, few things command so much of our attention as planning for retirement. I think part of that has to do with our culture in the United States. We worship youth, and our elderly are often pushed aside to fend for themselves. Extended family isn't what it used to be in this country and still is in many other nations.

We also are consumed by our work and our careers. When we meet people one of the first questions is, "What do you do?" It's a question that rarely comes up in conversations in many parts of Europe. We define ourselves by our work and spend longer hours working than do people in most other countries. We work longer days, longer weeks and take shorter vacations. Perhaps it's no wonder that so many people are so eager for retirement and so fearful of whether they will have sufficient incomes to live the way they hope to without working.

Despite all the time we spend thinking and talking about saving and investing for retirement, Americans are notoriously bad savers. Our saving rate pales in comparison to saving rates in other countries.

The only place to begin to tackle this subject, so fraught with expectation, is with how much you should save or invest to retire in the style you desire.

### WANTS VERSUS NEEDS

Most discussions of retirement planning begin with an estimate that you will need 70 percent of your working income when you retire. That's the wrong place to start. Don't let anyone tell you what you might *need* in retirement. You start the discussion by telling them what you *want*.

What's the point of planning, saving, and investing? If you begin where many industry experts and consultants advise, you may already be planning to fail. Don't start with *needs* planning. Needs planning is very popular and is the prevalent planning methodology in the financial industry today. It's one of the worst things you could do—and suggests a financial outlook that I constantly fight. If you base your planning on what you need, you are aiming too low. In the late 1960s the Rolling Stones sang, "You can't always get what you want . . ."—but why would anyone plan for anything less?

## THE EEYORE SCHOOL OF FINANCIAL PLANNING

If you don't have young kids around, you may have forgotten about Eeyore, the donkey in the wonderful Winnie the Pooh books. Eeyore walks around with a cloud over his head; he's always pessimistic. Eeyore's philosophy of life is, "If something can go wrong, it probably will." The world is full of needs planners, and their alma mater was the Eeyore School of Financial Planning.

Here's how needs planning works: You decide that it is time to plan for your retirement. You make $50,000 a year working and, following traditional financial thinking, decide that you need 70 percent of that income for retirement. Therefore, instead of $50,000, you decide you will need $35,000. Now that's a "Gloomy Place," as Eeyore's meadow is called.

At retirement your cost of living may be lower than ever, but isn't that the time to enjoy the fruits of your years of labor? How much fun can you have on $35,000 per year? My point is this: You may *need* only $35,000 per year, but how much do you *want*? Your financial plan should be designed to help you get what you want, not just what you need.

Why limit yourself to your perceived need rather than realizing your full financial potential? You should attempt to determine accurately your need and then exceed it. If you're embarking on a 100-mile car trip and your car gets 20 miles per gallon, you need five gallons of gas in your tank. My advice to you, however, would be to fill your tank before you leave. What if you encounter a traffic jam, a detour, or bad weather?

Needs planning is based on several assumptions that you are average—and we have already established that you are not and do not want to be.

## False Assumption #1: You'll Spend Less on Discretionary Items in Retirement

How exactly will you spend less in retirement? Maybe you will if you are happy to sit at home year round and read books borrowed from the library. Most people, however, have big plans for retirement, the first time in their adult lives that they can do precisely what they want to do. They plan to travel, play golf whenever they feel like it, pursue their hobbies. But all of those activities require money—probably more money than you'll save by not having work-related expenses.

Even social life changes for many people when they retire. The social aspect of work is lost; the camaraderie of the work place is gone. To make up for it, people get together with friends more often. But where do they go? They meet for lunch or dinner—and probably spend more on eating out in retirement than ever before.

Many people assume as well that they'll spend less on possessions. After all, don't they already own the furniture, the TV, all their kitchen appliances? True, but what of the next generation of technological advances? Will you buy a computer? Maybe you already have one, but will you want to upgrade it so you can watch movies on it—any movie, any time—and use it as a videophone to talk to and watch your grandchildren? Or will you be content to stick with older technology and just replace your old VCR with a new DVD player?

Technology advancements and planned obsolescence will certainly continue to change everyone's lives. Think of our many "necessities" today that were luxuries yesterday. When did telephones become a necessity? When will portable or cellular phones be viewed the same as old rotary telephones once were? What will the next 10 or 20 years bring? What new conveniences will become commonplace? Will you keep up to date? Will it matter? To most people it will, and they will buy the new conveniences. That takes money.

Before you plan to retire on an income based on a needs-planning target of 70 percent of your income, I challenge you to do some calculating. If you're making $50,000 now, as in our example above, and plan to retire on $35,000, figure out how you are going to spend $15,000 less every year. Your Golden Ager's discount at movie theaters is not going to cut your cost of living by 30 percent.

## False Assumption #2: Your Housing Costs Will Be Much Lower In Retirement

If your mortgage is paid off, your housing costs could drop significantly. That will be true for many people who have lived in the same house for the past three decades and paid for it—which is not many people in this day and age. But even that is no guarantee that your housing costs are going to plummet. Maintenance on older homes is an ongoing proposition, and property taxes increase. I know of people who have had to sell their homes because their retirement income wasn't high enough to pay the property taxes. They had the "misfortune" of owning a home in a desirable neighborhood where property values skyrocketed and their property taxes followed. Of course, they made some money by selling their houses, but they loved their homes and their neighborhoods; it was painful to leave.

### WANTS PLANNING: REALIZE YOUR POTENTIAL!

Needs planning is great advice for the masses—those who aren't planning at all now and need some place to start. It's a great way to convince people that they should save something, but it's pitiful advice for people who want to do better than get by. Don't settle for mediocrity in your investment planning. Try to excel. It is fine to set a floor or a minimum for what you'll need to get by, but then aim a little higher—and plan to get there! Become a "wants" planner.

Many of my clients retire with higher annual incomes than when they were working. My own personal plan is designed to exceed my average annual working income. Don't be satisfied to be one of the "70 percenters"—people striving, to use the word lightly, to retire at 70 percent of their working income just because they have been brainwashed to believe that's what they'll need.

## What Do You Want?

Instead of planning to meet your needs based on some percentage of your working income, ask yourself what you want from life: What life have you imagined? What is your dream? Few people hesitate when asked about their dream. For some the dream is a secure retirement, perhaps early, with the time, comfort, and good health to enjoy family and friends. Others imagine the opportunity to pursue passions: art, music, travel, perhaps even the infuriating white dimpled ball or the wily walleye. Perhaps you dream of education and security for your children or grandchildren, leaving a legacy in your community, or improving life for future generations. Your financial plan begins with your dreams, because they are the true currency of your life.

If I do my job well, my clients should not have to curtail their lifestyle in retirement—and many do not. The whole purpose of financial planning is to provide adequate resources so that people don't have to pinch pennies. How much will be enough for you? That depends on your lifestyle, your dreams, and, in most cases, the people you love.

## Don't Settle for Half a Plan

Once you have determined what you want in retirement, you have made a good start. You at least know where your financial plan has to take you. And then you start investing to accumulate as much money as possible to help you get to some magical figure that will provide the income you have chosen. Well, yes, partly. That's a third of a financial plan.

Everyone focuses on how they can accumulate enough assets to carry them from retirement until they die, but almost no one thinks about how they will distribute those assets. What impact will distribution have on how and how much you save and invest? How will you liquidate your investments? Will there be costs associated with that? What will be the impact of taxes on your distributions? Will you be in a higher or a lower tax bracket? Will you be taxed at ordinary income tax rates or capital gains tax rates?

If you die before your spouse, will your spouse collect life insurance? How will that affect the distribution of other assets? Will there be anything left for your estate? What will the tax bite on those assets be for your heirs?

Remember the three phases of financial planning I introduced in Chapter 6: accumulation, distribution, and legacy. All three are needed for a complete plan for most people. Problems arise because one cannot devise an efficient distribution strategy after the fact. In other words, the way you accumulate assets very often determines how they can be distributed. Efficient distribution strategies can't undo some steps taken years earlier. By the time you retire you may have to live with the results of your accumulation strategy.

Of course, some vehicles such as trusts for distribution and legacy can be established at any age and are a valuable tool. But as we discuss in Chapter 19, trusts do require a certain level of assets to be efficient. We can also provide useful advice on the timing of distributions from vehicles such as IRAs.

---

■ **EXAMPLE:** A 63-year-old man came to us for assistance in planning distributions from his IRA. He did not anticipate needing to use his IRA funds for the foreseeable future. He wanted to know if he should delay distribution until age 70½ when the IRA requires it. We recommended that he begin to take distributions from his IRA at the most advantageous tax rates and also to factor in the likely appreciation of his IRA before he reached 70½.

If his IRA continued to appreciate at historical average rates for equities—over 10 percent a year—his IRA would double in value before he reached age 70½. Many seniors have found that those types of returns in the time between retirement and mandatory distribution push their income from an IRA into a higher tax bracket—which really defeats the purpose of tax-deferred accounts.

We determined that the potential appreciation could push his income into a higher tax bracket and recommended that he begin taking distributions annually to "soak up" his present tax bracket. That meant he began immediately to take distributions from his IRA to the extent that it would push his income to the highest level of his present tax bracket without pushing him into a higher one. Just for illustration, let's assume that the top of his tax bracket was $50,000 in income. If he anticipated income from other sources to be $35,000, he would want to take a distribution from his IRA of $15,000. He would gradually reduce his IRA account that way so that he could reduce the likelihood that mandatory distributions from his IRA would push his income above $50,000 in later years. In addition, he shifted assets into personal accounts, which may not be subject to taxes when he dies.

---

Why don't more people plan for all three phases? The answer is found partly in the financial institutions of our country. They make their money largely from selling you products and taking commissions on helping you accumulate assets. Far fewer of them provide much assistance with distribution or legacy. The services they do provide in those fields are targeted primarily at the very rich. The reason is fairly simple: It takes considerably more expertise to provide good advice on distribution and legacy strategies. Anyone can recommend a hot stock. Devising an efficient distribution strategy is quite a bit more complicated and requires a great deal more knowledge.

Of course, all three phases of a financial plan are determined by individual goals. There is no such thing as a universal plan. You should view with great skepticism any advice that is given as appropriate for everybody. I have yet to find any financial instrument that fits everyone's needs.

For the remainder of this chapter I would like to take a closer look at some of the most widely used tools to save and invest for retirement. Most people will retire with assets in some mixture of these types of retirement accounts. I would urge you to diversify your retirement accounts much as you want to diversify your holdings within investment accounts. The greater diversification you have within your retirement plan, the greater the distribution options you are likely to have, even if you wait until you are just about retired to create a distribution strategy.

## SOCIAL SECURITY

Social Security is the one form of retirement investment in which we all participate. We have no choice. And even if Social Security is over-hauled in the near or distant future, it is likely to remain a universal program, meaning everyone will participate in some form. Every working American pays Social Security taxes. One American in every six at present receives some sort of monthly Social Security benefit, and that rate will increase as baby boomers start retiring in droves.

Social Security originally came into being and was signed into law by President Franklin Delano Roosevelt on August 14, 1935. The reason for his action was the Great Depression and the need it created in the United States for government intervention. Social Security was the first federal government program that dealt with the economic security of its citizens. It created a social insurance program. This social insurance program has helped to keep millions of Americans out of poverty.

Social Security offers protection four different ways: disability, survivor's benefits, retirement benefits, and Medicare health insurance. Roughly 6 million people currently receive Social Security disability benefits, and those benefits are equivalent to a $233,000 disability insurance policy. More than 7.5 million Americans receive survivor benefits equivalent to roughly a $354,000 life insurance policy.

Social Security is funded by the taxpayer; 7.65 percent of a worker's gross salary is deducted from his or her paycheck. This is known as FICA. Up to $87,000 of your earnings in the year 2003 were subject to this tax. The employer matches this tax dollar-for-dollar. Social Security taxes go into two different trust funds: 85 cents of every dollar pays present monthly benefits to retirees and their families and 15 cents of every dollar pays present benefits to the disabled and their families. Surplus dollars not used to pay administrative expenses or benefits are invested in U.S. government securities. These dollars are intended to be available to pay benefits in the future.

As you work and pay taxes, you earn Social Security credits. You get one credit for each $870 in earnings up to a maximum of four credits per year in 2002. Most people need 40 credits to qualify for benefits, or 10 years of employment. It's the earnings though, and not the number of credits, that determine your overall Social Security retirement benefit. Your benefit is based on your date of birth, your type of benefit, your Social Security number, and your earnings over your working lifetime.

The following formula is used to calculate future Social Security benefits:

**Step 1:** List compensation under Social Security wage base for each year worked.

**Step 2:** Adjust each year's wages for inflation.

**Step 3:** Determine the average indexed adjusted monthly earnings based on the number of years in Step 1.

**Step 4:** Multiply your average indexed adjusted monthly earnings by percentages in a formula specified by law.

The result of this formula is your primary insurance amount or the amount you are eligible to receive.

Most people now receive a statement of their projected benefits sometime around their birthday each year. If you're like me, you get that statement and realize that your benefits will not go too far in covering your living expenses.

Social Security was never intended to be anyone's sole source of retirement income. Social Security is intended to replace about 53 percent of income for low-wage earners, about 40 percent for average-wage earners, about 32 percent for high-wage earners, and about 24 percent for those who earn more than the maximum wage base.

To retire and be eligible for Social Security benefits you must be fully insured, meaning you have at least 40 credits, be at least age 62 and have filed an application for retirement benefits. Another thing that many Social Security recipients do not realize prior to receiving benefits is that Social Security benefits may be taxable. If you are an individual income tax filer and your income exceeds $25,000 a year, you will be subjected to income taxes on your Social Security income. In fact, from $25,000 to $34,000 up to 50 percent of your Social Security benefit may be taxed at your ordinary income tax rate. If you file a joint return and your combined income exceeds $32,000, but is less than $44,000, again, you may be taxed on up to 50 percent of your Social Security benefit at your ordinary income tax rate. If you're a single filer and your income exceeds $34,000, or if you're a joint filer and your combined income exceeds $44,000, up to 85 percent of Social Security benefits may be taxed at your ordinary income tax rate.

Social Security benefits were never intended to replace your working income or be your sole source of income at retirement, and with the benefits incurring significant income tax liability for many people, almost all Americans need to have alternative sources of retirement income. You must save and invest for your own future. You cannot depend on the government to give you your full retirement income—regardless of how Congress tinkers with Social Security now or in the future.

## DEFINED-BENEFIT PENSION PLANS: BEWARE!

Perhaps you're not worried about having to live on a meager Social Security retirement income because you're covered by a defined-benefit plan at work. I suggest you start worrying—and start planning for retirement life without the pension benefits you have expected to be there.

The world of defined-benefit pensions is changing rapidly. They are fast disappearing from the scene. Some of the only people who still have them are teachers, the military, and members of public employees unions.

These types of pension plans promise a specific pension income—a defined benefit—usually based on years of service and income level in the last years of work before retirement. In the past, they have provided very comfortable income for retirees, often providing pension income at 70–80 percent of a person's income before he or she retired. Add Social Security to that, in many cases, and retirement income for those covered did not drop off—and in some cases increased—from when they were working.

What has happened to that model? Employers have decided that it is too expensive. As life expectancy has increased and medical costs for retirees have skyrocketed, many companies have underfunded their pension plans. Now in many cases they are finding that they simply cannot catch up on their obligations to their pension plans without going into bankruptcy. In 2005, the airline industry (United, Northwest) was the largest of many employers that simply said they could no longer meet their obligations to retirees—and future retirees who expected to be covered by those pension plans. Even the icon of American industry, General Motors, has been rumored to be contemplating a similar move.

Pensions for employees of those companies will not be completely lost, because a quasi-governmental agency was created to address the issue and will pick up some of the obligations. But those people who thought they knew what their pension income would be will now get a payment far smaller—in some cases 70 percent less—than they had expected.

In the future, defined-benefit plans will just about disappear. Those that still exist will not be on the rock-solid footing that they were a generation or two ago. Most people who are now enrolled in a defined-benefit plan in the private sector should begin to make alternate plans in case their employer chooses to set aside their pension obligation.

Those defined-benefit plans will be replaced with defined-contribution plans, which are already the norm in most industries. Under those types of pension plans, the employer makes no guarantees as to the future value of a pension plan, they only agree to contribute a certain amount to a retirement account for each covered employee. In essence, the payout of those plans will be determined by investment returns on each employee's account.

The most common form of those defined contribution plans are 401(k)s or other tax-deferred plans. Those types of retirement accounts come with their own problems, as we will look at in some detail below.

I have devoted time to Social Security and defined-benefit pension plans to underscore that you should count on no one—*no one*—neither government nor employers, to provide a living income when you are older and can no longer earn income. Your financial future is yours, and yours alone, to manage.

I know many people who are nearing retirement age who already understand that they will have to work well past age 65 to get by. The truth of the matter is that 65-year-olds are not as old as they used to be.

Many people in their 60s want to continue to work. They are healthy, energetic, and have no desire to spend their days playing golf for 20 years. I applaud them. What I want for you, however, is the financial freedom to choose how you will spend your days when you reach 65 or 67 or 72, whatever age you want to leave your career. It is inescapable that the only way you can do that is to take personal control of your financial life early enough so that you have that freedom. Your retirement planning is solely in the hands of you and your spouse.

## Tax-Deferred Plans in Detail: Beware, Too!

One way that you may be planning for retirement is through a tax-deferred retirement plan. They are the primary vehicle for retirement investing these days. IRAs, SEPs, Keoughs, and 401(k)s all allow you to invest money in a retirement plan and defer taxes on that money until you withdraw it. The assumption is that when you withdraw that money, supposedly in retirement, you will have less income and you may, therefore, have to pay a lower tax rate on that money. Don't count on it.

In my opinion, we rely far too heavily on pretax plans, which suffer from two potential problems:

1. Failure to consider a distribution strategy; and
2. Tax rates that are currently at historical lows and are more likely to rise than fall.

What you have to keep in mind is that the taxes on these retirement accounts are deferred, but they are not tax-free. Although they do not count against your income when earned, and any earnings on those assets also are not taxed when earned, you will have to pay taxes on those assets and earnings when they are withdrawn from the account, usually in retirement. Even your heirs will have to pay a tax when they receive the balance after you die in many cases.

The prevailing wisdom is that you should take full advantage of these plans to the extent that you are eligible to do so. In other words, everyone should invest the maximum allowed, which varies from one plan to another. Look at the reduction you can get in taxes immediately. What more do you want?

It is certainly worth considering, but many people should reject those plans. For many people, pretax retirement plans are a very *inefficient* strategy to achieve their financial goals.

While many self-anointed experts who get time on TV or space in newspapers consider my position blasphemous, my question to them is, "How can the same financial solution apply equally well to everyone's financial situation?" The answer is simple: It doesn't!

How did society get to the point where virtually everyone believes we should pour our money into pretax retirement plans? To answer that question, consider who benefits if we all follow that course of action.

Contributions to these plans, by their design and because of tax treatment, remain in place for a very long time. If you begin making contributions while you're in your 30s, you're unlikely to take any distributions until you're age 59½ or older. The custodian of the money has the account for 20, 30, even 40 years. Do banks, insurance companies, mutual fund companies, brokerage houses, and other financial institutions like this arrangement? Of course they do! Think how they can use that money over that length of time. Do you think they might devote some of their marketing budget to convincing investors that these accounts are good? I think it's safe to conclude that financial institutions love pretax retirement accounts and spend a great deal of money convincing the public that they should love them, too.

But are they really such a great deal? Let's look at their supposed advantages—which for many people can turn out to be disadvantages.

### Presumed Advantage #1: Tax-Deferred Plans Avoid Taxes

Many people tell me they participate in these plans to avoid taxes. But they don't avoid taxes at all. They simply defer taxes until that income is received. You can pay now or you can pay later—but you will pay.

### Presumed Advantage #2: You Will Be in a Lower Tax Bracket in Retirement

The assumption is that when the income is actually received and the tax on the income is due, the investor will likely be retired and in a lower tax bracket. While that may be true for people who plan to have 70 percent of their working income in retirement, I think you should set a higher target. The only reason for being in a lower tax bracket in retirement is that you didn't save and plan for retirement as well as you could have.

But even the assumption that with a reduction in income you will be in a lower tax bracket is faulty. If you're married and together you and your spouse have combined taxable income of $70,000 per year while working, you're in the 28 percent federal tax bracket. Following the needs planning strategy promoted by graduates of the Eeyore School of Financial Planning, the outlook is always gloomy: You would then strive to retire at 70 percent of your working income—or $49,000 a year. Now we'll check our tax tables and—whoops!—that's still in the 28 percent federal tax bracket. By following the prevailing wisdom, you would retire with 30 percent less income but still be in the same tax bracket. Where's the advantage in that?

Furthermore, how do we know what future tax rates will be? We don't. What we do know is that present tax rates are low when compared to the historical average. The top federal bracket as of this writing is 38.6 percent. Reviewing federal income tax rates back to 1913, the average top rate is about 58 percent. In other words, we are at present almost 20 percentage points *below* the historical average.

Do you trust politicians to continue to try to balance budgets or pay off our rapidly growing national debt? My suspicion is that even if budgets are balanced, our debt won't be paid down very soon. What happens if the recovery rate of our economy slows? What happens if the recovery fizzles completely? Will growth projections be as rosy as some would have us believe? Will we continue to spend billions to rebuild Iraq? The estimated cost to rebuild New Orleans and other parts of the Gulf Coast following Hurricane Katrina exceeds $200 billion. We have gone from estimated federal government surpluses of $500 trillion to estimated deficits of more than $500 trillion in a couple of years. Will economic growth pull us out of this deficit, or do you think Congress might be tempted to raise taxes? It's the quickest way to increase revenues.

While we don't know what future tax rates will be, we do know we presently have very low rates compared to the past and that government spending outpaces revenues. Would you bet that your future tax rate will be higher or lower than it is now? My bet is higher—for all of us.

If tax rates go up, deferring tax on your pretax retirement plan will be counterproductive. Even if you are not in a higher tax bracket in the future, but retire with income in the same tax bracket that you are currently in, there is very little advantage to delaying the tax.

### Presumed Advantage #3: You Have an Immediate Gain through Tax Deferral

Another misconception with regard to pretax retirement plans is that the tax savings are somehow available to you. For example, in a 34 percent federal tax bracket, a $4,000 contribution to an IRA would save $1,360 in taxes. But that savings doesn't come to you; it's in the plan and you can't touch it without penalty—and that remains true until you reach age 59½. You can't use that money—not for your cost of living, not even for investments beyond the narrow range of equity investments that most plans offer. In truth, your spendable income has decreased by $2,640, because you had to spend $4,000 to save the $1,360.

If you are putting all of your investable income into your pretax retirement plan, what will happen if you have a family emergency that requires you to withdraw it? You will pay a 10 percent penalty, plus the full amount withdrawn (even the 10 percent paid in penalty) will be taxed as income in the year it is withdrawn. Or what if you come up with a great idea for a business, but you need money to get it off the ground? No, you can't withdraw from your pretax retirement plan without paying the penalty. Pretax retirement plans offer almost no flexibility. They were designed for one thing only: to encourage people to create a nest egg for retirement.

The effect of some people's contributions to pretax plans is that they live as if they are poor now so they won't have to live as if they are poor later. That's not a very appealing trade-off, especially if other retirement planning strategies are available that may not force such a drastic choice. Sure, an effective investment strategy and retirement plan may require some sacrifices in the shorter term, but they should be balanced against an expected reward. And those sacrifices will be reduced with an effective strategy for the future.

I already wrote about a couple who had good income but couldn't qualify for a home mortgage because they had more than $100,000 in credit card debt. Here's the kicker to their story: They also had more than $400,000 in 401(k) plans. Their 401(k)s were doing pretty well, too, delivering a return of 12.5 percent a year. But that means they were *losing* 3.5 percent a year on their pretax retirement plans, because they were paying 16 percent on their credit card debt! Now, *that's* a bad investment—and a cautionary tale for those who are scraping money together for their contribution to a pretax plan.

There is one significant exception to my skepticism about the wisdom of pretax plans. If your employer matches what you put into the plan, it is too good to pass up for most people—at least up to the level that your

### WHO NEEDS PRETAX PLANS . . .

Pretax retirement plans do make sense for essentially three types of people, those who:

1. Have their contributions matched by their employer.
2. Are already in the highest tax brackets and have a reasonable chance of being in a lower tax bracket in retirement.
3. Do not have the discipline to save or invest without the plan. With all of their shortcomings for many people, pretax plans are still far better than saving and investing nothing.

### . . . AND WHO DOES NOT

Everyone else, but especially those who:

1. Have any outstanding consumer debt. Pay it off before you contribute to a pretax plan.
2. Are saving for a down payment on a home. Your mortgage interest deduction will probably provide a bigger tax deduction than your pretax plan even as you build equity in an asset and lock in your housing costs, which you can't do with rent.
3. Are disciplined savers and investors.
4. Invest in strategies that are tax-free, allow other tax deductions, or generate tax credits.

PLANNING FOR RETIREMENT ■ 167

employer will match. Many employers will match your contribution up to 3 percent to 4 percent of your income. Employers who do this calculate that contribution in determining your overall compensation, so it's really part of your pay. You should make every effort to qualify for that match, because your money immediately doubles and you still get the tax deduction. Whether you contribute the maximum you are allowed, however, above any amount that your employer matches, requires careful scrutiny.

## SUMMARY OF PRETAX PLANS

Without knowing the specifics of your situation I can't say for sure whether your pretax retirement plan is the best way for you to save and invest. I can say with certainty, however, that pretax retirement plans:

- Do not actually avoid taxes. They merely defer taxes by deferring income.
- Provide no additional spendable income. The tax savings generated by the contribution are in the plan. In fact, spendable income actually decreases.
- Will not necessarily be taxed at a lower rate when distributed to you. We don't know what future tax rates will be. However, a compelling argument can be made that they are unlikely to be lower than they are now.
- Are heavily promoted by large financial institutions that benefit greatly by holding your money for a few decades.
- Are inefficient to die with because the beneficiary is also fully taxed.

Be sure to evaluate pretax retirement plans in the context of your overall financial picture. Is retirement saving and investing your top priority? On one hand, an early start to retirement planning can make an enormous difference as we saw with Jack and Jill in Chapter 3. Other financial goals may take priority, however. Can you save to make a down payment on a house at the same time you're putting money into a retirement plan?

How do you resolve competing priorities? These questions cannot be answered without considering your life situation and the people you love.

Consider pretax plans alongside all other options for retirement planning. For most people pretax plans should not be the only investment vehicle for retirement.

Finally, maintain control over pretax accounts after leaving a job. You can take it with you, and you should. Keep as much control of your retirement accounts as you can. If you leave it behind with a former employer, the managers of those funds may make decisions you don't like. Shift the account to your control and make the decisions yourself—or with your financial adviser.

## DON'T OVERLOOK THE STEPSISTERS OF INVESTING

In Chapter 3 we looked closely at a possible alternative for retirement planning: variable annuities. We have also discussed in Chapter 8 the possible advantages of variable universal life insurance as an investment alternative.

As I have noted, variable annuities and permanent life insurance can be very effective tools in a financial plan. They cost more than mutual fund investments, which is why they are often overlooked, but they provide value that may justify the cost.

They may provide better returns than mutual funds because the managers of those funds do not face some of the same market pressures that mutual fund managers face. They provide easy and inexpensive ways to rebalance your portfolio. And they both offer distinct advantages for estate planning.

I would encourage you to review those chapters and the arguments they present in favor of considering those retirement planning vehicles if you are currently invested only in tax-deferred retirement accounts.

The other retirement vehicle that I would strongly encourage you to consider is the Roth IRA. You do not get a tax deferment on your contributions to a Roth IRA, but the earnings in your investment account do accumulate tax-deferred. A Roth IRA is an excellent complement to traditional tax-deferred accounts.

## PLAN TOGETHER

The first step in planning for retirement with your spouse is to reach agreement on your primary objectives. Without that, a strategy is impossible, or at least a lot more complicated and expensive

I have been amazed at how often I've interviewed new clients, couples creating a financial plan, who have fundamental disagreements on what they want from retirement. Sometimes they don't even realize their differences until I ask them both to write down their ideal retirement. I get back one piece of paper from Mars and one from Venus.

As in all other things with your spouse, communicate clearly and never assume. Lay out precisely what each of you wants and decide how you can make those desires work together. Be specific. I advised one couple that was confident they shared a similar vision of retirement, a home on the beach. Only after I probed further did we all learn that he wanted to live in Florida and she wanted to live on Martha's Vineyard. Both were shocked, and neither would budge. They had always talked about a beach home, but had never gotten around to specifying which beach.

As part of your review of your financial plan you might also want to confirm that your partner's plans or wants have not changed. You wouldn't want to find out years from now that your spouse decided long ago that his view of an ideal retirement had changed, but he had forgotten to tell you.

# PART III

# Money and Children

Financial planning has a clear impact on children. Through efficient planning, children may be protected financially in the event of your disability or death. Careful planning is also a must for most people to pay for at least a portion of a child's education.

Perhaps the most important reason to plan, though, is the effect it has on you. For one, a good plan may help you worry less about money. That alone can have a positive impact on your home life and your children. Moreover, if you let a financial adviser do much of the planning work, and the worrying, you will have more time to spend with your children. Wouldn't you rather have an expert figure out ways you can increase investable income, or reduce taxes, than spending tedious evening and weekend hours trying to decipher investment prospectuses and state and federal tax codes? You could be playing ball with your kids or getting to the recital early—and relaxed.

Effective financial planning may help you live more of your life without plans—or at least without such a tight schedule. A friend of mine tells the story of the Saturday morning he spent with his five-year-old daughter. He was sitting on his front steps, contemplating his long "to-do" list for the day, when his daughter came out and sat down next to him with a handful of pistachios. Before long they were setting nuts on the sidewalk and watching chipmunks come up and snatch them. The little girl then got a big oak leaf and set out a bunch of nuts on it. She called it a "platter" at "Talia's Nut Restaurant." The two tried desperately to stifle their laughter so they wouldn't scare the chipmunks running up and stuffing their cheeks with nuts. Between chipmunk forays to the "platter," they watched a spider weaving a web in the railing on the steps. An hour-and-a-half passed as they sat there. Finally the little girl turned to her dad and said, "This is the best day ever."

My friend's "to-do" list wasn't shortened that day—he never got to it, and he was glad he didn't. None of those chores could have ever resulted in the time he had with his daughter.

Money is about securing a future with innumerable "best days ever." And for so many of us, our children, or our prospective children, are a large part of our future.

I am the proud father of two fantastic kids. Being a parent is the most rewarding, challenging, and important aspect of my life. I would not trade the experience for anything. But economically, kids are the single greatest cost most of us will ever encounter. Boy, are they expensive: diapers, baby food, formula, candy, school, hobbies, and clothes, especially shoes, which they seem to outgrow every few weeks. The list of expenses is endless. And do you want to pay for their college education? Wedding? First car? First house? You will spend hundreds of thousands of dollars in your lifetime for each child you have.

People who never have children or haven't yet (begin planning now!) have a huge economic advantage over those of us who do, but my kids have added immeasurably to the richness of my life. The return on my investment in my children is incalculably high. But children, those you have or intend to have, offer one of the most compelling reasons to create an efficient financial plan—not just for when you are still living, but also for transferring your wealth to your children when you die.

Our financial relationship with our children will go through many stages as they, and we, age. I'll write about four of those stages—with a brief comment on a fifth stage that I hope you will be able to avoid with proper financial planning. The four key stages of your financial relationship with children are:

- **Protector and provider:** What you provide for your children.
- **Teacher:** What you teach your children. I have definite ideas about what and how to teach children about money and life. I was trained as a teacher in college, but student teaching convinced me that teaching in a school wasn't my calling. My ideas

on teaching children about money come not, however, from an academic background but from my experience as a parent and financial adviser. I have seen many clients and colleagues impart their ideas about the role of money to their children, intentionally or not. Whether you are an eager or reluctant teacher, you will certainly teach your children about money as their role model.

- **Financier:** What expenses you pay for your children. College—and more.
- **Benefactor:** What you leave your children.

In almost all cases, these stages will overlap. As your children grow up you simply play more roles. Your roles as provider and teacher certainly will overlap for some time. When you are no longer the provider for your children, you will remain, at least in your view, their protector—even if not financially. And you will always be a teacher. The only change is that as they mature into adulthood, your children will probably become more willing to listen to you; you will gradually grow wiser in their eyes. Even the financier stage of the relationship may extend well beyond paying for some or all of their education. You may help them buy a car or a home. You may pay for a wedding, which these days can be a significant cost. You may help them pay some of the costs of raising their own children, from braces for their teeth to summer camps or travel.

A potential fifth stage in our money relationship with our children is best avoided—and can be with good planning and good fortune. That is the role of financial dependent, needing financial assistance from your children in your later years. I have addressed this issue in the next chapter on our financial relationship with our parents.

The possibility that one may have to provide some economic assistance to parents is an important contingency in financial planning for many younger people. For those who are already elderly and facing financial burdens or obligations they cannot meet, financial planning can't achieve the same successes. As always, the time to plan is as soon as possible to avoid the challenges that arise when parents become financially dependent on their children.

# 11

## PROTECTOR AND PROVIDER

■ ■ ■

The biological imperative that we propagate our genes and ensure their survival makes us natural-born protectors and providers. What separates us from our distant ancestors, however, is that for most of us the survival of our offspring is never really in question. In the developed world, we don't have to scrape and claw to keep our children clothed and fed. We are more concerned with their comfort and their happiness. Our focus is on helping them lead happy, productive lives instead of just staying alive.

Will you always be able to provide for your children until they can provide for themselves? I hope so. But hope is the last refuge of failure. It is better to plan than to hope. An important part of any financial plan for your children is financial protection for them if anything should happen to you.

### LIFE INSURANCE

You will probably have to overcome some serious biases, from both conventional wisdom and some financial advisers, when considering life insurance. The bottom line is that your family probably needs some financial protection in the event of your death or the death of your family's primary income earner. That much is agreed upon by nearly everybody.

If you are looking for purely financial protection for your family in the event of death, the best life insurance for you may be what is called *term* life insurance. With term insurance you pay a premium for a set amount of time for a set amount of coverage. If you die, your family collects the insurance. If you don't die during that term, you receive no benefit except peace of mind. If you ever quit paying the premiums—maybe your children have grown and you no longer need the protection for your family—your policy lapses or is canceled. Pretty simple—if all you want is protection.

But let's look ahead a bit as well to your continuing role in the financial life of your family to the point at which you may become financier or benefactor. In other words, let's look at your longer-term financial plan.

As part of an overall financial plan I prefer permanent life insurance. Term insurance, however, may be an economic necessity for some. If you can't afford as much death benefit as you would like on a permanent basis, it's better to get enough term insurance to protect your family. But permanent life insurance is more efficient in the long run. With the competitive returns and other advantages of variable universal life insurance, permanent insurance is more attractive than it once was. Most people will have a successful financial plan if they put a significant portion of their investment money into permanent life insurance. If you do acquire term insurance due to economic necessity, I recommend that you convert it to a permanent policy as soon as your economic situation allows.

Buying term life insurance to protect your family is not throwing money away—if it's the only life insurance you can afford. I don't like term insurance because it's unlikely that you will ever collect on it. A study at Penn State University revealed that only 1 percent of term policies ever pay a claim because most people quit paying premiums before the term ends, often because their children grow up and they no longer need the protection. What makes better financial sense is variable universal life insurance, which combines a death benefit and an investment account that has several advantages over other investments. If you can afford variable universal life insurance, that's what I would recommend.

If you go back a couple of decades, the money invested in permanent insurance, above the cost of the death benefit, was in fixed-interest investments that provided low returns. That changed, however, in the late 1970s, when a new type of permanent life insurance—variable universal life—was created. With variable universal life, the cash value of life insurance is invested in equity portfolios called subaccounts that can be compared to mutual funds. With that change came the potential to earn competitive returns within the life insurance policy. But old prejudices die hard. I think the lesson is, don't accept conventional wisdom. Do your own research—on insurance and everything else. (For a more detailed discussion of life insurance see Chapter 8, "Planning for Emergencies.")

## Disability Insurance

For most families, a long-term disability would be far more detrimental financially than even a premature death. However, disability insurance policies are owned by far fewer parents than life insurance, partly because of its cost and partly because so few people understand it. Taking the time and making the effort to understand disability insurance and its potential impact on your life and future is obviously the first step. In your role as protector and provider for your children, purchasing disability coverage may be one of the most important financial decisions you will make. (See Chapter 8, "Planning for Emergencies," for in-depth information on disability insurance.)

## A Plan for the Unimaginable

We always assume that if anything happens to us at least our spouse will be able to raise our children and provide for them, ideally with the help of the financial protection we have left behind. But, heaven forbid, what happens if both you and your spouse are unable to provide for your children? I would highly recommend that you discuss that distant possibility with family or friends. Make arrangements for the care and protection of your children, and make them in writing, should you be unable to care for them.

A will is not simply a way to divide your assets, it is a way to designate disposition of your assets to care for your younger children. Equally important, it establishes your choice of legal guardians for your children and how your assets can be used for their benefit. It is difficult to imagine someone else raising your children. It is easier if you have made clear in a legal document your choice of loving, caring legal guardians for them.

# 12

## TEACHER

■ ■ ■

As a parent, you probably want your children to have a better life than you had growing up. It is a universal wish, and it is admirable. If you are able to fulfill that wish, however, how do you instill ambition in your children and keep them from getting spoiled? How do you teach them the value of what you earned and to be good stewards of what you are able to give them? How do you raise financially smart children? How do you give them all you can without creating disincentives to their own productivity?

Many parents, especially those blessed with affluence, fear that wealth will rob their children of ambition. According to a 1996 survey by U.S. Trust, half of the country's wealthiest parents worry that material advantages will undermine their children's initiative and independence.

I have a client who recently cashed out his stock in a dot-com start-up. He walked away with roughly $10,000,000 after taxes. That didn't put him on the Forbes list of the richest people in the world, but to him and his family it was an enormous sum after years of toiling with little reward to get a business off the ground. I was surprised to hear that he had not yet told his teenage kids of his financial success. In fact, he said he didn't know when—or if—he ever would. Before he and his wife told the kids anything, they wanted to have an estate plan in place, which was why they came to me.

The couple told me they had gone through a lot of soul-searching about what to do with the money and how it would best benefit their children. They continually weighed the advantages that money could bestow on their children against the harm that such a nest egg could do to their children's drive and ambition. The fact that they were concerned about the issue demonstrates that they themselves have strong values and have probably passed those values on to their kids—which means the kids will probably do well regardless of the parents' decision.

I have had people tell me that too much money limits children, that it serves as a disincentive and leads them into nonproductive, dysfunctional lives. My own opinion is that too much money does not hurt children. There's no such thing as too much money; there's only too little character.

Your role as teacher in all things financial begins with teaching your children about life, work and play and, only then, where money fits in. The first lessons we give our children are the most important and stay with them for life. We teach them how to love, we teach them values, and we teach them how to pursue their own happiness. If they learn those lessons well, they will find the appropriate place for money in their lives.

I believe most children are inclined to learn those invaluable lessons, but to be sure we teach them well we have to give them time. No one learns anything of any importance without putting in time on the lessons. There is no substitute for time. We often hear the phrase "quality, not quantity" in regard to time with our children. I disagree. Our children need quality *and* quantity. The key, I believe, is to invest time, as well as money, in your children's lives. You can't let devices and activities manage your children; *you* have to.

In my opinion, a lot of trust fund kids who lead unproductive lives while living off the family money were not given time and affection by their parents. I envision the parents jet-setting off to France, summering in Europe or sending the kids off to summer camp and not including them in their own plans. I believe that if you parent—if you love your children and tell them and show them by spending time with them—you can instill in them the character to handle the financial advantages you can give them.

## RULES FOR RAISING RESPONSIBLE KIDS

I would suggest three basic rules that parents should remember when teaching their children to understand the role of money in their lives. I think they apply regardless of your personal financial circumstances.

## Rule #1: Teach Values First

Whether you have a great deal of money or very little, your children have the same basic needs: security, love, and guidance in how to live in a crowded world. If we lived in isolation, we would have no need for money. It's because we share the planet with so many others organized into communities, tribes, and nations that we even have a use for currency, something of value to exchange with others.

If you teach values to your children—self-esteem, commitment to excellence, respect and concern for others, accountability to themselves, their community, school, faith community, and world—you certainly can teach them about money and its role in their lives. I believe with great conviction that if you parent your children, if you teach them values and set a solid foundation, they can learn to use money, as well as the other tools they have, efficiently and responsibly.

Two concepts pervade every discussion I have about money: responsibility (using resources wisely) and finding what makes you happy (pursuing your own goals with passion). The same essentials apply to almost every childhood activity from school to play to spending money. You can never separate discussions of money from the core values you teach your kids. They are pieces of the same jigsaw puzzle.

Of course, to teach, you have to communicate effectively. Effective communication is the glue of all interpersonal relationships, whether it's with your spouse, your parents, your children, your colleagues at work, or your neighbors. Ineffective or inefficient communication nearly always plays a role in the breakdown of a relationship. We communicate with our children in three essential ways. We need to pay equal attention to all three.

### What We Do

Actions speak louder than words, and children are the world's best mimics. If you really want a confused kid, a kid who learns to distrust you, say one thing but do another. Our kids are learning our values even when we say nothing.

Showing our children our values begins with the big picture—how we live our lives. The priorities we set for ourselves are often the priorities our kids adopt. These lifestyle lessons require more thought than we often give them.

Your income and how you earn it are lessons in themselves to your children. How do your work life and income fit with your home life? How do you choose to balance the need to provide money for your family with the need to provide them time? Very simply, that is the greatest complication in many financial plans. And I think it is one the best reasons to create a thoughtful financial plan: It forces you to focus on what your priorities are and to determine how money can help you achieve your goals. A good financial planning process tries to synchronize your values and your money, because the two are inextricably woven together. Some people mistakenly view financial planning as a way to have more money. On the contrary, some of the best financial plans I have helped to create were intended to help people live better on less money. Our goal was to align money and values.

In my life, my family is my top priority. Virtually anytime I'm not at work, I'm with my children. I tell clients and I tell our staff that as much as it would be politically correct to say they come first, the reality is that they do not. My children, my family, come first. My employees, the people who make me smarter and better than I actually am, come second, and clients come third. But if all three of those groups are happy, then I'm in a pretty good place.

Our actions also include how we expose our children to the world beyond the narrow confines of our family, friends, and neighborhood. To the extent we can, it's important that we help our children understand the wide range of people who live in our world. That may come through the books we read to them or the TV shows we allow them to watch. Our children also see from our involvement in church, school, and community what we value. Are we active participants in organizations that we value?

We try to expose our children to the "real world" so that they see how other people live. We drive through neighborhoods where the homes aren't so nice and we talk about what those people have to do to make ends meet. The basketball league at our school plays in areas where people are not as economically fortunate as those in our neighborhood.

We also sponsor children in Third World countries. We get letters and pictures from them so that our kids can learn how people live in other parts of the world.

Diversity is one of the popular words of our time and it usually refers to people of different races or ethnic backgrounds, but economic or financial diversity is also an important concept for kids to understand. I believe our children have an advantage if they see the world not in narrowly defined groupings of race, class, and even religion, but in terms of individuals who live in many circumstances and make a wide variety of choices about how they live their lives.

I can remember filling out my own college financial aid forms. My parents lacked the education to assist me and I remember how low our family income was, so I've never forgotten where I came from or what my background was, and I make sure that my kids understand that, too. When we talk about vacations, I remind our kids that we are fortunate to take a vacation every year. When I was a child we never took vacations because we couldn't afford it. When you come from humble beginnings, as I did, you never forget it and you want to share that message with children. I try not to pound them with it, because I don't want them to view my reminiscences as a history lesson about life in ancient times and have them think that I'm almost as old as dinosaurs. But I do want them to know that enjoying what money can buy is a privilege, not a right. For young children, it can be an eye-opener to learn that not every child has what they have or does what they do.

### How We Listen

Next in communication priority comes how we listen. It is an especially important skill with children because their world is so immediate. But it's not only children; everybody wants to be heard. However, leaders—and financially successful people tend to be leaders—sometimes are more accustomed to giving orders than to listening. High achievers must discipline themselves to take the time to truly listen to the members of their family, as the experience of being heard is critical to validating a child's personal worth.

We have a friend with a son about our son's age. The father is basically a good guy, but he's one of these people who talks over everybody. He seems to believe that what he has to say is more important than what anyone else could say. You can just see the impatience in him when someone else has the floor in a discussion. He can hardly wait for that person to take a breath so he can jump in. Frequently he doesn't wait; he interrupts and takes over the conversation.

The man's son is constantly shouting. Even when there's no one in the room and he's the only one talking, he's shouting, shouting, shouting all the time. We believe it's because his dad doesn't listen to him. His dad is a talker, not a listener. We have speculated that the child shouts to be heard by his dad, who otherwise ignores him and is too wrapped up in his own thoughts and words to listen to his child.

Your willingness to take time from your busy schedules to listen to your kids without criticism and without interruption gives their self-esteem an immeasurable boost.

You also need to listen to yourself. Try to hear your words through a young child's ears. Do you ever hear yourself? Try this at home after you read this section of the book. Keep track of how many things you say that are positive, such as, "Oh, thank you so much for that, I appreciate your help," compared to negative things like, "I can't trust you," or "You're always talking too loud."

If we're honest in completing this exercise we may be surprised by the number of interactions with our kids that are negative instead of positive. Self-esteem is built on the positives. That's not to say that parents shouldn't correct or discipline kids for inappropriate behavior. Discipline is most effective, however, when focused on the undesired behavior and conveyed in neutral terms. If you're quick to criticize, be equally or more generous with praise.

### What We Say

Even though your actions will speak louder than your words, kids need to hear the words, too. You need to consider carefully what you tell your children about money so they understand from the time they are very young what money can and cannot do for them and how you believe it should and should not be used.

Parents should never substitute money and possessions for love and affection, but money can be a powerful teacher. It's a tool. Parents have to work together to answer some questions: What values do we want our children to learn? What will we provide for our children? What do we expect them to do in return? This is a parental discussion, and it does not involve the children. Your decisions will determine what you say about money. Perhaps the most important things we say about money are two words, "yes" and "no." Obviously, both refer to your response to your kids' requests, demands, or pleadings that you buy something for them. Don't be afraid to say no. But when you do, give them the real reason for your answer. When you say yes to your children's requests, don't be afraid to attach some strings to the generosity.

As an adult I have encountered two statements about money that make a lot of sense to me and have helped me come to grips with my own financial success—and that have influenced what I tell my children about money. The first is from John Wesley, the founder of the Methodist Church: "Make all you can, save all you can, give all you can." The other quote that has stayed with me is from former British prime minister Margaret Thatcher: "No one would have remembered the Good Samaritan if he'd only had good intentions. He had money as well."

I believe both quotes are powerful. The point of each is that it matters

---

### MY FAVORITE SAYINGS

Almost every day I use phrases and expressions with my kids that I hope are reminders for them (and me) of how I want to live my life and how I would like them to live their lives. You could ask my kids, who would probably roll their eyes because they hear them so often.

"No one can ruin your day without your permission. Make it a great day."
"The best way to escape a problem is to solve it."
"No excuses offered, none accepted."
"You can achieve what your mind can conceive."
"Cheaters never win, winners never cheat."

what you do with your money, the values that guide your use of money. And I believe it is implicit in both expressions that money must be earned ethically and honorably.

I tell my children that they'll become what they think about and I encourage them to think positively. Positive thoughts are the beginning of a chain that has been explained like this:

Watch your thoughts because your thoughts become your words.
Watch your words because your words become your actions.
Watch your actions because they become your habits.
Watch your habits because they become your character.
Watch your character because it becomes your destiny.

There are, however, some things you should *not* tell your kids, in my opinion. A few frequently heard statements from parents to children can have unintentional harmful effects.

**"We can't afford it."** How many times have we heard that? In addition to perhaps being dishonest, the response may cause unnecessary anxiety for small kids. If you're going to say no to something your child wants, be prepared to give the real reason. Don't just say, "We can't afford it." Tell them instead what you intend to spend your money on—even if it's the gas, water, or electricity you use in your home.

What do you say to your kids when you know the "We can't afford it" excuse isn't true? You could punt, you could pray, you could give them everything their hearts desire—but more effective is getting them to imagine what they want to contribute to the world. Teach young children that no one gets everything he or she wants. Life is about making tough choices. Set expectations about what you can and can't provide or will or won't provide. As an example, my daughter asked for a phone for her room. Well, obviously we could do that, but then we'd have no idea of who's calling. We're just not willing to do that, even though economically we can afford to get her a phone.

**"We'll pay you for every A on your report card."** This is really a form of bribery, and it sends the wrong message. Children should be taught to achieve goals for intrinsic reasons like self-satisfaction in achievement and a commitment to excellence—not for monetary rewards.

**"Time is money."** It really isn't. Equating time spent on anything with its monetary value sends an unhealthy message that your time and your money are equal, and, as I have noted, there is no substitute for time spent with your children. In fact, time in my life has a much higher value to me than money.

**"They're disgustingly rich."** Or, as my parents used to say, "They were born with silver spoons in their mouths." Using words like "disgustingly" or "filthy" or "stinking" to describe someone's wealth encourages a child to see wealth negatively. And it isn't negative. Going back to my own personal situation, when I was able to achieve in my career a certain level of financial success, it actually took me awhile to come to grips with it because of the way I was raised. My parents were envious of anyone who had money. I learned from them to be distrusting and resentful of people who had money and, frankly, to be intimidated by them.

In my hometown there was an affluent area that people from my neighborhood called "Snob Hill." Throughout my childhood I believed that anyone who lived in that neighborhood was somehow bad. As I got older, I got to know many of those people and I came to realize that many were kind and generous—the type of people that I wanted to associate with.

Teaching your children that affluence is a bad thing is not only discriminatory and unfair, but could be detrimental to your child. The viewpoint could be an obstacle to your child's happiness and success and the financial rewards that could come with it. In my opinion it's far healthier to teach your children how to appreciate and be good stewards of whatever they may have in life. Will money make them happy? Certainly not. Will money come as a result of doing what *does* make them happy? Very possibly.

**"Be thankful you don't live there."** This statement implies that happiness can't exist in a neighborhood or a house that isn't as comfortable as the one your children live in. It is the flip side of "disgustingly rich" comments. Teach your children to value human qualities rather than net worth or lifestyle, and I think they will be much happier and better able to adjust to whatever circumstance life throws at them. Money is neutral in terms of values. It can be used for good or bad. Neither having a lot of money nor having little money will make your children good or bad, happy or sad. For them to have a healthy relationship with money, they need to know this. They will learn it from listening to you.

Your children never have to learn to read stock tables or exchange rates to be wealthy or to use money efficiently. They do have to learn to work hard, have fun, save some of their money, and respect themselves and others. They have to learn values. It's worth repeating: There's no such thing as too much money; there's only too little character. It's our job as parents to make sure our children have character. It's too important a task to be left to others.

### Rule #2: Teach Children the Joy of Work

You teach kids the joy of work, first, by enjoying work yourself. If you don't, it's probably time for a change of jobs. Your kids need to see you excited about your own work and life. Your everyday actions speak far louder than any serious sit-down discussion about work and money, no matter how carefully and artfully you choose your words.

Second, I believe you teach your kids that whatever they do, work or play, they should put all their energy into it. If they are playing, play hard. If they are studying, study hard. If they are laughing, laugh hard. Live life to the brim. It's a lesson they'll learn from you long before they earn their first paycheck. One of the great qualities of extracurricular activities—drama, music, sports—is that kids learn the value, the joy, and the rewards of hard work. It is, however, up to you to keep the values, joys, and rewards balanced—and to be sure your children are pursuing their goals, not yours.

Third, let your kids experience the joys of work—overcoming obstacles, enjoying the "I did that" of a finished project—by including them in work around the house. Kids are usually delighted to help, and they love praise for their part in a completed project. Help children and explain things if they need help, but don't do their homework for them. Kids don't learn if you do it for them. And they don't get the self-satisfaction, sense of achievement, and sense of responsibility of having done a task themselves. As a parent you're there to help, you're not there to do it for them. I can think of nothing that is more likely to give our children self-confidence than achieving a goal themselves and enjoying the fulfillment of completing a task—and being praised for it.

Many affluent families possess sufficient wealth to ensure that their children can live a comfortable lifestyle without ever doing anything productive in order to pay the rent. I believe these children need to experience the inner satisfaction of achievement so that this natural high is its own reward and productivity will continue regardless of the dollars available. For this reason, allowing kids to experience delayed gratification becomes vitally important. When the "I want" demand sounds, parents should insist that the child add this demand to a future wish list that's only visited on special occasions like birthdays and holidays. "No" is an appropriate word in the parenting vocabulary.

Help your kids understand the difference between needs and wants. So many Americans spend beyond their means because of things they want. So, we tell our kids that it's okay to want things, but there are certain things they need. There's a difference, for instance, between school supplies and a new video game. You need one and want the other.

I think this is a particularly difficult challenge for people who want to provide their children with things and experiences they didn't have when they were young. It is a wonderful and powerful feeling to be able to indulge your kids, but it may be detrimental to them. There's a fine line between providing for and spoiling.

When we immediately indulge our kids' continually changing demands, we're doing them an incredible disservice. Spoiled kids never learn how to delay gratification or appreciate the things that they have. They become seriously infected with the disease of entitlement, the misguided belief that privilege is our birthright. Some level of frustration remains a necessary ingredient for achievement. The overindulged child does not tolerate the discomfort of not being instantly gratified and, therefore, will not stick with a task long enough to develop mastery and experience the pride and pleasure of achievement. When the going gets tough, they go.

I think the primary way you avoid creating disincentives for children by giving them too much is to help them develop a sense of self-esteem rooted in reality and in your love for them. How do you do that? You begin by providing your children with realistic and reasonable expectations. Then you cultivate competency. And you always communicate effectively.

A child develops a sense of accomplishment if expectations are realistic. Sometimes people who are very successful financially place high and even unreasonable expectations on their children. They're used to demanding a lot from their coworkers or employees—and probably from themselves as well. It can be especially difficult for highly motivated people not to succumb to the belief that they can push and pressure their kids to achieve the levels of performance that they desire for them. Because kids naturally want to please their parents, when they fall short of expectations it diminishes their sense of being loved unconditionally and impedes the development of self-esteem. Naturally, we all have high expectations for our kids and that in itself is not harmful as long as our expectations are reasonable—and based on the children's abilities, learning styles, and personalities.

Motivation is a self-regulated drive that occurs when the activity in which a child is engaged creates a positive feeling. Children avoid situations that cause stress, frustration, or disappointment. One area in which unrealistic expectations frequently create difficulty is school. Especially if we were good students, we want to see our kids succeed with good grades. However, not every child can be a straight A student. The love of learning is one of the critical life skills that I think enables each person to achieve his or her own potential and succeed in the long term. Accordingly, we as parents should stress academic responsibility and the love of learning as a motivator, rather than grades. Some kids can work really hard and put all their effort into it and not achieve, and other kids can phone it in and get A's. I would bet on the former children in terms of long-term success, the ones who have to work for what they get, as opposed to the kids who are able to coast.

Kids acquire competence through the experience of dealing with tasks independently. However well meaning, powerful parents and people who are financially successful are often very self-assertive. Sometimes powerful parents will involve themselves excessively in all aspects of their kids' lives. Operating on the misguided belief that they can prevent their kids from experiencing frustration or disappointment, they continually make important decisions for them. This approach to parenting, I believe, breeds passive, dependent children who often grow up unable to function independently.

A young child naturally tries to handle many tasks independently. Of course, physical safety does require restrictions on some of the kid's independent desires. But too many parents give too much help, and I think, frankly, sometimes I'm guilty of this. I'm too quick to jump in if my kids struggle with something. One way to control the natural desire to assist is to stop and ask, "Could my kid perform this task, or any part of it, independently?" If so, let him or her do it. This begins with self-care: brushing your teeth, washing your hair, taking a shower, getting dressed, and so forth. And then progresses to problem solving, dealing with homework, handling interactions with schoolmates, and giving their opinion on a variety of issues.

Finally, I believe it is positive, when the time comes, for kids to get summer or after-school jobs. Yes, they do have their whole lives to work, but there is a great sense of accomplishment when they earn their first money. They also learn to interact in a workplace with coworkers and boss in quite a different way than they interact with you.

I had my first job when I was 10 years old. On weekends I cleaned bathrooms, vacuumed, straightened tables, and generally cleaned up in a restaurant. The only reason I remember how old I was is because one weekend when I was working my boss told me to come and look at the TV. A man was walking on the moon—not something you quickly forget seeing. That tells me the year was 1969. By the next summer, at the age of 11, I worked in fields detasseling corn, which is a very hard job. I learned the value of a dollar—and the value of working for it—at a very early age.

I believe it is also positive to encourage entrepreneurship in kids. To help kids earn money beyond their weekly allowance, you might want to suggest that they find creative ways to make money. The focus should be on "creative" rather than "money." We encourage our kids to do special chores above and beyond the usual responsibilities for which we might compensate them, like raking or mowing or watching a neighbor's pet or, in the case of my older child, she's getting to the age now where she's going to be babysitting. I've also had her come into the office and do filing for me. I've paid her a wage, and since that's a legitimate payment, we've put the money that she's earned into a Roth IRA in her name.

Teaching kids the joy of accomplishment, just like teaching values, is a continuous process. Neither can be learned in a 15-minute lecture; they take years. While those teaching tasks are ongoing, a third rule comes into play as your children begin to understand the concept of money and some basic arithmetic.

### Rule #3: Let Your Children Manage Money

The key to teaching kids about personal finance is to have them learn by doing. They learn the value of a dollar by doing things for themselves and spending their money how they want on what they want. The choice between a new trinket or baseball now and a coveted doll or game later effectively teaches kids to balance short- and long-term desires. They can learn early that saving for something they really want is worthwhile.

Experience is a good teacher that not all things—toys or treats—are as good as they look on television ads. That's one reason it's good for kids to have some discretionary money. And if it's discretionary, that means you can't veto how your kids spend it. You may want to point out the advantages or disadvantages of spending money a certain way, but if it's their money, let them make the final choice. You may have to grit your teeth as they buy some cheaply made Transmogrifying Reversible Talking Widget that you know will soon be gathering dust. But it's one way that they learn the value of wise buying decisions. If they spend their money and then want something else so badly it tugs at your heartstrings, remind them that they recently decided to buy the Gonzor ShrinkMonster. If they hadn't bought that, they would have enough to buy the Kiss-a-bye Baby.

It's important to reinforce the value and consequences of spending and saving decisions, but it's probably wisest to do it as a statement of fact. The point is not to make children feel stupid for buying something you didn't want them to—even if, in fact, it seemed stupid to you. Rather you want to be sure that they understand they made a choice and they have to live with it.

For almost all of us, our financial lives require constant "either-or" decisions. If you don't face those decisions daily, you either have more money than you can keep track of, are very deeply in debt, or are a candidate for sainthood. Kids can learn to address the "either-or" spending and saving dilemma with your gentle guidance. It's a lesson that applies to money—and to most other areas of our lives. It comes down to valuing our resources, whether that means money, time, or even trust. Actions always have consequences.

### Allowances

Money management begins with an allowance. There's a lot of debate about the appropriate age to start receiving an allowance. We started both of our children at the age of six. I think by first grade most kids can appreciate that money buys things.

We give our kids a weekly allowance. It's not a paycheck. We do not pay them to be a part of our household and do their share in maintaining our home or their rooms. We expect that without pay. Rather, we give them an allowance so that they can learn about money and have some measure of independent decision making. I believe kids need something that is theirs to control. Restricting an allowance should not be a punishment for inappropriate behavior. The allowance is what it is, to be used how they want. In effect, it's really Mom and Dad's money, but it's Mom and Dad's money that I think is well spent to teach our kids about money and independence.

Some parents feel that they don't have to pay allowances because they generously hand out money to their kids whenever their kids want it. But studies have shown that kids who got money from their parents whenever they wanted it tended to save less and were broke more often than kids who received allowances and learned to budget. Even when the total amount of money each group received was the same, the allowance and the responsibility that goes along with it taught kids the value of a dollar for later in life. Don't just hand out money to your kids whenever they think they want it.

We split our kids' allowances into thirds. One-third of the money can be used for anything they want in the short term—a toy or a game. They buy what they want with their own money. The second third is for bigger purchases, something that it will take some time to save for, like a new bicycle. To my kids' credit, they have both used this part of their allowance to buy presents for each other, which made me so proud of them. The third component of their allowance goes into long-term savings. We periodically empty the piggybank and deposit the money in a savings account at a local bank. When their long-term account reaches a certain level, we take the money out and invest it in mutual funds.

Recently my son was going to spend some of his money to buy a PlayStation 2 game. We went to the store and found that the game he wanted cost $49.99. His comment was, "Whoa, 50 bucks is a lot for a game. I don't know if I should spend 50 bucks on a game." He kept looking at various games and he found another game that sold for $29.99. He said, "Well, I think I can afford 30 bucks, but 50 bucks is probably too much to spend on a PS-2 game." He bought that game with his own money. To me it was confirmation that the lessons we're trying to teach him, at least to some extent, are working. He got what in his mind was a less attractive game, but one that was a "better deal." It gave him more bang for his buck. It was a rewarding experience for me, because I saw that he was getting it.

Another good idea used by many parents is to divide allowances even further so that a portion of the allowance is set aside for giving to a faith community or charity. We don't do it in our family, because all our charitable contributions are made from my wife's or my account. But setting aside a portion of the allowance to give to others can be an effective way to teach kids to share their good fortune and to reflect on those who do not have as comfortable a life as they do. Perhaps by doing so, they will appreciate more what they have. If you intend to do this with your child's allowance, I still think it's important that they have some choice in where their money goes. If you do make this a requirement for part of their allowance, they should have options for which charity gets their money. You could help them do some research, which is another good learning experience.

One of my partners uses an excellent money management teaching tool with his daughter, who is a senior in high school. He gave her a debit card. She puts money she has earned into the account, and my partner augments it with an allowance each month. So at the beginning of the month she has a set amount in her account from her parents in addition to her earnings. That is all she gets. When she needs to buy something, she can use her debit card. But when her account reaches zero, she can't use her card for more. It's not a credit card, so she can only withdraw what's in the account.

The first month she had the account she used up her money in a week. Of course, she asked her parents for more—and, of course, they refused. She had to learn to live on what she had. She figured out how to handle a budget and spend her money carefully, not frivolously. My children are still too young to have debit cards, but I like the idea so much that I plan to do the same with them when they get older.

As your kids get older and go to college you may want to try another tactic that helps them learn to manage money on a larger scale. If you are blessed with the wherewithal to pay for your kids' college, instead of paying tuition directly to the university from your account, deposit the money into your child's checking account and have him or her write the check. Writing a check for five figures has a big impact on a young person. It tells them that their education is important business and gives them a sense of responsibility to take education seriously and try to do well in college.

Soon after you start your child on an allowance, I think it's important to open a savings account in the child's name. One of the benefits of doing this is that it encourages your child to make saving a habit. Let your child know how much money he or she has. All the money our kids get from birthdays, Christmas, allowances, even the loose change I bring home in my pocket each night—goes into a piggy bank. As I've said, when the bank is full, we take the contents to the bank to be deposited in their savings accounts. When the savings accounts reach a certain figure, we withdraw the amount and invest it in a mutual fund. My kids know how much they have in mutual funds and how much they have in their savings account.

The sums they have saved are eye-popping to me as I remember the money I had at their age. Part of that is due to the different financial circumstances of my family when I grew up and my family now. But it's also partly due to "gift inflation." My kids get presents, sometimes money, from relatives and friends of ours. That would have been very unusual when I grew up. And the tooth fairy these days is pretty flush compared to when I was a kid.

### How Would You Like to Get Paid?

Once your kids are old enough to understand a bit about money, offer them this exercise to get them thinking about saving and earning money with their money. Ask them which way they would prefer to get paid if they were given a job for one month. They could either take $100 a day for their work, or they could get paid one penny the first day and their employer would double their pay every day for 30 days. If they accepted the $100 dollars a day, they could earn $3,000. What could they earn if they accepted a penny the first day and the amount doubled every day? They would end up with total pay of more than $10 million!

| | | |
|---|---|---|
| 1. $ .01 | 11. $10.24 | 21. $10,485.76 |
| 2. $ .02 | 12. $20.48 | 22. $20,971.52 |
| 3. $ .04 | 13. $40.96 | 23. $41,934.04 |
| 4. $ .08 | 14. $81.92 | 24. $83,886.08 |
| 5. $ .16 | 15. $163.84 | 25. $167,772.16 |
| 6. $ .32 | 16. $327.68 | 26. $335,544.32 |
| 7. $ .64 | 17. $655.36 | 27. $671,088.64 |
| 8. $1.28 | 18. $1,310.72 | 28. $1,342,177.28 |
| 9. $2.56 | 19. $2,621.44 | 29. $2,684,354.56 |
| 10. $5.12 | 20. $5,242.88 | 30. $5,368,709.12 |
| | | Total: $10,737,418.24 |

Of course, there is no way to get such a deal from anyone. In the real world, money doesn't double that fast. But this exercise is a good introduction for children to the concept of earning some kind of return on their money by saving it and investing it.

**Have your children write down what they want to do with their money.**
Writing down goals or plans has a unique impact on our subconscious.
Once we see something in writing, it becomes more concrete. It also
forces decisions. It's part of the "either-or" process that I mentioned earlier. Seeing in black and white that we can have one or the other, this or
that, focuses attention and energy. With kids, for whom the future often
means two hours from now, it helps them understand some of their options with money and life. I believe it's so important, at any age, to have
goals in writing that I ask all my new clients to go through this exercise as
well. Putting ideas on paper makes them more real. Writing them down
forces us to be precise and succinct, to sift through "it would be nice" to
get to "this is the most important thing."

We use goal setting with our kids in all aspects of their lives, not just
saving and spending. We ask them to think of what big thing that they
want to do this year, this month, or the next few years. My older child, who
is not yet in high school, is already thinking about where she might want
to go to college. I know she's likely to change her mind many times in the
years before she actually goes to college, but she's thinking about it now
and is developing a vision of the kind of college she might like. She and her
mother took a trip to New York, and she fell in love with the city and wants
to go college in that area. That's fine. She's setting goals already—concrete
goals beyond "what do you want to be when you grow up"—which I believe is appropriate for her age. She is aware of a future and has begun to
understand what might be required of her to achieve what she wants.

**Get kids interested in money early.** Money is a great way to get kids
interested in arithmetic. When they were very young—even three or
four—we showed our kids how to tell different coins apart. I have always
brought my change home with me every day. All the loose change in my
pocket gets split evenly between the kids, according to the number of
each type of coin, and they put it in their piggy banks. Very quickly both
of my kids learned that if they had four quarters or ten dimes that was
one dollar. They learned to do the math and knew roughly in their heads
how much money they had.

**Keep discussions of money in the family.** I've had to point out to my
kids that many other kids do not have the same things—and money—

they have. Having some money saved is not something to brag about to friends. Whether you and your kids have money or not is simply a fact of their lives. It has nothing to do with character, it has nothing to do with friendships, and it has nothing to do with the people they are becoming. It is a tool that should be respected and valued.

I also always stress to my kids that our discussions of money are to remain in the family. How much money they have or even the cost of something they have is not a proper subject to discuss with their friends or others. I try to keep discussions of money very general, too, especially in terms of income.

---

### LESSONS I WANT MY CHILDREN TO LEARN

**Lesson #1: Life is not fair, get used to it.** One of daughter's favorite expressions is, "That's not fair." My response? "Life's not fair. Who said it was. Get used to it." Depending on the circumstances, of course, I may elaborate. I don't want the phrase to become a cliché or have her resent or ignore it, so we'll talk about what is fair and how we can make something fairer or more reasonable. But the bottom line is that life often isn't fair.

**Lesson #2: The world doesn't care about you.** The world expects you to accomplish something before it cares about you. I stress that I always care about them, but they shouldn't expect others to.

**Lesson #3: No honest job is beneath your dignity.** Dignity is a personal, internal characteristic. Doing a job, any job, well is an expression of our personal dignity. Flipping burgers or delivering pizza is not beneath your dignity. I delivered pizzas after I got married. I did whatever I could to make ends meet and to pay the rent. Some people would call it opportunity.

**Lesson #4: If you goof up, it's not someone else's fault.** Don't whine about your mistakes, learn from them. The quickest way to end criticism for a mistake, and begin to repair any damage, is to own up to it.

**Lesson #5: TV is not real life.** In real life people actually leave the bar or coffee shop and go to work.

Kids don't need to know how much money you make. Younger children don't have any relative concept of numbers. To them, $100 isn't much different from $100,000. All they need to know about your family's income is that it's enough to buy what your family needs, perhaps as well as an occasional treat or gift. Especially if money is tight in your family and your kids hear you discussing paying bills or saving and investing, they need reassurance that you have enough money to provide for them. Money worries should not be a part of your children's lives. As minor as their worries may seem to you, they already worry about a lot. Don't let them think that your family is in any danger or facing hardship.

## TEACHING GENEROSITY

At the risk of sounding arrogant, my wife and I are blessed in that we've been fortunate enough to earn a good income and accumulate significant financial assets. I say this not to boast; it is simply what it is. As thankful and as blessed as I feel and as fortunate as I feel, I also believe that you give back what you get. Part of the reason we've been blessed with economic success is because we've focused on doing things the right way, doing the best we can for our clients. I firmly believe that when you do well for others, you are rewarded in return. Our focus and our priorities have always been on our clients' success, not on our own financial gain. The financial gain has been a result of doing our jobs well.

My wife is a leader for our daughter's Girl Scout troop, and recently during the holiday season they held a fund-raiser. Their profits were lower than in previous years for a variety of reasons. In the past the troop had always given a significant amount of the money they raised to buy toys for Toys for Tots around Christmastime, with the remainder of the money going to troop functions and a pizza party. Because the profits were down this year, the girls were reluctant to give money to charity as they had in the past. My wife encouraged them to still give money to charity even though the troop would have less for itself than in previous years. "You get back what you give," she told them.

To the girls' credit, they talked about it and decided my wife was right. So they donated $25 of their $75 profit to Toys for Tots. A couple of days after this decision, the troop was out caroling for the holiday season and a local merchant was so impressed by their voices that he asked them to stay on in his store. His customers apparently enjoyed the carols, too. Before the girls finally left, he made out a check as a donation to the troop. The amount? The same $25 the girls had donated to a worthy cause. Of course, my wife did not waste the opportunity to share this lesson with the girls. They had been generous and had gotten back what they had given. She added, naturally, that the exchange is usually not so immediate and precise.

## Beware the Love of Money

Money is an important tool that our children need to understand, and yet financial literacy is one thing that's not taught in school. Compound that lack of education with our society's confusing messages about wealth—from a reticence to flaunt wealth, true at least here in the Midwest, perhaps less so elsewhere, to images of conspicuous consumption on TV and movies—and you are left with the difficult job of teaching your children to appreciate, yet not worship, money. Both the Old and New Testaments in the Bible contain warnings about the dangers of the love of money. It's important to note that money itself is not deemed to be dangerous but rather the love of money, which in 1 Timothy is called the "root of all evil."

In my experience, most kids except the richest and poorest grow into their teen years assuming their financial circumstances are the norm. Their own life is all they know, and all but a few people in the world know others who have either more or less than they have. What matters most when addressing the issue of money with your children is not how much you or they have. The most vital issues are teaching them your values, of which money is a small part, and letting them learn to enjoy giving their full energy to their activities.

# 13

## FINANCIER

■ ■ ■

The "financier" stage of our relationship with our children really begins for most of us when they finish high school and go to college. College tuition is probably the first expense related to raising children that will require advance planning, investing, or borrowing.

The escalating costs of higher education have been staggering, matched only by the increases in medical care in the past 20 years. Paying for college has always been an important consideration for parents, but with increases in tuition far higher than the general inflation rate, it has now become a serious planning issue for many families.

### SAVING FOR COLLEGE

Saving for the children's education is a goal that is often contemplated but less often acted upon. A college education for your kids will probably be the second-largest investment or purchase you make in your life after your home. There is no shortage of reasons to save for your children's education.

First among them is the breathtaking increase in the cost of post-secondary education. In recent years, college costs have increased at a rate far greater than the general rate of inflation. As of this writing, the cost of a college education can vary greatly depending upon whether you're going to a public or private institution. In 2002, the average cost of a state institution ranged from $10,000 to $12,000 per year. These annual costs included tuition, fees, and room and board. Books and supplies, transportation, and other personal expenses would be additional.

At private institutions for 2002, the average was far higher. If you look at universities like Yale, Northwestern, and Stanford, you can expect between $30,000 and $35,000 a year. Assuming an increase of 4 percent per year, by 2009, we will see public institutions cost in excess of $15,000 per year and private colleges around $45,000 a year. Clearly, the cost of an education is profound and needs to be planned for properly if it's a priority for you as a parent to pay for your kids' college—or at least assist them with education costs.

Perhaps the most effective way of comparing the increases in college costs is to look at the amount a young person can contribute to the cost of college by working. When I went to college in the 1970s, it was nearly possible to pay a year's tuition with a good summer job. A year of college at private institutions now takes almost the median income for a family of four in the United States! Young people are far less likely today to be able to pay even a substantial portion of their tuition by their own labors. Most will need considerable financial assistance.

The second important reason why kids need more help today to pay for education is the years they will probably spend studying before they move into the world of work and paychecks. Many careers now require more than four years of college. Call it degree inflation. Employers in many professions that once required only a bachelor's degree now insist upon, or at least prefer, a master's degree. Moreover, many students today take more than four years to earn their undergraduate degrees.

Is it worth the effort to save and invest to assist your child with college costs? I believe it is. First, let's look at your child's future earning power. According to the U.S. Statistical Abstract 2001, men with a four-year college degree earn an average income of $66,810, while men with only a high school diploma earn an average of $30,414—an annual difference of $36,396. If you multiply that by the estimated years that one will work as an adult, the potential lifetime difference is more than $1.4 million. For women with a four-year college degree—and these numbers reflect the continuing pay inequities between men and women—the average annual salary with a four-year college degree is $36,755, whereas with a high school diploma, the average annual salary is only $18,092, less than half. With the average work-life expectancy for a woman, the difference between a college degree and a high school diploma is well over $500,000.

College provides more than a professional credential, however; it also provides young people the opportunity to sample many subjects and discover their true "calling." Many have discovered a field of interest in college, often in the classes of a favorite professor who has changed their view of the work they would like to pursue. As I have already noted more than once, the discovery and pursuit of that "passion" are perhaps the most important aspect of one's life—even in purely financial terms. I have seen over and over again that financial success is the result of pursuing a passion, not money. Not all people who are passionate about what they do are wealthy in financial terms (though many lead rich lives), but very few people become wealthy if they have no passion for what they do.

Also, the college experience broadens the horizon of most young people both socially and intellectually. They expand their contacts and friendships beyond what most have in high school. Most of us learned lessons in college that have served us well for many years since. College is a learning experience that little else can equal: how to budget time, how to solve problems, how to think, how to take responsibility for our actions. It is a critical transition into the adult world, not only the professional world.

Despite the increased emphasis these days on college as preparation for a career, its primary value, in my opinion, remains that young people emerge from college with critical thinking skills and an awareness of the world they did not have when they entered. And it is only the most exceptional people who learn those lessons without the benefit of post-secondary education. This has not changed from when I went to school; it has remained one of the most important benefits of a college education.

A friend of mine renovated his home recently. The two carpenters he hired, as well as his concrete contractor, had four-year college degrees. Another friend hired a landscaper to redesign his yard. His contractor had a master's degree. All valued their college education highly and believed that it had given them advantages in their lives and their occupations.

Certainly the same is true for me. I was an education major and even student-taught in a high school during my senior year in college. The experience proved to me that I was not going to enjoy teaching. Were my college years wasted? Far from it. What I learned in those years I could not have learned another way. My life is richer for studying history, literature, mathematics. I don't remember many of the details I learned in those classes, but they helped me immeasurably, shaping my view of the world. I wouldn't trade them for any other experience.

## PLANNING FOR COLLEGE COSTS

Saving and investing for college is just like any other investment activity: Time is your greatest ally. The sooner you start, the less you have to invest. It may seem a distant goal when your child isn't even in kindergarten yet, but saving for college is much easier if you begin early. Obviously, if you begin saving before they can spell "college" (or any other word), you will have an easier time budgeting for it than if you put it off until they begin looking at college brochures.

### Step #1: Estimate What College Will Cost When Your Child Is Ready to Go

A financial adviser can help you with this projection, or you can consult Table 13.1. You can also find Internet sites that can help you calculate college costs. Factor in things such as the current cost for a year of school, the number of years until your child will begin college, how many years you think it will take him or her to get through college, and an estimated rate of inflation of college costs. Once the total cost is known, the amount of monthly or annual savings required to meet that goal can be calculated.

### Step #2: Compare Available Cash Flow with the Savings Required

You need to determine how much financial help you may realistically provide to defray your children's college costs. Paying for four years of college for your kids may not be within the realm of possibility for you. It isn't for many Americans. One caller to my radio show said she had saved enough to pay for two years of college for her daughter and was wondering about her options for financing the last two years. Before I dug into her options I congratulated her on saving as much as she had.

TABLE 13.1. PROJECTED COST OF COLLEGE

Four-Year Public College

| Child's Age | Year Entering College | Total Goal | Lump Sum | Contribute Per Year | Per Month |
|---|---|---|---|---|---|
| 1 | 2022 | $186,786 | $44,934 | $4,561 | $394 |
| 2 | 2021 | $177,891 | $46,218 | $4,835 | $417 |
| 3 | 2020 | $169,420 | $47,538 | $5,142 | $444 |
| 4 | 2019 | $161,352 | $48,896 | $5,492 | $474 |
| 5 | 2018 | $153,669 | $50,294 | $5,892 | $508 |
| 6 | 2017 | $146,351 | $51,730 | $6,356 | $549 |
| 7 | 2016 | $139,382 | $53,209 | $6,901 | $596 |
| 8 | 2015 | $132,745 | $54,729 | $7,552 | $652 |
| 9 | 2014 | $126,424 | $56,292 | $8,344 | $720 |
| 10 | 2013 | $120,403 | $57,901 | $9,329 | $805 |
| 11 | 2012 | $114,670 | $59,555 | $10,592 | $914 |
| 12 | 2011 | $109,209 | $61,257 | $12,269 | $1,059 |
| 13 | 2010 | $104,009 | $63,007 | $14,612 | $1,261 |
| 14 | 2009 | $99,056 | $64,807 | $18,117 | $1,564 |
| 15 | 2008 | $94,339 | $66,659 | $23,950 | $2,067 |
| 16 | 2007 | $89,847 | $68,563 | $35,600 | $3,072 |
| 17 | 2006 | $85,568 | $70,522 | $70,522 | $6,086 |

Paying for two years of college is no small accomplishment. It probably entailed considerable forethought and frugality. It was a wonderful gift to her child. The same may be true for you. Perhaps your child will have to borrow money or work part-time to pay for the rest. That's not all bad.

The key is deciding what you can spare from your weekly, monthly, or yearly budget to contribute to a college fund and begin to put that money away as soon as you can. As you can see in the preceding hypothetical example, you don't have to contribute thousands a year to pay for four years of college. If you can save something, it will help your child enormously. It's better to save what you can, rather than throw up your hands in frustration at the impossibility of paying for all college costs. If your children are still very young, you may be surprised to find out what you may be able to accumulate in a college fund before they reach

## TABLE 13.1. PROJECTED COST OF COLLEGE (CONT.)

**Four-Year Private College**

| Child's Age | Year Entering College | Total Goal | Lump Sum | Contribute Per Year | Per Month |
|---|---|---|---|---|---|
| 1 | 2022 | $241,613 | $58,123 | $5,900 | $509 |
| 2 | 2021 | $230,107 | $59,784 | $6,254 | $540 |
| 3 | 2020 | $219,150 | $61,492 | $6,652 | $574 |
| 4 | 2019 | $208,714 | $63,249 | $7,104 | $613 |
| 5 | 2018 | $198,775 | $65,056 | $7,621 | $658 |
| 6 | 2017 | $189,310 | $66,915 | $8,222 | $710 |
| 7 | 2016 | $180,295 | $68,827 | $8,927 | $770 |
| 8 | 2015 | $171,710 | $70,793 | $9,769 | $843 |
| 9 | 2014 | $163,533 | $72,816 | $10,793 | $931 |
| 10 | 2013 | $155,746 | $74,896 | $12,068 | $1,041 |
| 11 | 2012 | $148,329 | $77,036 | $13,701 | $1,182 |
| 12 | 2011 | $141,266 | $79,237 | $15,871 | $1,370 |
| 13 | 2010 | $134,539 | $81,501 | $18,900 | $1,631 |
| 14 | 2009 | $128,132 | $83,830 | $23,435 | $2,023 |
| 15 | 2008 | $122,031 | $86,225 | $30,980 | $2,674 |
| 16 | 2007 | $116,220 | $88,689 | $46,050 | $3,974 |
| 17 | 2006 | $110,685 | $91,222 | $91,222 | $7,873 |

*Contributions assume 8 percent rate of return per year.*

*College costs used in these calculators are based on data from the Annual Survey of Colleges of the College Board and Data Base, 2004–2005. Assumes four years of expenses.*

*Costs assume tuition, fees, room and board, books and supplies, and increase 5 percent per year.*

college age. Be sure to include in your projections any funds the family may have already saved.

## Step #3: Determine What Financial Aid May Be Available. Be Realistic!

Don't count on athletic scholarships. Kids are better off studying than playing sports, because far more financial aid is awarded to good students than to good athletes. A tiny fraction of kids have the physical skills to earn an athletic scholarship, yet playgrounds are full of parents pushing their kids to excel in the hope that they might earn one. The unrealistic notion of earning athletic scholarships has corrupted a lot of youth sports—a pet peeve of mine. As a former college athlete, I understand how unrealistic expectations can be on this subject. A metro area as big as Minneapolis–St. Paul produces only a few dozen Division I athletes a year, at most, if you include all sports for boys and girls. Don't put pressure on preteenage kids to excel at a sport in the hope that it may pay for their college. Accept that pressure yourself—and put a plan in place to do what you can to save for their education. You'll enjoy Little League baseball games much more, and so will your kids, if you don't put that pressure on their backs.

When colleges determine eligibility for financial aid, they look at savings in your child's name, but they won't consider some investments in your name, if structured properly. An example is the cash value of life insurance. Money in retirement plans is usually also excluded.

## Step #4: Decide How to Invest the Money

Many financial advisers will recommend that money saved for college be placed in relatively low-risk investments. I recommend a more aggressive approach if you have a long enough time frame. In that case, savings may be placed initially in higher-risk or growth types of investments. As the time for college gets closer, the accumulated funds can be shifted from growth-oriented assets into more conservative choices, such as fixed-income assets. We typically recommend that for an infant, who has 18 years before college, the investments be made primarily in equities. However, if your child is already 15, and you are just starting to save for expenses that are only three years away, you might stick with fixed-interest investments.

The ultimate decision depends on a range of factors, such as the number of years until college begins, the amount of money available to invest, and the family's tax bracket, risk tolerance, and investment experience. Regardless of how you save or where you put the money, the key to successfully saving for your children's college education is to begin as early as possible. I also recommend that you seek professional advice. Developing a plan to save for college education can be complicated. Questions can and will arise involving income, estate and gift taxes, as well as investment issues.

## EDUCATION SAVINGS PLANS IN DETAIL

A number of tax-advantaged strategies are available to accumulate funds for college expenses. The rules surrounding these strategies can be complicated, and I recommend that you review them carefully with a financial adviser.

### The Section 529 Plan

I think one of the most efficient ways of saving for a child's college education is the Section 529 Plan. Section 529 Qualified Tuition Plans (QTPs) were established under the provisions of Internal Revenue Code Section 529. They provide a tax-favored framework within which funds may be accumulated to pay for a beneficiary's qualified higher education expenses at an eligible educational institution. In other words, you can get a tax advantage if the money is ultimately spent for post–high school education. QTPs allow you either to prepay a student's tuition or to contribute to a savings account established to pay the student's qualified higher education expenses. Both prepaid tuition plans and savings account plans may be established by all of the 50 states. Eligible private institutions are also authorized to establish prepaid tuition plans.

One type of QTP is a prepaid tuition plan. Contributions are made to a qualified trust, which invests the funds to offset increases in tuition costs between now and when the child attends college. The contract allows one to purchase a number of course units or academic periods that are redeemed when the beneficiary becomes old enough to attend college.

In a second type of QTP, a higher education savings account plan, contributions are made to an account established for a named beneficiary. A mutual fund typically manages the investments. The amount available to pay higher education expenses depends upon the growth in the account during the period between which the contribution is made and when you are ready to make withdrawals for college. Contributions to these programs are not tax deductible; however, the earnings in these accounts grow tax-deferred. If the funds are used for qualified education expenses, earnings are taxed at the beneficiary's tax rate when withdrawn.

Contributions to a QTP must be in cash and may not exceed the amount necessary to provide the beneficiary's qualified higher education expenses. Program sponsors will specify maximum total contribution amounts based on factors such as the beneficiary's current age, current education costs, projected inflation, and anticipated investment returns. In some programs, up to as much as $240,000 may be contributed for a beneficiary.

### Eligibility

Generally speaking, qualified higher education expenses include tuition, fees, books, supplies, and equipment required for attendance. Room and board is also included if the student is attending school at least half-time. Qualified higher education expenses also include costs incurred to allow a special-needs beneficiary to enroll at and attend an eligible institution. (Note: The cost of beer does not qualify.)

In general, accredited post–high school educational institutions offering associate, bachelor's, graduate level, or professional degrees are eligible. Certain vocational schools are also included.

The beneficiary must be identified at the time the account is created. As a general rule, the person who contributes to the account is the owner. The account owner may change the beneficiary. If the new beneficiary is a member of the same family as the original beneficiary, there's generally no current federal income tax. Qualifying family members include the beneficiary's spouse, son, or daughter, a son's or daughter's descendants, stepson or stepdaughter, brother, sister, stepbrother or stepsister, father or mother, or ancestor of either, stepfather or stepmother, son or daughter of a brother or sister, brother or sister of a father or a mother, spouse of any person listed above, and first cousins.

More than 50 different 529 plans are available, one for every state. A change in investment strategy is typically permitted at least once each year or if a new beneficiary is named. Amounts accumulating in a QTP operated by one state generally may be used at educational institutions in a different state. In fact, you could reside in one state, and your beneficiary could reside in the same state as you or a different state. You could take the 529 plan from yet another state and attend school in yet another state.

### Distributions and Taxes

For federal and state tax purposes, funds in a QTP are normally not included in the donor's estate. However, any amounts in a QTP when a beneficiary dies will generally be included in the beneficiary's estate. In other words, if grandparents want to assist a grandchild with college education and they make a gift to the 529 QTP, they not only get a tax advantage for the beneficiary or the grandchild, they also effectively remove some dollars from their estate. It can be an efficient estate-planning tool because it removes assets from the estate.

Another thing to consider with a QTP is that these assets may affect the student's eligibility for financial aid. The U.S. Department of Education has advised that assets in a savings account plan are considered assets of the parent for the purposes of the Free Application for Federal Student Aid. The assets in a prepaid tuition plan are generally considered to reduce the student's need on a dollar-for-dollar basis. Private institutions may also take QTP assets into account when considering financial aid.

In my opinion, the Section 529 Qualified Tuition Plan offers the best benefits if you know your child will ultimately attend a post–high school institution of higher learning. It is the most efficient due to the tax advantages if the distributions qualify as higher education expenses. However, like everything else with financial planning, flexibility is important, and QTPs are not very flexible apart from the fact that you can change the beneficiary within your family. If the funds are not used for higher education, a big tax bill could result.

## Coverdell Education Savings Accounts

Another excellent choice for saving for your kids' college education is the Coverdell Education Savings Account. The Coverdell Education Savings Account offers tax-free withdrawals for higher education and has done so since 1998. The annual contribution limit has now been boosted from the previous $500 per year to $2,000 per year. Coverdell accounts, unlike 529 Qualified Tuition Plans, can now be used for elementary and secondary education and even academic tutoring and education-related computer expenses.

Not everyone is eligible to establish these accounts. If your income exceeds certain limits, you will not be eligible to fund a Coverdell account. Additionally, because annual contributions are limited to $2,000, it can be difficult to accumulate a large amount of money unless you start very early. If you do qualify, the payoff for investing in Coverdell accounts could be substantial. For example, if you contribute $2,000 each year from your child's first year to his or her 18th birthday, and you could earn a hypothetical 8 percent per year on your investment, the account would grow to more than $80,000, which should at least make a serious dent in the total cost of four years of college.

## Custodial Accounts

Another type of account used to be very popular but is less attractive today—the Uniform Gift to Minor (UGMA) or Uniform Transfer to Minor Act (UTMA), which are custodial accounts in the child's name. For many years, these accounts were the only substantial savings vehicle for education expenses. As a result, many people have built up sizable amounts in custodial accounts. Unlike Coverdell accounts, there are no income or contribution limits. At least part of the earnings on the investment may be exempt from federal income tax, or some or all are taxed at the child's lower rate if the child is under the age of 14.

Money can be withdrawn at any time for the benefit of the child—not only for education—with certain limitations. Contributions to UGMAs and UTMAs are irrevocable, meaning that once the money or other property is given or put in, the donor cannot change his or her mind and withdraw the gift. And the child assumes control of the account upon reaching the age of majority, which is 18 or 21 in most states. I consider this the major drawback to custodial accounts.

I prefer to see education savings remain in the parent's or grand-parent's names. If the custodial account is in your son's name, he could spend it on a new car instead of college once he reaches age 18 or 21. If it's in your name, the decision is yours. The tax benefits of accounts in a child's name are relatively small and are not an important factor. Moreover, money in the child's name is usually considered when determining financial aid, whereas money held by the parents in some accounts may not be counted in calculating need-based financial aid.

## BORROWING MONEY FOR EDUCATION

As I wrote in Chapter 1, in the section on debt, I believe borrowing for education is one of the only good uses of debt. Student loans typically charge very low interest rates, are amortized over a long period of time, and are used to buy an appreciating asset. As I have noted earlier, a college degree, on average, leads to higher lifetime earnings. It is a good investment.

I have often been asked, however, if it makes sense to borrow from a 401(k) or other pretax retirement account to pay for college. In my opinion, it does *not* make sense and I would recommend against it. Borrowing against retirement savings should be a last resort for paying college costs.

One reason is that you could face severe penalties if you had a financial emergency that caused you to miss payments on loans against your pretax retirement account. The IRS would then treat the entire amount you borrowed, even amounts already repaid, as an early withdrawal. You'd have to pay penalties and income taxes on all of it. It's not a risk I would recommend, if there's any alternative.

Instead of borrowing against your retirement account, I would recommend the option of not contributing to your 401(k) for a couple of years and putting that money toward college costs.

If you do need to borrow money for college, beyond student loans, I would prefer that you borrow against any equity in your home before you borrow from your retirement.

A final option for financing college that too few people consider is variable universal life insurance (VUL). It can be an excellent way to save for college for parents who are somewhat young and healthy, so the cost of the death benefit is relatively low. Most policies allow borrowing against the cash value of the policy at attractive interest rates. Another advantage of investing within a VUL is that most colleges don't consider the cash value of life insurance when determining eligibility for financial aid. Moreover, there are no limits on the amount that can be invested each year, unlike IRAs and most 401(k)s. For a detailed discussion of VUL, refer to Chapter 8.

# 14

## BENEFACTOR

■ ■ ■

Each of us leaves a legacy to our children. Producing your own personal legacy is an art form, like writing a symphony. And like the composition of a symphony, your wealth management solutions will require thought, planning, and creativity. Estate planning is about living. What you do with your estate is not just a matter of death and dying. How you plan the distribution of your assets helps define who you are, how you think of yourself, your aspirations, and your sense of purpose in life.

Who will benefit from your life's work? Will it be the people you want to benefit? How can you be sure they will receive what you want them to receive when you're gone? Your estate plan helps answer these questions. If you haven't created an estate plan, you may be surprised to know you actually already have one. Anyone who doesn't create an estate plan has a default plan imposed by the probate and tax laws of the state that you live in. But this plan does not necessarily ensure that your assets are given to the people you love.

The purpose of your estate plan is to distribute the property you've accumulated over a lifetime exactly as you wish. Your goals may include ensuring that you have a solid retirement program, providing for your surviving family members, or supporting the work of charitable causes. Your concerns may include determining who needs or deserves your gifts most, whether your gifts will be used prudently, and how to reduce losses from taxes.

For example, it's possible to set up a trust for your heirs, contributing to your peace of mind and expressing your love and concern. It's also possible to donate property to charities while retaining lifetime ownership and use. When working with the right team and taking into account your personal vision, estate planning can be one of the most fulfilling projects you will ever undertake.

## WHERE DO YOU START?

At my company, we approach estate planning differently from most. We do it almost backward from how it's traditionally done. We look first at our clients' income needs for the lifestyle they want. Only then do we look at how they can use what remains to create an estate for their children or others. We base estate planning on their excess cash flow, money they don't need and wouldn't spend anyway.

For instance, paying a premium for life insurance in order to give more money to charity or to benefit your children may be generous, but we don't want our clients to be saddled with costs, overhead, or premiums that are going to diminish their lifestyle. A cash flow analysis ensures that they can live as they want in their later years, which we believe is more important than the size of their estate. So we always do an analysis of cash flow needs first, and we look at buying insurance for estate planning only if they can pay the cost of the insurance without detracting from their lifestyle.

### Inventory

To start estate planning, you need an inventory of all your holdings and their fair market value. You need to list all the debts and expenses, including mortgages and other loans. Additionally, you should project funeral expenses and administrative costs. Typically, property is owned outright by an individual. How the property is owned is important because this will control how it passes to your heirs. For example, property held solely in your name or as a tenant in common will pass according to the provisions of your will. Property held jointly with rights of survivorship, however, will pass automatically at your death to the surviving tenant and will not be controlled by your will. Once you've listed your assets, you can begin to see how much you have. You will also see which assets can be transferred directly, which must be divided or converted to cash before they can be transferred, and which require special administration in order to reap any economic return.

As you go about taking inventory, think of how you can make the management of your estate less stressful for your heirs. If assets can be easily centralized into a few accounts instead of many, do it. If you own valuable personal property that is locked away somewhere, especially illiquid things such as art, jewelry, or antiques, consider disposing of all but the items you still hold dearest or that still give you pleasure. Then your heirs won't have to try to calculate what they are worth, or dispose of them under duress when they may get only a fraction of their value.

The mother of a friend of mine was once an antique dealer, and although in her 80s, still has room after room of valuable antiques. She has even rented warehouse space to store some of her treasures. She has not even looked in those spaces for years. Those things that she values, but doesn't enjoy, will be a monstrous headache for her children someday. And her children, not willing to put in the months of work it would require to obtain fair value for her collection, will likely sell it by the truckload for a fraction of what the woman knows it to be worth. Her unwillingness to part with her possessions now will be a boon later, not to her children, but to antique dealers and scavengers who will offer pennies on the dollar for them.

## The Estate Planner's Tool Kit

Here are some of the basic instruments used in estate planning to meet each individual's goals and those of their children.

### Unlimited Marital Deduction

If you are married, the unlimited marital deduction allows spouses to transfer an unlimited amount of property at the first death without incurring a federal gift or estate tax. This deduction can help alleviate the estate tax burden on the survivor; however, state inheritance and estate taxes may still apply. The deduction does not help you avoid the tax; it only delays it until the surviving spouse dies. At the death of the surviving spouse, all the property that was previously shielded from taxation will be considered part of the taxable estate and the toll will have to be paid by your children or grandchildren. Of course, any property that was spent prior to the second death will not be taxed.

### The Unified Credit

In 2000, federal law allowed you to transfer cash or property to another party during your lifetime or at your death up to $675,000 without incurring any federal, state, or gift tax liability. In 2005, that amount has been ramped up to $1.5 million. The estate tax rates and the exclusion allowed per person up to 2011 are shown in Table 14.1. The exclusion amount is the value of an estate that will not be subject to estate taxes. In other words, in 2006, if your estate is worth less than $2 million, your heirs will not be subject to estate taxes. That $2 million exclusion also applies to each person, so, for example, a couple can effectively have an estate of $4 million without paying estate taxes, $2 million each for husband and wife. In 2011, unless the law is changed or extended, estate tax rates and exclusion amounts will return to where they were in 2000 when the estate tax was revised.

TABLE 14.1. ESTATE TAX RATES

| Year | Exclusion Per Person | Tax Rate on Amount over Exclusion (in %) |
| --- | --- | --- |
| 2005 | $1.5 million | 47 |
| 2006 | $2.0 million | 46 |
| 2007 | $2.0 million | 45 |
| 2008 | $2.0 million | 45 |
| 2009 | $3.5 million | 45 |
| 2010 | No estate taxes | |
| 2011 | $675,000 | 55 |

The only thing I can tell you for sure about the estate tax law is that is unlikely to survive the way it currently is through 2011. Congress is debating whether to extend the elimination of the estate tax beyond 2010. I believe that is unlikely. Where the exclusion amount and the tax rate will settle is anybody's guess.

## *Annual Gift Program*

A lifetime program of gift giving can increase the amount of property you can transfer without being taxed. In 2005, current law allows individuals to give up to $11,000 per year to a person without incurring any gift tax. This amount may increase in future years. In most cases, these gifts will not be included in the donor's estate and so will pass completely free of estate taxes as well. Another advantage of making annual gifts, particularly to young children, is that they result in income tax savings for the family. The future income from the gifted property will be taxed to the children at their income tax rates, which are usually lower than those of their parents or grandparents.

The other advantage of distributing assets prior to death is that the gifts may be more valuable to your children while you are alive than after you die. Children saving for a home, planning a big purchase, or simply facing financial difficulties may find the smaller sums allowed as tax-free gifts more helpful than the larger sums you may leave them when you die.

## *Wills*

The basic instrument of estate planning is the will, a legal document in which you state who will receive what portion of your property, as well as when and under what conditions they will receive it. A will also allows you to designate a guardian for your children and an executor or personal representative who carries out the terms of the will. If you die intestate—without a will—the executor and guardian are appointed by the court, and your assets are disposed of according to state law. In all states, however, at least part of your estate will go to your children, and in many states they will receive more than your spouse. A will that is complete and current, one that names all those legally entitled to a share in your estate, accounts for assets, and pays all creditors, will ensure that the administration of your estate proceeds quickly according to your intentions. Keeping those close to you informed of your plans, especially if your financial or family situation changes, can help avoid litigation, costly delays, and unnecessary conflict.

### Trusts

Trusts are vehicles that shelter your assets from taxation and manage the property that you leave to your heirs. Simply put, you transfer property in the name of a trustee who manages it for the benefit of a third party, the beneficiary. One of the great advantages of trusts is their flexibility. They can be adapted to fit a wide variety of situations. In fact, as our attorneys at Wealth Enhancement Group say, "Trust is not the key word. Trust doesn't tell you that much." What *precedes* the word trust tells you everything. The most important aspect of trusts is that they allow property to be managed according to the donor's specific wishes, far into the future. Living trusts allow you to control trust assets; irrevocable trusts take away control but offer many attractive estate tax implications and more. Your advisers can help you determine which type of trust best suits your situation.

### Life Insurance

Life insurance is a flexible estate planning tool that can be used to create an estate, replace a financial loss caused by death, provide liquidity to fund a business buyout agreement, pay estate costs, or replace the cost of a charitable contribution. Life insurance benefits are generally received income tax free and with careful planning can also be received estate tax free. Since life insurance passes by contract, it avoids the delays and expenses of probate. A survivorship or second- or last-to-die insurance policy provides an ideal low-cost foundation for a married couple's estate plan. This type of insurance contract is specifically designed to cover the costs of estate taxes and fees while insuring two lives under the same contract and paying a benefit only upon the second or last death. Most sophisticated estate plans make optimal use of the unlimited marital deduction and so defer the payment of estate taxes until the death of the surviving spouse. A survivorship life insurance policy dovetails perfectly with these plans by providing the benefit when it is really needed. It provides a customized solution to the dilemma of estate taxes and the need for liquidity.

## Paying Costs

Even the most efficient estate planning will not totally eliminate state settlement costs. After using the tools that will minimize taxes and administration costs you need to consider the alternatives for financing the costs that remain.

Four possible sources of funds can be used for these expenses: cash, credit, sale of assets, and life insurance.

**Cash.** Most estates don't normally have large reserves of cash. Additionally, using cash resources costs the estate 100 cents on the dollar to pay off taxes.

**Credit.** The executor may go to the bank and obtain a loan at current interest rates. In certain cases, estates of closely held business interests may qualify for a loan from the federal government for a portion of the estate settlement costs. With the interest total, estate settlement costs increase to more than 100 cents on the dollar.

**Sale of assets.** Having to sell nonliquid assets, such as securities, business interests, or real estate, can result in disastrous losses if markets are unfavorable. Additionally, commissions and other sales expenses may be incurred. Furthermore, if you're in an estate stress sale and the buyers know that you're desperate, you are unlikely to get fair market value for the assets you're trying to sell.

**Life insurance.** A life insurance policy provides cash immediately and can be structured so that the proceeds pass free of income, gift, and estate taxes. The result is that life insurance typically costs just pennies on the dollar to provide immediate funds to cover estate settlement costs.

A tool for life insurance often used in estate planning is called the irrevocable life insurance trust or ILIT. Here, the trust, rather than an individual, owns the life insurance policy. ILITs offer many potential benefits, including:

- Death proceeds avoid federal estate tax, generation-skipping taxes, or transfer taxes.
- Relatively small premium payments maximize the value of the annual gift tax exclusion since the entire policy proceeds will be sheltered from transfer tax.
- Estate liquidity problems can be solved.
- The estate left to heirs can be enhanced.
- Trust assets invested in life insurance avoid income tax.
- Death proceeds avoid the expenses and publicity of probate.
- Death proceeds are managed for heirs by a trustee according to the grantor's directions.
- Flexibility is still possible if the ILIT is properly designed.

One of the difficulties associated with life insurance trusts is that they are irrevocable. However, there are some methods that can be employed to increase flexibility. This may be particularly important if Congress amends the estate and gift tax laws, which I fully expect it to do before 2010. Today, ILITs can be structured in such a way that the proceeds are effectively removed from the estate but are simultaneously accessible for living expenses. Clearly, the goal would be not to have to spend these assets, and they probably would be the last assets someone would spend. You wouldn't want to take distributions from the trust unless it was a last resort. But the fact is that these trusts can now be structured in such a way that money is accessible.

## LIFE VERSUS LEGACY

Before leaving the issue of your role as benefactor to your children, I want to make two important points. Your legacy to your children can't make up for your failures as a provider, protector, or teacher. Your children will probably get along just fine without your money after you die. They won't do nearly so well if they don't get your time, your values, and your love while you're alive. Your first and most important legacy to your children is the way you lived and your relationships with them. Money will not mend fences that were broken long ago. If amends need to be made, don't rely on your estate to do it.

Second, consider the impact of your estate and your will on those you leave behind. Wills can leave bitterness among family members when assets are bequeathed inequitably. Will your estate unite or divide your family? Leaving an estate to your children should be your last act of love for them, not a parting shot in a long-running argument. If you have good reason to divide your estate in certain ways—perhaps one child provided your care in your later years—you can always take the time and summon the words to express your wishes and your reasons.

Estate planning isn't always easy, and some people are not comfortable talking about the things that make it difficult: our fears, our hopes, and family conflicts. It's easy to feel overwhelmed by estate planning. Many people find it difficult to think about dying and about how things might be when they are gone. For some, estate planning can be an isolating experience, especially when family situations arise that can't be resolved easily. Treating death as an intensely private topic to be avoided at all costs takes an emotional and spiritual toll. Creating your estate plan, knowing that you have found a smart way to pay estate taxes, enrich the lives of those you love, or support the causes that mean the most to you, can be an opportunity to break the silence and to better understand the rich fabric of family and social relationships that make up your life.

# 15

## MONEY AND YOUR CHILDREN'S CHILDREN

■ ■ ■

The relationship between grandparents and their grandchildren is unique, and it can be loving and rewarding for all. This special relationship often results in grandparents wanting to assist their grandchildren financially.

That desire is admirable. Even more admirable is a willingness to give them your time and love. Babysit your grandkids. Play catch. Teach them to fish, to golf, to play a musical instrument. Take them to the theater. Give them your time and love, and chances are they'll make you proud and use your financial gifts to better themselves and make the gift more rewarding for you.

As your grandchildren grow up, don't overlook the benefit to them of your experience. You may be able to give them advice or help them with problems that they may not be as willing to address with their parents. You will probably have few chances in life to be as revered as a role model as you are with your grandchildren.

I think it is the unique prerogative of grandparents to spoil their grandchildren—with one caveat. Include your children in any discussion of how to assist your grandchildren, financially or otherwise. Despite your love for your grandchildren, you still have a "grand" in front of your name. You are not the parents and should not make decisions without their input.

Loving grandparents who want to help financially can do a lot. But there are some things that cannot be done or are inadvisable. Let's consider some of the possibilities.

## GIFTS

Cash gifts of up to $11,000 per year can be given to a grandchild without gift tax consequences for the child. I don't believe it is appropriate, however, to put large sums of money in an account in a young child's name. You have no control over how it is spent.

## UTMA/UGMA

Uniform Transfer to Minors Act (UTMA) and Uniform Gift to Minors Act (UGMA) accounts were more efficient strategies prior to 1986. The Tax Reform Act of 1986 eliminated most of the tax benefits of putting assets in a child's name. There are two primary disadvantages to UGMA/UTMA accounts. First, money in the child's name decreases their chances for college financial aid more than if the money were in a parent's or grandparent's name. Second, when the child reaches the age of majority (18 for UGMA, 21 for UTMA), he or she can do anything they want with the money. Many 18- to 21-year-olds are not fiscally responsible and may not use the money the way you intended. Furthermore, once the account is opened, even prior to the age of majority, the custodian of the account must manage the account in the child's best interest. Translation: You can't spend it on yourself.

## IRA

When a grandchild can legitimately earn income and receive a W-2 or 1099, the grandparent may contribute to an IRA in the grandchild's name of up to $4,000 annually. *You may not open an IRA or Roth IRA in the name of a child who does not have earned income.* One must have earned income in order to contribute to an IRA. I had clients who wanted to open a Roth for their three-year-old granddaughter. What is a three-year-old going to do to generate earned income? Employing the child in a family business or to assist you is a legitimate way for the child to earn income toward the $4,000 threshold—as long as actual work is done and is compensated at realistic rates of pay.

## Real Estate

I have encountered this situation on several occasions: A grandparent wants to put a grandchild's name on the deed to property to ensure the grandchild receives the property on the death of the grandparent. You shouldn't do this for two reasons. One, by making a grandchild a co-owner, he may have to pay gift tax on a portion of your home's value. Two, if you make him co-owner now, it could be more expensive for him if he ever wanted to sell the house. His basis in the house would be its value when *you* acquired it, which increases the likelihood that he would pay capital gains taxes. The simplest solution is to designate in your will that you want him to have the house. For tax purposes, he would then acquire the house at its value when you die, making it less likely that he would pay capital gains if he sold it.

### EDUCATION

Helping to pay for post–high school education is a priority for many grandparents. You have several options to help out.

## Education IRAs

Grandparents can contribute up to $2,000 per year per grandchild with no tax liability for the grandchild, if used for education. One note of caution: $2,000 per year, even if started at infancy, is only a total investment of $36,000 ($2,000 x 18 years). Even with excellent investment results, it won't cover college costs for long, given the rate of increase of education expenses.

## Qualified Tuition Plans (QTPs) or 529 Plans

As described earlier, these college savings plans are state-sponsored investment programs. Anyone can contribute to a QTP for a child, with a maximum contribution of $55,000 per person. All earnings accumulate tax deferred, and withdrawals for qualified education expenses may be tax free. These savings plans can be an efficient way to defray education costs, especially for grandchildren who are unlikely to qualify for financial aid.

QTPs offer an advantageous way for grandparents in high tax brackets to transfer assets to their grandchildren.

## Transferring Highly Appreciated Assets

Giving highly appreciated assets to a grandchild over age 14, or their educational institution, can be tax efficient. The alternative of selling the asset and then making a gift may cause a huge tax liability to the giver.

### LEGACY

Many grandparents choose to transfer assets directly to their grandchildren when they die. Doing so can be done efficiently as an act of love, as an investment in your own gene pool, and as a way to shield some of your estate from taxes.

## Roth IRA

Name your grandchild the beneficiary of a Roth IRA. When you die, he or she then receives the proceeds income tax free if distributions don't occur until after you reach age 59½ or at least five years after you open the account. While you could also make your grandchild the beneficiary of a regular IRA, the proceeds of that IRA would be subject to income tax for your grandchild. You can only make contributions to a Roth IRA, however, if you still have earned income. If you have earned income of at least $4,000 per year, you can contribute up to $4,000 per year to a Roth. The same is true for your spouse.

## Variable Universal Life Insurance

Variable universal life insurance (VUL) can be an extremely effective strategy for transferring assets to grandchildren. The grandparent applying for the insurance should be healthy and able to fund the VUL for at least 10 years for it to be efficient. Distributions and the death benefit may be income tax free. The VUL may also be beneficial to the grandparents in their estate planning by creating an infusion of capital that their heirs could use to offset estate tax liability.

# PART IV

# Money and Parents

A financial relationship between an adult child and his or her parents has steadily become a more important issue in my business—from the perspective of the child. The inexorable rise in life expectancy is one of the primary reasons for that increasing interest from a financial planning perspective.

Your parents will most likely live considerably longer into your adult years than parents did in the past. It is not uncommon now to find retired people who have one or both parents still alive and healthy. Parent and child may both be senior citizens, which often means that both parent and child are living off fixed incomes, either through pensions or retirement savings. The possibility that your parents, probably among the handful of people you love the most, may need financial assistance from you when you are no longer earning an income from your skills or labor increases the need for preparation and planning before you reach that stage.

The need to consider the financial relationship between parent and adult child has also been accentuated by the phenomenal rise in medical and health care costs in the past couple of decades. Some of the medical advances that have contributed to greater longevity are very expensive. This increase in medical costs, which can sap a life's savings in no time, has increased the need for financial planning for parent and child alike.

Finally, the financial relationship among parent and adult child has changed for many others owing to the truly staggering sums of money that today's adult children will inherit in the next few years from their parents. Children are not responsible for planning the passing of wealth from one generation to the next, but they will often be involved in that planning—and will certainly be required to manage the inheritance when it passes to *them*.

Based on my experience working with a wide variety of clients I see three important financial issues involving money and parents, one of which you will likely have to address with your parents or on their behalf. Those three issues are:

- Caring for elderly parents;
- Wills and estate planning; and
- Managing an inheritance.

You will see one persistent theme through the next three chapters: communication.

Communication between parents and children on these issues is often difficult. If there is one thing that families talk about less than family finances, it is death in the family. So in this chapter I am asking you to talk about the two things that many families talk about least—and I'm asking you to combine the two in one conversation! Take heart. In most human interaction, the energy expended to understand another person is richly rewarded. And you have a huge head start: You love each other.

# 16

## CARING FOR ELDERLY PARENTS

■ ■ ■

One of the most difficult jobs you may face in life is caring for a parent, physically or financially. I say this not because of the strain it may place on your body, your schedule, or your bank account, but because of the fundamental emotional shift it requires. To become the parent to the man who tossed you in the air as a child, catching you in his unfailing big hands, or the woman who was your primary source of care and comfort, always there with wisdom or just the right touch to perk up your spirits, requires you to accept a world and a relationship that have turned upside down.

The key thing to keep in mind as you provide that care is that the relationship is as new and difficult for your parent as it is for you. Especially in this United States that so celebrates independence, self-reliance, and financial success, too many older people see any kind of dependence on their children as a sign of failure in their own lives. That is unfortunate, because in my view raising children who are sympathetic and empathetic and willing to give of themselves to others is one of the greatest successes any parent can achieve.

The prescription for parent and child in this situation is honesty and open communication—the same attributes that mark a healthy relationship between parent and child from early in their lives together. As a child, you have to be willing to talk about the difficult choices you have to make together. If you think you can help, offer. As a parent, you have to be honest about your own fears and worries. If you think you need help, ask. No subjects should be out of bounds for either of you, not long-term illness, not even death. Talk about your futures, and they will be less frightening for both of you.

Two subjects involving money are perhaps the most worrisome for children as they seek to provide assistance to elderly parents. One issue is how the parents are managing their money. The second is how they will be able to afford the longer-term care they may need, sooner or later.

## PROTECTING THE NEST EGG

It may sound selfish for children to worry about their parents' assets, but it is not. I have heard many people express concerns about their elderly parents' use of money, not because of their desire to inherit it, but because of their increasing protectiveness of their parents.

A friend recently admitted his concern that his 80-year-old father, a frugal hourly-wage earner his entire working life, was no longer content to have a couple thousand in his checking account. He was starting to maintain balances of $40,000 to $50,000. This uncharacteristic behavior of shifting retirement assets into a liquid account had my friend worried. He had no interest in an inheritance because he was very well positioned financially. What bothered him was that his father, who had spent so carefully and saved so religiously during his life, was in danger of blowing his nest egg. Of course, part of his concern was for his mother, who remained in better health than his father. But the other part of his concern was for his father's emotional state and the impact it would have on his father if he were to fall prey to a scam or throw away his hard-earned money some other way.

Some children in this position react in opposite ways. One says it's none of his business; his parents earned the money, saved the money, and can spend it however they wish. The other extreme is to initiate action to seek control over a parent's finances. In most cases, neither extreme is appropriate. A better reaction is to find a way to talk about your concerns in the context of your parents' financial plans, their ability to pay for long-term care, and their estate plans. You might suggest that they seek the advice of a financial professional to assist them or at least review their plans. Parents sometimes feel more comfortable talking about finances, which they consider family secrets, with a neutral professional.

Most important are your parents' health and happiness. If medical conditions are present, such as Alzheimer's, that may impair your parent's ability to make good decisions, perhaps then you should seek greater involvement in managing their finances. But if that is not the case, if your parents are simply being a bit profligate with resources they are pretty sure they can't outlive, maybe you should let them have their day.

## Elder Care

The second important issue for children assisting elderly parents is long-term care, a costly issue both financially and emotionally. The easiest solution for some people would be simply to purchase long-term care insurance. As I discussed in Chapter 8, however, long-term care insurance is not a feasible option for many people. Because of the cost, long-term care insurance is financially most efficient for those who are trying to protect their estate from being spent down.

The reality for some people is that by the time they look into long-term care protection, they have already encountered some type of medical problem that would disqualify them for long-term care insurance. By the time most children are involved in their parents' longer-term decisions, they are already in crisis-control mode.

Addressing a crisis requires first that we examine all of our options. To pay for nursing home care, hospice, assisted living, or elder care, you have essentially four choices: private pay (meaning the patient pays for it out of pocket), long-term care insurance, Medicare, and Medical Assistance.

If you are indeed facing a crisis, private pay is probably out of the question. We've already discussed the problems with long-term care insurance. That leaves us with Medicare and Medical Assistance.

Many people get confused about the difference between Medical Assistance and Medicare. Medicare is an entitlement program much like Social Security. In fact, you make regular contributions to Medicare, just like Social Security, through mandatory deductions from your pay. Medicare covers certain health care costs and will cover nursing home care costs under certain circumstances. Medical Assistance, on the other hand, is a welfare program. The person must qualify to receive Medical Assistance benefits, and, once eligibility is established, Medical Assistance will pay for all health care costs. Eligibility is determined by the assets a person has. That's the simple explanation. In reality, the criteria for eligibility are complex.

This is where we often turn to an attorney specializing in elder care. Elder care law is a relatively new term referring to areas of law that affect the elderly, including estate planning, probate, and trust administration. It can also include disability planning, advanced directives, guardianship and conservatorships, and, of course, long-term care planning.

## A Plan for Parents

For some of us, planning for the care of our aging parents is a legitimate contingency in our financial plans. Most children have at least a vague idea of whether their parents will require financial assistance or guidance from them well before they reach the age when it may become a crisis. But there is only one way to know for sure: Ask. Talk about finances with your parents early enough to get a clearer picture of how their needs may affect your finances and planning. Your questions may be met by silence or diversions, but they may not be. It's a safe bet that your parents think about their financial situation often. Who doesn't? They probably have a pretty good idea of their financial future and will give you at least a glimpse of it.

For those of you who have adult children, I would recommend that you initiate the discussion. Let your kids know if you have worries about your finances or if you have sufficient assets that they should never have to consider assisting you. Tell them whether you have a financial plan. If you find it difficult to discuss your specific finances with your children, at least give them a clue. Just remember how infuriating it was when they were teenagers and they never seemed to communicate with you—even on matters that you thought were important. Don't behave like an old teenager with your own children. Talk to them. They probably want to know but may not know how to ask, just like you years ago.

# 17

## WILLS AND ESTATE PLANNING

■ ■ ■

It's not your money yet, but there are still things you can do to help your parents manage their finances—if they allow it.

I have addressed wills and estate planning in greater detail in Chapter 14 from the parents' perspectives, but the same issues can also be important from adult children's perspectives as they look to the financial future of their parents.

The most important thing you can do with regard to your parents' finances is to encourage them to have a written, legal will. The rationale you can present to them is simple: Don't make us guess what you want us to do with your estate, and don't leave it to the courts or state law.

Laws in your state may divide your parents' estate exactly as they would like. That's fine as long as they are making that choice. But sometimes leaving estates to law can be grossly unfair.

### CHUCK THE DAIRYMAN

Growing up in rural Minnesota in the heart of an agricultural county, I knew a lot of farmers. One farmer I knew and called upon but who never became a client was "Chuck." Chuck was a very successful dairyman and breeder of Holsteins.

Chuck was always going to get his estate in order and work with me "as soon as they quit screwing around with tax laws and we know what we're dealing with."

One day I got a call from his son, Bob. He informed me that his dad had died, and he wanted to know if we had done any planning together. I offered my condolences, but told him that Chuck had never done business with me or anyone else that I knew of. Bob was very upset. He thought his dad had planned his estate. Bob was one of eight kids, but the only one to stay on the farm. He thought he was working for his future and would be justly rewarded, but now his seven siblings were all going to share equally in the estate. Chuck's dairy farm was a huge operation.

Unfortunately, it is all gone now. The cows were sold, the real estate was sold, a huge tax was paid. Bob, who had been a critical component in the growth and the success of the operation, was left with little and had to start over. He no longer speaks with any of his siblings, who received the same benefits he did from the estate.

Could Bob have done more while his father was alive? He probably could have, although given the culture of silence about family finances in that type of community, any efforts by Bob to suggest an equitable division of an estate might have been met with silence from Chuck. Perhaps Bob could have proposed becoming a formal partner in the ownership of the farm or some of its assets, which might have stimulated a productive discussion. The fact that Bob did not know whether his father had made any plans suggests to me that he was not as aggressive as he could have been in divining his father's plans and not as astute as he could have been in accumulating some assets in his own name.

## THE NEED TO KNOW

Adult children should know whether their parents have made provisions for their later years and their estates. Asking if your parents have made those plans is appropriate. It is not prying. Of course, the parents are free to reveal as many or as few details as they are comfortable doing.

The primary motive in asking should not be to ascertain how much of an inheritance you will receive so that you can plan your purchase of a new lake home. Rather, the point in asking, and you should make this clear, is that you would like to know if assisting your parents at some point is a contingency you should consider in your financial planning. There is a strong likelihood that one of your parents will live for some time after the death of the other. When your father or mother is alone, their needs may change and they are also more likely to rely on you for input and advice on their financial plans. It would be helpful for both of you to have some idea of what to expect your surviving parent's situation will be.

Second, you may have more knowledge of estate planning tools (especially after reading this book!) and may be able to suggest some useful options for your parents to consider. If your parents do reveal enough of their finances and thoughts on their estate to you that you know you will inherit some assets, you should bring to their attention any estate-planning options that could be beneficial to both of you.

One of the best ways for you to ensure that your parents' finances in life and death are in the best shape they can be is to encourage them to formalize their plans with a financial adviser. That takes the onus off you to manage their finances, but gives you some assurance that they will receive good advice and may be introduced to efficient planning options they may not have considered. They maintain their independence, and you get some peace of mind that their lives will be lived as they wish and that their financial legacy to their family will be all that it can be.

## A LIVING WILL

Addressing the eventual death of your parents is not easy, but you know it will happen. Discussing estate issues is not morbid. It is but one of the topics surrounding death or serious illness that it is healthy for families to talk about. I think you should also know your parents' wishes about the extent of medical treatment they wish to receive if they suffer serious illness or injury. These wishes are often referred to as a "living will" and are also best put in writing. Do your parents want to be resuscitated in a medical emergency? In what circumstances? Would they want to be kept alive by a respirator and feeding tube? They can make known their wishes for such possibilities in a living will. You should know where your parents keep a copy of their living wills in the sad event that they should be consulted.

Although it is not necessary to have it in writing, as with a living will, you should also know your parents' wishes for their physical remains. Do they want to be buried? If so, where? Have they made provisions for burial already? Or do they want to be cremated? They may even have clear preferences for the type of funeral or memorial service they want. A friend of mine, whose father is a retired Methodist minister, has received explicit instructions from his father: He wants to be cremated; there should be no public funeral and no open casket. Rather, he wants a memorial service that would consist mainly of singing joyous Christian hymns such as "How Great Thou Art." My friend is in the enviable position, by the grace of his father, of not having to make a lot of difficult decisions at a time of loss and grieving. His father has spared him that by relating exactly what he wants upon his death. Good for him.

The issue of living wills is often a nonthreatening opening to talk with your parents about their "other" will and their estate planning. In my opinion, you have an obligation and a right to know your parents' wishes for their lives, their deaths, and their legacies. And you can tell them I said so.

# 18

## Inheriting Money

■ ■ ■

We will conclude our discussion of money and parents on a positive note. What will you do with the money you may inherit from your parents? It's a question many have not considered.

We probably all know people who will inherit a few million from parents who were very successful. Far more of us will inherit, not those large sums, but still substantial assets that could have a significant impact on our own lives and those of our children. Consider this: In more than 70 percent of inheritances of $100,000 or more, the money is completely spent in less than two years.

In the next few years we will see the acceleration of an unprecedented transfer of wealth that has already begun. People often speak of baby boomers as the generation that has driven much of our culture and behavior for the past 50-plus years. While that may be true, what enabled baby boomers to be the driving force in our society was the unparalleled economic success of their parents. This "greatest generation," to use Tom Brokaw's term, did far more than win World War II. They provided the energy for a period of tremendous prosperity following the war, a period that, one could argue, has continued with only minor hiccups until the present day. That long period of prosperity, combined with the frugality of the generation—many grew up in the Great Depression—led to an accumulation of wealth, even among average working people, that is now being passed down to their children. I'm surprised that we have not seen more research on the topic, more analysis of the historical forces that created it, and more speculation on the impact it will have on our society.

Given this enormous transfer of wealth, some estimates put it at over

$10 trillion, many of us will wrestle with what to do with an inheritance, perhaps unexpected in its size.

## THE FIRST REACTION

Inheriting money, particularly life-changing sums of money, can spark financial and emotional reactions and problems for people who have never thought about or prepared for it. Some of the potential difficulties include:

- **Grief.** Inherited money usually comes at a deep personal cost: the death of a loved one. This personal pain can cloud your financial and emotional judgment.
- **Guilt.** Experts who work with inherited wealth say guilt is a far more common and more powerful emotion among heirs than people realize. It's often the cause for doing nothing with an inheritance or even disclaiming it. Heirs often ask themselves what they did to earn the money other than win the gene pool lottery. Some also have philosophical differences with how the money was acquired, considering it dirty money.
- **Anger.** Anger often complicates grief and financial decisions. Anger can arise when someone doesn't receive as much money as they thought they would or thought they deserved. Perhaps they feel there is an inequitable distribution among several heirs, including their siblings. Heirs sometimes measure the benefactor's love by the size of the inheritance. Ironically, some heirs are angry for a quite different reason: They receive well more than they thought they would, but they become angry because they've lived frugally and could have used the money years earlier.
- **Inadequacy.** Wealth is often created by talented, resourceful, dynamic people. An heir may feel inadequate or unworthy of the inheritance because he or she doesn't possess the benefactor's talents.
- **Paralysis.** People who are not financially competent or experienced, commonly people who inherit at a young age or never

learn good money management practices, may simply be paralyzed by what to do with inherited money. For example, the deceased may have handled all of the family finances and the surviving spouse or child doesn't know what to do, so they do nothing or they spend it immediately and recklessly, which results in regret or financial hardship later.

■ **Conflict with spouse.** Spouses can disagree over what to do with an inheritance, especially if they have conflicting money personalities. The heir may feel it is his or her money and not want to share it with the spouse, or the nonheir may feel inadequate because the partner has brought disproportionate wealth into the household.

In each of these cases, time is often a cure. To the extent that you are able, you should try to separate your reaction to a death and decisions about an inheritance. Give yourself time to grieve. Some financial issues may need to be addressed soon after a death, but try to defer your big decisions until you have had a time to grieve that is appropriate for you.

Avoid making all financial decisions that can be deferred until you are ready to deal with them.

If you are fortunate, other than inheriting a considerable sum of money, your parents will have engaged in some long-range planning before death. They may have established trusts to control their estates; they may have given away some of their money while still alive; or, at least, they may have given you some explanation of what you might expect to inherit and perhaps even why.

## Surprise!

What if you inherit money without adequate preparation from the benefactor?

First, do as you would if you were to win the lottery. The key is to think before acting.

Don't do anything for a while, maybe even as much as six months. Put the cash in a money market account; don't sell off any inherited stock right away unless there's a serious risk that it will lose significant value;

keep the business or the farm running as usual; and maintain any property. Take time to make sound decisions.

Make a list of what you could do with the inheritance. Let your mind roam freely. You'll probably soon realize how quickly your list eats up all the inheritance. At that point, begin to do some realistic prioritizing. Think about what you can do with this money that matches your own values—values that in most cases were learned from the parent bequeathing the money to you. Perhaps you want to donate a portion of it or put some toward college for your kids. If you have problems with how the money was acquired, consider "cleaning" what you think of as dirty money by donating it to a charitable cause instead of merely disclaiming it.

Most important, develop a plan for how you will use the money. Incorporate it into your existing financial plan. Even if the sum of inherited money is substantial enough to change the way you may live, it's a good idea to stick to the basic objectives of your earlier plan. If that plan reflects your values and your goals, as it should, new money shouldn't change that. Instead, look at the new money as a way to go further down your list of goals or to strengthen parts of your plan.

Do not let more money, however acquired, change your core values, the way you think you should live your life and your relationships to the people you love. Let me repeat: Money is one of many tools that may help you accomplish your objectives in life. When you inherit money, whether a pleasant surprise or well anticipated, take the time to put the new resources in their proper place in your life.

Second, seek professional advice. Perhaps you really need the services of a counselor, pastor, or mental health professional to help you come to terms with the inheritance—and your relationship with your benefactor. Then a qualified financial adviser can help you make sound financial decisions. Sadly, heirs are frequently targets for investment schemes and scams. A financial adviser can help you deal with those unscrupulous people. Most important, a financial adviser can help you create a plan that will make your inheritance an asset in reaching your dreams and goals as well as those of the people you love. An efficient financial plan that makes wise use of your inherited resources is often one of the best ways to honor the person who chose you to be the steward of his or her financial legacy.

A financial adviser can also help you negotiate the tangled tax laws that address estates and inherited property. Estate tax laws have been the subject of considerable political and legislative debate in both Washington, D.C., and many state capitals, as we discussed in Chapter 14. But even without estate taxes to worry about—and the vast majority of people won't have to, regardless of whether estate taxes are repealed—many other potential tax questions arise for those who inherit assets.

---

▪ **EXAMPLE:** A client's father recently died, and the client sold his father's home for $250,000. He received a 1099 form reporting that as income. He wondered if he had to pay income tax on that amount. He did not. He will have to report that 1099 income on Schedule D on his tax return, but he will also be asked his "basis" in the property, the value when he acquired it, to determine whether he realized a gain on the sale. In fact, his basis was the same, $250,000, as the price for which he sold the home. The result was a gain of zero, creating no income tax. In this case, the father's total estate was not subject to estate taxes.

---

## INHERITING RESPONSIBILITY

Most of us who stand to inherit some money from our parents will get it only when both parents have died. In most cases, one parent's assets will pass to the spouse when they die. Statistically, the first to die is usually the father. And for many couples of the "Greatest Generation," the man managed most of the finances as we discussed in Part II. That may mean that if your father dies first, your mother may want or need help to manage her assets. The money is still hers, her financial situation may not have changed at all with the death of your father, but she now has a responsibility she didn't have before.

It is not inappropriate to ask your mother if she needs any help or to offer your assistance. You may find, as I have seen with clients, that she may be more comfortable discussing her finances, even admitting her own sense of incompetence in financial matters, with a financial adviser than with her children. Do not be offended; secrecy regarding family finances among those of a certain age extends even to their children. The best assistance you might provide in this case is to help your mother find a competent financial adviser that she can trust. It may be the best protection you can offer her, especially in that most vulnerable time after she has lost her lifelong partner and is probably overwhelmed by grief and trepidation at the thought of life alone.

# PART V

# Money and Others

For many people, the desire to share our wealth or good fortune with others beyond the tight circle of those we love most dearly is a strong motivation for financial planning. That compelling sense of responsibility for others, even those we may not know, appears to be an innate drive in most human beings. It is one of the principal tenets of every major religion and nearly every society, whether primitive or modern. It is an acknowledgment of the spiritual nature of people that provides a common bond—we are all God's children—and the intensely social nature of human beings—no man is an island.

We saw many examples of the desire to help others in 2005. The first was the devastating tsunami in the Indian Ocean. The flow of contributions to relief efforts was staggering. The empathy we so obviously felt for those few who survived in many coastal villages even compelled Congress to take the extraordinary step of allowing contributions to tsunami relief made up until January 31, 2005, to be deductible on 2004 tax returns. Another example of altruism we witnessed in 2005 was the G-8 summit, a meeting of the leaders of eight of the most prosperous large countries. Those leaders, with widespread public support in their home countries, agreed to forgive the debt of more than 20 of the world's poorest countries, most of them in Africa. I am not enough of a cynic to believe that debt relief served the selfish interest of the nations involved. Rather, it was perceived as the right thing to do. Most recently, as I write, the ongoing efforts to assist the victims of Hurricane Katrina provide another example.

## CHARITIES, FAITH COMMUNITIES, COLLEGES AND CAUSES: LITTLE PLANNING REQUIRED

Our propensity to share our wealth with others finds its expression most often in support of charities, faith communities, colleges, and causes. The motivation for most people is purely altruistic. I have had many clients make very generous contributions to each of these types of organizations simply because they believed it was right to share their wealth. In most cases they had had no personal contact with those they were helping and they expected nothing in return. If there was any self-interest involved in most of those cases, it was simply that they wanted a better world for themselves and their children to live in.

Most charitable giving is a matter of routine for many people. They plan each week, month, or year to contribute a certain amount of money to an organization or cause that is important to them. Even if they are "tithers" who regularly give 10 percent of their income to church or charity, that giving is a matter of course for them. Many view it as nondiscretionary spending. It is as a much a part of their financial obligations as paying their utility bills every month. They treat giving much as I recommend you treat investing: They set aside a percentage of their income every month before they address other spending or saving possibilities.

In that respect, giving is for most people not necessarily a part of their financial planning process. It becomes a more important issue in planning, however, for those with greater personal net worth who want to make larger gifts or bequests to the organizations they favor. They can establish trusts or foundations that make their contributions more efficient for them as well as the institutions they give to. As I will discuss in the following chapter, unless you have at least $100,000 to establish a trust, that form of giving will probably be inefficient for you. I would recommend that you continue to make your regular, usually tax-deductible, gifts as you see fit—and I commend you for your generosity. The very nature of most giving is the reason why this section of the book is shorter than the others. It is not because I consider it less important to share your wealth than to spend it on yourself.

Yet I would encourage you to investigate the tools that may be available to you if you are facing a major financial event—such as the sale of valuable property or inheriting money—to see if there are ways to include organizations you like in your good fortune. The example of Howard and Betty in Chapter 5 is a good one for people who don't consider themselves wealthy, but have a one-time windfall.

The other prime opportunity to investigate a giving strategy is when you prepare your will. If you wish to leave some portion of your estate to a charitable organization, consult your financial adviser or the organization directly to find out how to make that gift most efficiently for both of you. Most charities, faith communities, colleges, and causes have their own experts in gift giving and how to make it work for you and for them.

## Giving Your Time and Energy

Another form of sharing your wealth may benefit significantly from careful financial planning. Especially in retirement, many people want to be able to do volunteer work in which they can share their energy or expertise. Volunteer work is an important priority for many of my clients as they plan for retirement. Volunteering your time in retirement presumes that you have planned well enough to retire at an age when you are still sufficiently healthy and secure to devote time and energy to a cause that is important to you. That can be a vital element of your financial planning process.

In the following chapter, I will address briefly some of the ways that you and your causes may benefit from the establishment of charitable trusts.

# 19

## CHARITABLE TRUSTS

■ ■ ■

Charitable trusts were provided for in the U.S. tax code for one simple reason: to encourage you to contribute to organizations that address our nation's or our world's needs, so that governments may not have to. Our leaders over many decades have recognized the national interest we have in private citizens and nonprofit organizations addressing the pressing needs of our society and our world. That is why charitable giving is tax deductible and that is why rules for giving through trusts were created by our federal and state governments.

Like everything else in our tax code, the rules for charitable trusts are complicated. But it is worth playing by IRS rules because you may gain significant tax advantages by giving through a trust. Does that lessen the altruism of your gift? Not at all. In fact, the tax benefits inherent in giving the IRS way likely enable you to give more than you would otherwise feel comfortable doing.

A gift made to an eligible organization is deductible on your income taxes however it is made, as an outright cash gift or as part of a charitable trust, within some percentage limits. Gifts made to charitable organizations in almost every form may also reduce the size of your estate, whether given during your life or through your estate, and may therefore reduce any estate tax your heirs might have to pay. Gifts made through trusts may also offer the advantage of avoiding capital gains taxes on highly appreciated assets.

One of the primary advantages of charitable trusts is that they may allow you to make charitable gifts during your lifetime instead of waiting to make a contribution through your estate. The dilemma for many people who would like to make significant donations to charities is that they may depend on income from their assets to meet their daily needs. Or with an unpredictable future, they can't be sure what resources they will consume in their lifetime. They could keep their assets and simply specify in their will that they want so much money to go to such and such organization. The advantage of a charitable trust created during your lifetime is that your gift goes to work sooner for the beneficiary of your trust; you have the opportunity to see your gift at work and the tax benefits accrue to you rather than just your estate.

That is why split-interest gifts are allowed through trusts. You'll remember from Chapter 5 that split-interest gifts refer to assets that have two valuable parts: One is an asset, the other is the income that asset is able to earn. In a split-interest gift, one portion is given in trust for the charity, and the other portion is retained. In other words, you may give an asset to a charity through a trust, but retain the income that asset earns until your death. This is called a remainder trust. When you die, or after a set period of time, the asset and the income become the property of the charity. The other possibility is to give the income from the asset to charity—a lead trust—but retain ownership of the underlying asset that earns the income.

---

■ **EXAMPLE:** Let's say you bought 10,000 shares of some cheap stock in 1965. That stock has split many times and pays a handsome dividend now that provides much of your retirement income. It has appreciated in value many times over. If you established a remainder trust using those shares of stock you would enjoy many benefits:

- You would still receive the dividend income from that stock for your lifetime in order to pay your living expenses.
- By donating the stock you would not have to pay capital gains tax on the huge appreciation of that stock since you bought it.
- You would be able to claim a charitable deduction on your taxes for the full value of that stock in the year you establish the trust even though you didn't pay tax on the gain and you still receive income from that asset. The likely result is a reduction in the income tax you owe.

- You have reduced the size of your estate, so your heirs will owe less estate tax, if any.
- You have given a valuable asset to your favorite charity that it will own when you die—asset, income, and all.

Those are significant benefits for you and the charity and well worth getting the professional assistance required to establish a trust.

## TYPES OF TRUSTS

The U.S. tax code provides for a wide variety of trusts to meet the financial situations of many different people. We have already noted the difference between a "lead" and a "remainder" trust. Another important distinction is between a "unitrust" and an "annuity" trust. The primary difference is in the form of income paid by an asset. A unitrust pays out a fixed percentage, while an annuity trust pays out a fixed dollar amount. These terms can be combined in many ways to give you a list of the most commonly used types of trusts:

- Charitable remainder annuity trust (CRAT)
- Charitable remainder unitrust (CRUT)
- Charitable gift annuity
- Charitable lead annuity trust (CLAT)
- Charitable lead unitrust (CLUT)

Each of these trusts is appropriate for quite different financial circumstances, which is why establishing a trust is not a do-it-yourself activity. Professional assistance is required, either through your financial adviser or through the financial people at the organization to which you wish to donate.

## HOW MUCH DO YOU NEED?

Unless you have $250,000 to put into a trust, it probably would not be efficient. A trust is a separate legal entity that must file its own tax returns and requires other paperwork, which will probably cost at least $2,000 a year. With less than $250,000 in the trust, these costs probably take too high a percentage of the trust's value to justify them.

An alternative to establishing your own trust is to contribute to a pooled income fund (PIF). PIFs operate like a trust, but combine the gifts of many people. If you would like to make a contribution to a charity through a trust, but have insufficient funds to justify the administrative costs on your own, check with your favorite charity to see if it has already created a PIF to which you could contribute. Many charities have PIFs, would welcome your contribution, and will make it very easy for you to contribute.

## PLANNING WITH THE CHARITY OF YOUR CHOICE

Whether you choose to create a trust yourself or take part in a pooled income fund, your favorite charity will happily provide assistance. Such organizations know the rules and can explain the benefits and procedures. Why do charities like to be the beneficiaries of charitable trusts and often prefer them to cash gifts? It's quite simple from their perspective as well: A trust establishes a dependable income stream on which the charity can base future plans. A trust provides some predictability regarding the money it has to work with. So the charitable organization will be as helpful as possible in removing any obstacles between you and your potential gift.

One word of caution on establishing charitable trusts with the assistance of the charity itself. Unlike a personal financial adviser, the financial pros at your charity may not fully understand your overall financial goals and plans apart from your desire to make a charitable contribution. Even with the best of intentions, they may not have a good enough grasp of your financial big picture to help you make your gift as efficient as possible for you and for them.

# PART VI

# Money and Financial Professionals

Okay, I don't expect you to love your financial adviser. That's asking too much even for those of us in the profession who are lovable! But even if you have no intention of loving your financial adviser, you will develop a personal relationship that is as at least as intimate as your relationship with any other professional who serves you. Money has a way of drawing people together, especially when the relationship is as it should be.

A financial adviser cannot serve you well unless he or she gets to know you well. A financial plan, revolving as it should around your most dearly held goals and aspirations, requires a level of knowledge and insights into your personality and life that you would likely reveal to at most a handful of others. If some personal affinity is not present, I would suggest you may have hired the wrong person to help you with your financial planning.

This section of the book may seem self-serving, but I believe in the services I provide and the value I deliver. I've shared in these pages some guidelines that I believe are important to your financial life, but I can't cover every subject or every contingency in a book such as this. I sincerely believe that for you to be in the best possible financial health, you need the expert advice of a qualified and competent financial adviser.

I hope this section gives you some of the information you will need to find the right person to advise you and play an integral role in helping you achieve your dreams.

# 20

## THE FUTURE OF FINANCIAL SERVICES

■ ■ ■

The world of financial services has changed dramatically in the past decade, and change will continue. Consolidation of the big financial service providers also is likely to continue. Those service companies will focus on speed and technological efficiency, often at the expense of person-to-person service. Their focus will remain, simply because of the size required for efficiency in that arena, on the execution of financial transactions, whether writing a check or buying a stock, for people who already know what they want. But those companies are ill suited to providing personal advice to clients.

The nature of companies that have traditionally provided narrow advice in the investment arena will also change. For instance, I believe that stockbrokers will become obsolete. I know this is a bold statement that many people, especially brokers, will disagree with. But I stand by my prediction. In the not-too-distant future, stockbrokers will disappear. Their focus is too often on specific investments without regard to strategy, portfolio, or long-term financial planning goals. Stockbrokers who are bullish on a particular investment call all the clients in their database and recommend it. But for many clients, the investment may be totally inappropriate.

Moreover, with technological advances and the public's increasing familiarity with those technologies, primarily the Internet, investors are able to do their own research and make their own trades far more cheaply than they can through a broker. If brokers serve primarily as simply the executors of trades, they offer little value for their charges.

The method by which brokers are compensated is also inherently flawed: It promotes trading activity, rather than success. If your broker sells some of your ABC stock, they are compensated based on the transaction. If they use that money to buy XYZ stock, they are compensated again. How either stock performs does not affect their compensation. Most brokers are paid when and only when they execute trades. That is a poor platform from which to help their clients meet their long-term goals.

People who rely on stockbrokers are placing greater importance on picking stocks than on their overall financial strategy, which I hope you've come to realize does not give you the best chance of success financially. Successful financial planning requires much more than deciding which stocks to buy. To increase the efficiency of your money, you probably don't need stock-picking advice as much as you need expertise on the U.S. tax code or advice on a wider variety of investments that offer advantages you may not find with traditional equity investments. Those are areas in which most brokerages do not provide much assistance to any but the wealthiest clients.

The accounting industry has already gone through an earthshaking change, with the largest firms consolidating and one, Arthur Andersen, disappearing in the wake of charges of complicity in the Enron debacle. The behemoths of the industry will continue to serve primarily corporate clients with smaller firms targeting smaller businesses and individuals.

By the process of elimination, the future of personalized, comprehensive financial services is me—and many others like me. In my company I can draw on the expertise of accountants, lawyers, and investment managers, as well as experts in insurance, to give you comprehensive financial planning and management services under one roof. We are big enough to have expertise at our fingertips, even when not in our heads, yet we are small enough to be able to spend time with you, get to know you, and tailor plans to your unique needs.

## THE VALUE OF A FINANCIAL ADVISER

The reasons for choosing someone to help formulate and execute a financial plan to achieve a dream will vary from one person to another as much as the dreams themselves. Whether you lack the time, the expertise, or the stomach for worry to create your own financial plan, a professional should be able to provide valuable assistance.

Choosing a financial adviser is intensely personal. You will reveal information to your adviser that you would reveal to very few others, and you will give that person an extraordinary responsibility for helping you achieve your dream. Beyond the empirical or factual evidence of a financial adviser's ability to meet your needs, you have to trust that person and place your confidence in him or her. All facts being equal, trust your intuition. If you actually like the person and enjoy your interaction with him or her, the process of achieving your dream will be much more enjoyable—and never forget that enjoying life is the ultimate purpose of money.

Whether you use a financial adviser or create your own plan without expert assistance, always remember that you are in control of your money. Someone else may sweat the details, someone else may take the worry of day-to-day money management off your shoulders, but you are the CEO of your money. When you hear or read advice from any source about how to create wealth, think carefully about what you're hearing or reading and whether it applies to you and your situation. A lot of conventional wisdom does not apply to you, whether you hear it from your friends, your relatives, or your financial adviser.

## ADDING VALUE IN MANY WAYS

A good financial adviser can add value in many ways:

- **Creating additional investable capital.** Many consumers have inefficient strategies in place. A good planner can suggest strategies that can free up more investable capital without detracting from one's lifestyle.
- **Being objective.** Many otherwise intelligent people can have a hard time being objective about their own personal finances.
- **Identifying goals.** A good planner can help clarify a vision of one's future.
- **Saving time.** Many people are so busy with the day-to-day

demands of work and family that they want to delegate responsibility for their money.

▪ **Worrying about your money for you.** Most people realize they don't have the desire, time, or aptitude to manage their own money efficiently. Therefore, they worry about it. I tell clients that it's my job to worry for them, and if they are still worrying after I'm on board, maybe they should hire someone else.

Why do many of my clients hire my services? Because I'm smarter than they are? I don't believe that—and neither do they! They hire me for what I know, even though they are capable of learning what I know. It's just not how they choose to spend their time.

In my office, on the street, at parties, and on my radio show, I'm asked one question more than any other: *How do I determine the best way to take distributions from my retirement plan?* The frequency with which I'm asked this question in the many forms it takes underscores the need to work with a professional adviser. If you think the purpose of financial planning is only to accumulate assets, you aren't seeing half the picture. Good financial planning not only helps you accumulate assets efficiently but also helps you distribute them efficiently.

Many of my clients are just beginning to think about distributions in their 50s, a time when it is already too late to avail themselves of some of the most effective accumulation and distribution strategies. If you're in your 50s or 60s, you can still make smart decisions to enhance your life and your wealth, but if you're in your 20s or 30s, you have so many more investment tools and vehicles to use. I think financial advisers serve a very useful purpose if they do nothing more than get younger people to begin considering options and strategies. Begin planning your distribution strategy as you are planning your accumulation strategy.

As I wrote at the beginning of this book, the goal of enhancing your wealth is to enhance your life—however you choose to do it. A whole-life planning approach, a plan for your accumulation years as well as your distribution years, will help you do that. That's why you need the services of a good financial adviser.

And by the way, I can't answer the question on distributions very effectively unless I know your full financial profile and your goals in life. That's because, like most people, you are not "average"—and taking advice aimed at "average" investors can be risky, as I have tried to point out.

## YOU CAN DO IT YOURSELF (MAYBE)

If you devote the time and energy to it, you may be able to create your own financial plan—with one very important exception: You probably will *not* be able to integrate effective tax strategies into that plan even if you do consider the tax liabilities of your investments. Taxes are the big complication, but tax strategies also present an enormous opportunity to use your money more efficiently. Taxes are likely the largest single cost in your life.

I would strongly advise you to determine how you can reduce taxes as much as possible. Pay what you must, but pay no more. So even if you do create your own plan, hire the services of a qualified professional who can examine the tax consequences of your plan and perhaps recommend alternative strategies that will reduce your taxes.

You might think that you don't have enough assets to qualify for tax-reduction strategies, but you may be surprised at how little you need to invest to avail yourself of these opportunities—especially if you don't concentrate simply on reducing taxes *this* year. Too many people rely too heavily on tax-deferred plans, which we discussed in Chapter 1, in a sometimes shortsighted effort to reduce taxes *now*. They get a tax deferment this year, but it may not help at all in years to come.

Tax deferment in pretax plans may be nothing more than seeking instant gratification at a greater cost in the long term. In that sense it's not a lot different from spending your money on something you want, instead of investing it with the intention of getting a bigger reward at a later time. Just because you can reduce your taxes this year, don't think that you're avoiding them. You may not be.

Plan for the longer term. Assess the tax consequences of your plan several years out or into retirement. That's what real planning does: It examines all the variables of your finances well into the future. Professional financial advisers should be better at this task than you are.

## How You Will Pay

There are two options. You pay an adviser a fee for services, or you pay commission on the sale of products—or perhaps both. The advantage of working with an adviser who charges fees instead of earning commissions on products is that you avoid conflicts of interest because he or she is not trying to sell you anything. However, because fees are the sole profit center, they may be high. Moreover, a fee-only adviser has no motivation to inspire you to implement a plan, so it may collect dust. If a financial adviser earns commissions on the sale of products to you, look for someone who is independent, instead of an employee of a financial products company. Find an adviser who can offer products from a variety of companies so that you get the best products to meet *your* needs—and not what a parent company pushes your adviser to sell.

A financial adviser should be able to provide value that justifies the cost of services, and he or she should be willing to explain that value. Financial authors and magazines that are critical of various planning and investment strategies for reasons of cost frequently overlook the benefits purchased by that cost. In hiring a financial adviser, as in determining the execution of your investment strategy, focus on value instead of just cost.

# 21

## HOW TO CHOOSE A FINANCIAL ADVISER

∎ ∎ ∎

I hope I have convinced you that using a financial adviser is a good idea. Now, how do you go about choosing one who will deliver the value that justifies the cost? A good way to start is with a personal referral from someone whose opinion you value. Even with a personal referral, however, you should still interview the candidate yourself. Ultimately, I think the decision will be instinctive rather than intellectual.

Over the years, I've been interviewed by hundreds of people looking for someone to help them manage their finances. In the course of those interviews, I've learned what is useful to them, and I've developed a keen sense of what questions elicit information that I would want if I were in their shoes. I've boiled the list down to 10 questions. The first nine are useful, but the last, which is frequently asked, reveals nothing that will help you.

**1. What professional designations does the adviser have?** The designation or lack of a designation does not necessarily indicate the competence of the planner. On the one hand, some people in the financial industry try to present themselves as financial planners in an attempt to enhance their credibility, even though they are not qualified. On the other hand, pursuit of a professional designation can demonstrate a commitment to the profession. The designations I deem relevant are:

- Certified Financial Planner (CFP)
- Chartered Financial Analyst (CFA)

- Chartered Financial Consultant (ChFC)
- Certified Public Accountant (CPA)
- Registered Financial Consultant (RFC)

**2. How many years has the adviser been working in the industry, and how did he or she get started?** There is a high attrition rate in the financial service industry. Many firms actually recruit representatives with the idea that the newly hired representative will establish accounts with friends and family and then ultimately fail and leave the industry, but the new clients will stay because they don't know where else to go.

**3. Has the planner ever been fined or suspended by a regulatory agency?** Consumer complaints are to be expected with an adviser who has practiced a long time with a lot of clients. But to be fined or suspended indicates wrongdoing. There may be a reasonable explanation. Find out.

**4. How does he or she get paid?** Financial advisers earn their compensation in two ways:

1. Fees
   A. Time
   B. Management
   C. Plan preparation
2. Commissions

It is also widely believed that if an adviser receives commissions, it will cost the investor more. That simply is not true. When you plan a vacation, do you call all the hotels in and around your ultimate destination? Do you personally check out all the times and costs of flights and then book your flight? How do you arrange your car rental? Many people make one call to a travel agent who will do all of those things for them. Furthermore, the cost is the same as (or even less than) if they arranged the trip themselves. Acquiring financial products is similar to planning a vacation with a travel agent. You can acquire products directly from the entity distributing the product or through an agent—the financial planner—and the fees and costs are often the same.

**5. Is the adviser captive to a larger corporation?** (Does he or she sell proprietary products?) Many so-called financial planners are really product salespeople. If they're aligned with a specific company, they may have a vested interest in selling that company's products. If I were a consumer shopping for a financial adviser, I would want one who is independent, with a fiduciary responsibility to me and not to a parent company.

**6. How many clients does the adviser have?** If the adviser has very few clients, you might wonder how proficient he or she is. If he or she has too many clients, you may wonder about the level of service you will receive. Find out what you can expect from your adviser. Then you will be able to measure whether or not he or she delivers.

**7. How many people does the adviser have to support him or her? And what is their expertise?** Ask a prospective planner how big his or her staff is today and how big it was last year and the year before. It's important to know whether the organization is growing and the ratio of support staff to advisers. The number of people in support roles will tell you something about the level of service you will receive. To give you a benchmark for evaluating staff support, my firm has six staff people for every financial adviser. I believe that's one of the best support ratios in our business.

**8. How does the adviser address issues on which he or she is not an expert?** As I freely admit, I don't know all there is to know about personal finance. But I have formal working relationships with people whose job it is to follow and track developments in specific fields, such as taxes and accounting. In my company, we have hired those experts for our staff, and they review every plan we put together. Their advice is invaluable to me, and I wouldn't be able to deliver the value I do to my clients without them. If the advisers you interview do not have formal working relationships with such experts, find out how those issues will be resolved—and what it will cost you if outside assistance is required.

**9. What is the average net worth of the adviser's clients or the range of clients he or she serves?** Financial advisers may have a specialty or a focus that may not suit you. An adviser who serves primarily clients who have net worths in the millions of dollars may not have the knowledge or the interest in working with those who have less money to invest. You may get lost in the shuffle of big-buck deals. On the other hand, if advisers work primarily with people who have less money to invest, they may not know the intricacies of more advanced planning and investing techniques such as trusts and tax-advantaged investments. Such an adviser may suit your needs now, but will he or she still be able to help you as your net worth grows?

Most of all, look for someone who listens to and understands what *you* want to accomplish. Less effective financial advisers are as likely to fall victim to myths and to old habits as the average consumer. In the day-to-day crush of work, they may rely on off-the-shelf, one-size-fits-all investment strategies that are little better than the myths embraced by your uncle Wilbur.

**10. Will the adviser provide references?** Of course. Every adviser will probably be able to provide names of clients who would give him or her a favorable recommendation. That's why I think asking for references is a waste of time. Don't bother. The adviser will give you the names of only those who have a good opinion of the services they receive—and you don't know whether *those* people are astute investors. Are they qualified to evaluate the services they receive? You can only guess.

# 22

## GETTING READY TO CREATE A PLAN

■ ■ ■

Choosing a financial adviser isn't the end of your responsibility. Regardless of whom you choose, you are still the CEO of your money, and it's up to you to ensure that you are gaining full value from your adviser's services. No good adviser can tell you what to do; he or she can only make recommendations. So you still need to supervise your adviser and your financial plan. On the next few pages, I provide a framework for your decision making.

Also, in recognition that some of you will still insist on giving a financial plan a try by yourself, the advice here will help you do it as well as possible—assuming that you enjoy all the disciplines involved in creating and implementing a good financial plan.

If you intend to create your own plan, however, you have to be brutally honest with yourself from the beginning. Many people have the best intentions when they sit down to create a plan and they might even do a pretty good job. But that's not where the biggest problems arise.

The real problems arise in the continuous management of that plan (bear in mind that these issues refer only to investment management, which is the tip of the iceberg in comprehensive financial planning):

- Preventing style drift in your portfolio or the funds in which you've invested;
- Rebalancing regularly to maintain the ideal asset allocation;
- Changing your allocation as your needs change;
- Keeping abreast of tax changes that could give you a window of opportunity to alter your plan to your advantage.

After a while, many investors get careless and begin to let their plans slide. Their portfolio no longer represents the asset allocation they selected. Or worse, their asset allocation accurately reflects their situation or needs of 10 years ago, even though their lives have changed dramatically. So think hard, not just about the knowledge you'll need to acquire or the time it will take to create a plan, but also about the commitment of time and energy to manage it effectively.

## DREAM A LITTLE DREAM:
## KNOW WHERE YOU WANT TO GO

Slow down. Before you even begin to gather all the information you'll need to create an investment strategy, sit down on the porch or patio or in front of the fireplace (with your spouse or partner, if you have one) and let your mind roam.

What do you really want from life? If you could do anything you want, what would you do? Don't put financial restrictions on yourself now. Dream. Stretch a little. Once you have that dream defined, once you know roughly where you want to go, you can begin to determine what role a financial plan can play in helping you live that dream.

## GATHER ALL YOUR FINANCIAL INFORMATION:
## KNOW WHERE YOU ARE

The second step is to gather all the information you'll need. You can't plan unless you know where you are. In my practice, I ask my clients to obtain the documents and provide the information noted below.

## Documents

Get together the following financial and legal documents:

- Federal and state income tax returns for at least two years
- Most recent pay stubs
- Statements from all investment accounts

- Documentation of all company retirement, investment, and insurance plans, including benefits and costs
- All personal life, health, disability, long-term care, and Medicare supplement policies and statements
- Estate planning documents such as wills, trusts, powers of attorney, and living wills (if you don't have a will, this is an excellent time to prepare one)
- Documentation related to involvement in all business or personal matters that could affect your personal financial situation, such as buy/sell agreements, noncompete agreements, consulting agreements, and deferred compensation plans
- Social Security and pension benefit estimates

### Assets and Liabilities

Make a list of all of your assets and liabilities. If you are planning with a spouse, be sure to note which assets are in whose name or whether they are jointly held.

When you list your liabilities, be sure to include complete information on your loans for your primary residence, second home, cars, boats, and other recreational vehicles. This information should include original balance, current balance, monthly payment, length of loan, and the interest rate, as well as whether those obligations are personal or jointly held.

For any fixed-interest investments, list the current value and the interest rate. For equity investments, list the average growth rate for each stock or mutual fund. List your taxable, tax-deferred, and tax-free investments separately. Be sure to include any insurance policies, including disability insurance, company-sponsored plans, and annuities.

For each asset that you own, also include the amount you add to that investment each month or each year.

### Income and Expenses

You're not finished identifying where you are yet, because you still have to determine all of your income and expenses.

Don't calculate only your present income; try to project expected annual increases as a percentage of your present income. You want to have as clear a picture of your future income as possible. Include wages and salary, bonuses, self-employment income, interests or dividends on investments, Social Security, rental property income, pensions, alimony, and any loans you have made.

Make a realistic effort to determine what your living expenses are for a year. It may be easiest to break it down monthly and then add those up to get your yearly expenses. This is a good exercise in financial discipline by itself, because most people don't think they're spending as much as they are. When determining your expenses, be sure to add any estimated major expenses you will incur in the future, such as college education costs for your children.

# 23

## THE LAST WORD: LOVE

■ ■ ■

With all the details and advice on the preceding pages still swimming in your head, I hope you will keep your focus on the critical constant in this book: the people you love. The rewards you get in life from loving them will far surpass and outlive the rewards of any money you accumulate, distribute, or leave as a legacy. The priority in your life should always be the people you love, never the money. Never reverse the order of importance. Those you love can thrive with less money if they have your love; they cannot thrive if they get your money without your love. Money is only one tool among many that can be used to manifest your love for them, to provide for them, to enrich their lives.

Money can benefit the people you love, and it provides the greatest benefits if it is used efficiently. You may have a lot of money, or you may have little. It doesn't matter. Whatever money you have can be used well or poorly in an effort to improve the lives of those you love.

I can summarize all I have written about finances here in ten simple guidelines:

1. Dream
2. Make a plan
3. Eliminate debt
4. Live within your means
5. Invest systematically
6. Allocate assets
7. Ensure investment efficiency

   8. Reduce taxes
   9. Adjust your plan as your life changes
  10. Enjoy life

I can summarize the underlying purpose of it all in only one word: love. Without love in your heart, for one or for many, money in the bank has little value.

# To order additional copies of *Money and the People You Love*

Web:       www.itascabooks.com

Phone:    1-800-901-3480

Fax:        Copy and fill out the form below with credit card information. Fax to 763-398-0198.

Mail:       Copy and fill out the form below. Mail with check or credit card information to:

           Syren Book Company
           5120 Cedar Lake Road
           Minneapolis, MN 55416

Order Form

| Copies | Title / Author | Price | Totals |
|---|---|---|---|
| | **Money and the People You Love /** **Bruce Helmer** | $16.95 | $ |
| | Subtotal | | $ |
| | 7% sales tax (MN only) | | $ |
| | Shipping and handling, first copy | | $     4.00 |
| | Shipping and handling, ___ add'l copies @$1.00 ea. | | $ |
| | TOTAL TO REMIT | | $ |

Payment Information:

| __ Check Enclosed    __ Visa/MasterCard | | |
|---|---|---|
| Card number: | Expiration date: | |
| Name on card: | | |
| Billing address: | | |
| | | |
| City: | State: | Zip: |
| Signature: | Date: | |

Shipping Information:

| __ Same as billing address   __ Other (enter below) | | |
|---|---|---|
| Name: | | |
| Address: | | |
| | | |
| City: | State: | Zip: |

**Praise for *Money and the People You Love:***

"This book is insightful, educational, and focuses on the things that matter most in life . . . our family, friends, and other loved ones."

*—Jay Feely, New York Giants place kicker and a Financial Adviser*

"Plain English" is a language seldom spoken in the financial services industry. Bruce Helmer, in my opinion, holds a Masters Degree in "Plain English" and that is what makes this book extraordinarily useful to the average person. He also points out that "wealth" is defined by the beholder and makes one realize that they need to follow their own passion. Bruce's motto is, "Do the right thing and the money will come." He has changed my life and I thank him for it.

*—Peg Chromy Webb, Senior Financial Advisor*

"Counting my nine years playing in the NFL prior to coaching, I have been around professional athletes my entire adult life. And, I can tell you that a pro athlete's primary motivation is not money. It is a commitment to excellence. It is desire, dedication and determination to win, to be the best. Bruce embraces that attitude in his life and financial planning philosophy. And, some of that comes through loud and clear in this book."

*—Mike Mularkey, Head Coach of the NFL's Buffalo Bills*

"There are many books written on personal finance. [Helmer] challenges conventional wisdom [and] gives examples that illustrate why following the "heard mentality" often times can be detrimental to your financial health. And he communicates in a way that is fun and informative."

*—John Castino, MBA, Financial Adviser,*
*former major league baseball player*